352.63076
C499
2017

DETROIT PUBLIC LIBRARY

P9-DKF-382

SHERWOOD FOREST LIBRARY
7117 W. 7 MILE RD.
DETROIT, MI 48221

CIVIL SERVICE EXAMS
POWER PRACTICE

MAR --- 2019

SF

Other Titles of Interest from LearningExpress

Firefighter Exam

Paramedic Exam

Police Officer Exam

Police Officer Exam: Power Practice

Postal Worker Exam

SHERWOOD FOREST LIBRARY
7117 W. 7 MILE RD.
DETROIT, MI 48221

CIVIL SERVICE EXAMS POWER PRACTICE

Second Edition

SHERWOOD FOREST LIBRARY
7117 W. 7 MILE RD.
DETROIT, MI 48221

LearningExpress®

NEW YORK

Copyright © 2017 LearningExpress.

All rights reserved under International and Pan-American Copyright Conventions.
Published in the United States by LearningExpress, New York.

ISBN 978-1-61103-089-1

Printed in the United States of America

9 8 7 6 5 4 3 2

Second Edition

For information or to place an order, contact LearningExpress at:
   224 W. 29th Street
   3rd Floor
   New York, NY 10001

CONTENTS

CIVIL SERVICE EXAMS
POWER PRACTICE

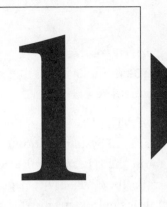

THE LEARNINGEXPRESS TEST PREPARATION SYSTEM

CHAPTER OVERVIEW

Taking any written exam can be tough. It demands a lot of preparation if you want to achieve a top score, and your rank on the eligibility list is often determined largely by this score. The LearningExpress Test Preparation System, developed exclusively for LearningExpress by leading test experts, gives you the discipline and attitude you need to be a winner.

Taking the civil service written exam is no picnic, and neither is getting ready for it. Your future career in civil service depends on you getting a high score on the various parts of the test, but there are all sorts of pitfalls that can keep you from doing your best on this all-important exam. Here are some of the obstacles that can stand in the way of your success:

- being unfamiliar with the format of the exam
- being paralyzed by test anxiety
- leaving your preparation to the last minute or not preparing at all
- not knowing vital test-taking skills: how to pace yourself through the exam, how to use the process of elimination, and when to guess
- not being in tip-top mental and physical shape
- messing up on exam day by having to work on an empty stomach or shivering through the exam because the room is cold

What's the common denominator in all these test-taking pitfalls? One word: *control*. Who's in control, you or the exam?

The LearningExpress Test Preparation System puts you in control. In just nine easy-to-follow steps, you will learn everything you need to know to make sure that you are in charge of your preparation and your performance on the exam. Other test takers may let the exam get the better of them; other test takers may be unprepared or out of shape, but not you. After completing this chapter, you will have taken all the steps you need to get a high score on any civil service exam.

Here's how the LearningExpress Test Preparation System works: nine easy steps lead you through everything you need to know and do to get ready for your exam. Each of the steps listed below and on the following pages includes both reading about the step and one or more activities. It's important that you do the activities along with the reading, or you won't be getting the full benefit of the system. Each step tells you approximately how much time that step will take you to complete.

Step 1. Get Information (30 minutes)
Step 2. Conquer Test Anxiety (20 minutes)
Step 3. Make a Plan (50 minutes)
Step 4. Learn to Manage Your Time (10 minutes)
Step 5. Learn to Use the Process of Elimination (20 minutes)
Step 6. Know When to Guess (20 minutes)
Step 7. Reach Your Peak Performance Zone (10 minutes)
Step 8. Get Your Act Together (10 minutes)
Step 9. Do It! (10 minutes)
Total time for complete system (180 minutes-3 hours)

We estimate that working through the entire system will take you approximately three hours. It's perfectly okay if you work at a faster or slower pace. If you can take a whole afternoon or evening, you can work through the whole LearningExpress Test Preparation System in one sitting. Otherwise, you can break it up, and do just one or two steps a day for the next several days. It's up to you—remember, you are in control.

Step 1: Get Information
Time to complete: 30 minutes
Activities: Independent research

Knowledge is power. The first step in the Learning-Express Test Preparation System is finding out everything you can about the types of civil service exams offered. For example, the Civil Service page of Federal Jobs Net (federaljobs.net/exams.htm) outlines the details about taking a civil service exam. *The Book of U.S. Government Jobs* (11th Edition) will have additional information for you on civil service exam requirements.

What You Should Find Out
The more details you can find out about the exam, the more efficiently you will be able to study. Here's a list of some things you might want to find out about your exam:

- What skills are tested?
- How many sections are on the exam?
- How many questions are in each section?
- Are the questions ordered from easy to hard, or is the sequence random?
- How much time is allotted for each section?
- Are there breaks between sections?
- What is the passing score, and how many questions do you have to answer right in order to get that score?
- Does a higher score give you any advantages, like a better rank on the eligibility list?
- How is the exam scored, and is there a penalty for wrong answers?
- Are you permitted to go back to a prior section or move on to the next section if you finish early?

- Can you write in the exam booklet, or will you be given scratch paper?
- What should you bring with you on exam day?

What's on Most Civil Service Exams

The skills that are tested on civil service exams vary from occupation to occupation. That's why it's important to contact your local state association to find out what skills are covered. Then, move on to the next step to get rid of that test anxiety.

Step 2: Conquer Test Anxiety

Time to complete: 20 minutes
Activity: Practice overcoming test anxiety

Having complete information about the exam is the first step in getting control of it. Next, you have to overcome one of the biggest obstacles to test success: test anxiety. Test anxiety can not only impair your performance on the exam itself, but it can even keep you from preparing properly. In Step 2, you will learn stress management techniques that will help you succeed on your exam. Learn these strategies now, and practice them as you work through the questions in this book, so they'll be second nature to you by exam day.

Combating Test Anxiety

The first thing you need to know is that a little test anxiety is a good thing. Everyone gets nervous before a big exam—and if that nervousness motivates you to prepare thoroughly, so much the better. It's said that Sir Olivier, one of the foremost British actors of the twentieth century, threw up before every performance. His stage fright didn't impair his performance; in fact, it probably gave him a little extra edge—just the kind of edge you need to do well, whether on a stage or in an examination room.

Stress Management before the Exam

If you feel your level of anxiety is getting the best of you in the weeks before the exam, here is what you need to do to bring the level down again:

- **Get prepared.** There's nothing like knowing what to expect, and being prepared for it, to put you in control of test anxiety. That's why you're reading this book. Use it faithfully, and remind yourself that you're better prepared than most of the people taking the exam.
- **Practice self-confidence.** A positive attitude is a great way to combat test anxiety. This is no time to be humble or shy. Stand in front of the mirror and say to your reflection, "I'm prepared. I'm full of self-confidence. I'm going to ace this exam. I know I can do it." Say it into a recorder, and play it back once a day. If you hear it often enough, you will believe it.
- **Fight negative messages.** Every time someone starts telling you how hard the exam is or how it's almost impossible to get a high score, start using your self-confidence messages. If the someone with the negative messages is you—telling yourself you don't do well on exams, that you just can't do this—don't listen. Turn on your recorder and listen to your self-confidence messages.
- **Visualize.** Imagine yourself reporting for duty on your first day of your civil service job. Think of yourself performing your job with pride and learning skills you will use for the rest of your life. Visualizing success can help make it happen— and it reminds you of why you're doing all this work in preparing for the exam.
- **Exercise.** Physical activity helps calm down your body and focus your mind. Besides, being in good physical shape can actually help you do well on the exam. Go for a run, lift weights, go swimming— and do it regularly.

Stress Management on Exam Day

There are several ways you can bring down your level of test stress and anxiety on exam day. They'll work best if you practice them in the weeks before the exam, so you know which ones work best for you.

- **Deep breathing.** Take a deep breath while you count to five. Hold it for a count of one, and then let it out on a count of five. Repeat several times.
- **Move your body.** Try rolling your head in a circle. Rotate your shoulders. Shake your hands from the wrist. Many people find these movements very relaxing.
- **Visualize again.** Think of the place where you are most relaxed: lying on the beach in the sun, walking through the park, or whatever relaxes you. Now, close your eyes and imagine you're actually there. If you practice in advance, you will find that you need only a few seconds of this exercise to experience a significant increase in your sense of well-being.

When anxiety threatens to overwhelm you during the exam, there are still things you can do to manage your stress level:

- **Repeat your self-confidence messages.** You should have them memorized by now. Say them quietly to yourself, and believe them!
- **Visualize one more time.** This time, visualize yourself moving smoothly and quickly through the exam, answering every question correctly and finishing just before time is up. Like most visualization techniques, this one works best if you've practiced it ahead of time.
- **Find an easy question.** Skim over the test until you find an easy question, and answer it. Getting even one circle filled in gets you into the test-taking groove.
- **Take a mental break.** Everyone loses concentration once in a while during a long exam. It's normal, so you shouldn't worry about it. Instead, accept what has happened. Say to yourself, "Hey, I lost it there for a minute. My brain is taking a break." Put down your pencil, close your eyes, and do some deep breathing for a few seconds. Then, you're ready to go back to work.

Try these techniques ahead of time, and see if they work for you!

Take the Test Stress Test on the following page to find out whether or not your level of test anxiety is something you should worry about.

TEST STRESS TEST

You need to worry about test anxiety only if it is extreme enough to impair your performance. The following questionnaire will provide a diagnosis of your level of test anxiety. In the blank before each statement, write the number that most accurately describes your experience.

0 = Never

1 = Once or twice

2 = Sometimes

3 = Often

_____ I have gotten so nervous before an exam that I simply put down the books and didn't study for it.

_____ I have experienced disabling physical symptoms such as vomiting and severe headaches because I was nervous about an exam.

_____ I have simply not showed up for an exam because I was scared to take it.

_____ I have experienced dizziness and disorientation while taking an exam.

_____ I have had trouble filling in the little circles because my hands were shaking too hard.

_____ I have failed an exam because I was too nervous to complete it.

_____ **Total: Add up the numbers in the blanks above.**

Understanding Your Test Stress Scores

Here are the steps you should take, depending on your score. If you scored:

- **Below 3:** Your level of test anxiety is nothing to worry about. It's probably just enough to give you that little extra edge.
- **Between 3 and 6:** Your test anxiety may be enough to impair your performance, and you should practice the stress-management techniques listed in this section to try to bring your test anxiety down to manageable levels.
- **Above 6:** Your level of test anxiety is a serious concern. In addition to practicing the stress-management techniques listed in this section, you may want to seek additional, personal help. Call your local high school or community college and ask for the academic counselor. Tell the counselor that you have a level of test anxiety that sometimes keeps you from being able to take the exam. The counselor may be willing to help you or may suggest someone else you should talk to.

Step 3: Make a Plan

Time to complete: 50 minutes
Activity: Construct a study plan, using Schedules
    A–D (pages 6–8)

Many people do poorly on exams because they forget to make a study schedule. The most important thing you can do to better prepare yourself for your exam is to create a study plan or schedule. Spending hours the day before the exam poring over sample test questions not only raises your level of anxiety, but it is also not a substitute for careful preparation and practice over time.

Don't cram. Take control of your time by mapping out a study schedule. There are four examples of study schedules on the following pages, based on the amount of time you have before the exam. If you're the kind of person who needs deadlines and assignments to motivate you for a project, here they are. If you're the kind of person who doesn't like to follow other people's plans, you can use the suggested schedules to construct your own.

In constructing your plan, you should take into account how much work you need to do. If your score on the sample test wasn't what you had hoped, consider taking some of the steps from Schedule A and fitting them into Schedule D, even if you do have only three weeks before the exam. (See Schedules A-D on the next few pages.)

Even more important than making a plan is making a commitment. You have to set aside some time every day for studying and practice. Try to set aside at least 20 minutes a day. Twenty minutes daily will do you more good than two hours crammed into a Saturday.

If you have months before the exam, you're lucky. Don't put off your study until the week before the exam. Start now. Even ten minutes a day, with half an hour or more on weekends, can make a big difference in your score—and in your chances of working in civil service.

Schedule A: The Leisure Plan

This schedule gives you at least six months to sharpen your skills and prepare for your exam. The more prep time you give yourself, the more relaxed you'll feel.

TIME	PREPARATION
Exam minus 6 months:	Start going to the library once every two weeks to read books, magazines, or websites in your desired field. Start gathering information about working. Find other people who are preparing for the exam, and form a study group.
Exam minus 5 months:	Take practice exam 1. See where your strengths and weaknesses lie.
Exam minus 4 months:	Take practice exam 2. Has your score improved? In which areas do you need more practice?

TIME	PREPARATION
Exam minus 3 months:	Take practice exam 3. Has your score improved? In which areas do you need more practice?
Exam minus 2 months:	Use your scores from practice exams 1, 2, and 3 to help you decide where to concentrate your efforts this month. Continue working with your study group. Find online and print resources to help you review relevant math and verbal skills.
Exam minus 1 month:	Take and review practice exams 4, 5, and 6. See how much you've learned in the past months. Concentrate on what you've done well, and decide not to let any areas where you still feel uncertain bother you.
Exam minus 1 week:	Take practice exam 7. Review any areas that are still giving you trouble.
Exam minus 1 day:	Relax. Do something unrelated to the civil service exam. Eat a good meal and go to bed at your usual time.

Schedule B: The Just Enough Time Plan

If you have three to six months before the exam, that should be enough time to prepare. This schedule assumes four months; stretch it out or compress it if you have more or less time.

TIME	PREPARATION
Exam minus 4 months:	Start going to the library once every two weeks to read books, magazines, or websites about civil service jobs. Start gathering information about civil service jobs.
Exam minus 3 months:	Take practice exam 1. Assess your strengths and weaknesses.
Exam minus 2 months:	Take practice exam 2. Has your score improved? In which areas do you need more practice?
Exam minus 1 month:	Take practice exams 3, 4, and 5. Use your scores to help you decide where to concentrate your efforts this month. Get the help of a friend or teacher.
Exam minus 1 week:	Take practice exams 6 and 7. See how much you've learned in the past months. Concentrate on what you've done well, and decide not to let any areas where you still feel uncertain bother you.
Exam minus 1 day:	Relax. Do something unrelated to your civil service exam. Eat a good meal and go to bed at your usual time.

Schedule C: More Study in Less Time

If you have one to three months before the exam, you still have enough time for some concentrated study that will help you improve your score. This schedule is built around a two-month time frame. If you have only one month, spend an extra couple of hours a week to get all these steps in. If you have three months, take some of the steps from Schedule B and fit them in.

TIME	PREPARATION
Exam minus 8 weeks:	Take practice exams 1 and 2.
Exam minus 6 weeks:	Take practice exams 3 and 4.
Exam minus 4 weeks:	Take practice exams 5 and 6.
Exam minus 2 weeks:	Take practice exam 7. Then, score it and read the answer explanations until you're sure you understand them. Review the areas where your score is lowest.
Exam minus 1 week:	Review the sample exams, concentrating on the areas where a little work can help the most.
Exam minus 1 day:	Relax. Do something unrelated to the civil service exam. Eat a good meal and go to bed at your usual time.

Schedule D: The Cram Plan

If you have three weeks or less before the exam, you may have your work cut out for you. Carve half an hour out of your day, every day, for studying. This schedule assumes you have the whole three weeks to prepare; if you have less time, you will have to compress your schedule accordingly.

TIME	PREPARATION
Exam minus 3 weeks:	Take practice exams 1, 2, and 3.
Exam minus 2 weeks:	Take practice exams 4, 5, and 6. Review areas you're weakest in.
Exam minus 1 week:	Take practice exam 7. Get a friend or teacher to help you with the section you had the most difficulty with.
Exam minus 2 days:	Review the results of your exams. Make sure you understand the answer . explanations
Exam minus 1 day:	Relax. Do something unrelated to the civil service exam. Eat a good meal and go to bed at your usual time.

Step 4: Learn to Manage Your Time

Time to complete: 10 minutes to read, many hours of practice
Activities: Practice these strategies as you take the sample exams.

Steps 4, 5, and 6 of the LearningExpress Test Preparation System put you in charge of your exam by showing you test taking strategies that work. Practice these strategies as you take the sample exams in Chapters 8, 9 and 10. Then, you will be ready to use them on exam day.

First, you will take control of your time on the exam. The first step in achieving this control is to find out the format of the exam you're going to take. Civil service exams may have different sections that are each timed separately. If this is true of the exam you will be taking, you will want to practice using your time wisely on the practice exams and trying to avoid mistakes while working quickly. Other types of exams don't have separately timed sections. If this is the case, just practice pacing yourself on the practice exams so you don't spend too much time on difficult questions.

- **Listen carefully to directions.** By the time you get to the exam, you should know how the test works, but listen just in case something has changed.
- **Pace yourself.** Glance at your watch every few minutes, and compare the time to how far you've gotten in the section. Leave some extra time for review, so that when one-quarter of the time has elapsed, you should be more than a quarter of the way through the section, and so on. If you're falling behind, pick up the pace.
- **Keep moving.** Don't spend too much time on one question. If you don't know the answer, skip the question and move on. Circle the number of the question in your test booklet in case you have time to come back to it later.

- **Keep track of your place on the answer sheet.** If you skip a question, make sure you skip on the answer sheet, too. Check yourself every five to ten questions to make sure the question number and the answer sheet number match.
- **Don't rush.** You should keep moving, rushing won't help. Try to keep calm and work methodically and quickly.

Step 5: Learn to Use the Process of Elimination

Time to complete: 20 minutes
Activity: Practice using the process of elimination on practice tests.

After time management, the next most important tool for taking control of your exam is using the process of elimination wisely. It's standard test-taking wisdom that you should always read all the answer choices before choosing your answer. This helps you find the right answer by eliminating wrong answer choices. And, sure enough, that standard wisdom applies to this exam, too.

Let's say you're facing a question that goes like this:

13. "Biology uses a binomial system of classification." In this sentence, the word *binomial* most nearly means
   a. understanding the law.
   b. having two names.
   c. scientifically sound.
   d. having a double meaning.

If you happen to know what *binomial* means, you don't need to use the process of elimination, but let's assume that, like most people, you don't. So, you look at the answer choices. "Understanding the law" sure doesn't sound very likely for something having to do with biology. So, you eliminate choice **a**—and now you only have three answer choices to deal with. Mark an **X** next to choice **a** so you never have to read it again.

Move on to the other answer choices. If you know that the prefix *bi-* means *two*, as in *bicycle*, you will flag choice **b** as a possible answer. Make a check mark beside it, meaning "good answer, I might use this one."

Choice **c**, "scientifically sound," is a possibility. At least it's about science, not law. It could work here, though, when you think about it, having a "scientifically sound" classification system in a scientific field is kind of redundant. You remember the *bi-* in *binomial*, and probably continue to like choice **b** better. But you're not sure, so you put a question mark next to choice **c**, meaning "well, maybe."

Now, look at choice **d**, "having a double meaning." You're still keeping in mind that *bi-* means *two*, so this one looks possible at first. But then you look again at the sentence the word belongs in, and you think, "Why would biology want a system of classification that has two meanings? That wouldn't work very well!" If you're really taken with the idea that *bi-* means *two*, you might put a question mark here. But if you're feeling a little more confident, you will put an **X**. You've already got a better answer picked out.

Now, your question looks like this:

13. "Biology uses a *binomial* system of classification." In this sentence, the word *binomial* most nearly means

  X **a.** understanding the law.
  ✓ **b.** having two names.
  ? **c.** scientifically sound.
  ? **d.** having a double meaning.

You've got just one check mark, for a good answer. If you're pressed for time, you should simply mark choice **b** on your answer sheet. If you've got the time to be extra careful, you could compare your check mark answer to your question mark answers to make sure that it's better. (It is: The *binomial* system in biology is the one that gives a two-part genus and species name like homo sapiens.)

It's good to have a system for marking good, bad, and maybe answers. We recommend using this one:

  X = bad
  ✓ = good
  ? = maybe

If you don't like these marks, devise your own system. Just make sure you do it long before exam day—while you're working through the practice exams in this book—so you won't have to worry about it during the exam.

Even when you think you're absolutely clueless about a question, you can often use the process of elimination to get rid of one answer choice. If so, you're better prepared to make an educated guess, as you will see in Step 6.

More often, the process of elimination allows you to get down to only two possibly right answers. Then you're in a strong position to guess. And sometimes, even though you don't know the right answer, you find it simply by getting rid of the wrong ones, as you did in the previous example.

Try using your powers of elimination on the questions in the Using the Process of Elimination worksheet, beginning on the next page. The answer explanations there show one possible way you might use the process to arrive at the right answer.

The process of elimination is your tool for the next step, which is knowing when to guess.

1. Ilsa is as old as Meghan will be in five years. The difference between Ed's age and Meghan's age is twice the difference between Ilsa's age and Meghan's age. Ed is 29. How old is Ilsa?
   a. 4
   b. 10
   c. 19
   d. 24

2. "All drivers of commercial vehicles must carry a valid commercial driver's license whenever operating a commercial vehicle." According to this sentence, which of the following people need **NOT** carry a commercial driver's license?
   a. a truck driver idling his engine while waiting to be directed to a loading dock
   b. a bus operator backing her bus out of the way of another bus in the bus lot
   c. a taxi driver driving his personal car to the grocery store
   d. a limousine driver taking the limousine to her home after dropping off her last passenger of the evening

3. Smoking tobacco has been linked to
   a. increased risk of stroke and heart attack.
   b. all forms of respiratory disease.
   c. increasing mortality rates over the past ten years.
   d. juvenile delinquency.

4. Which of the following words is spelled correctly?
   a. incorrigible
   b. outragous
   c. domestickated
   d. understandible

Answers

Here are the answers, as well as some suggestions as to how you might have used the process of elimination to find them.

1. d. You should have eliminated choice **a** off the bat. Ilsa can't be four years old if Meghan is going to be Ilsa's age in five years. The best way to eliminate other answer choices is to try plugging them in to the information given in the problem. For instance, for choice **b**, if Ilsa is 10, then Meghan must be 5. The difference in their ages is 5. The difference between Ed's age, 29, and Meghan's age, 5, is 24. Is 24 two times 5? No. Then choice **b** is wrong. You could eliminate choice **c** in the same way and be left with choice **d**.

2. c. Note the word *not* in the question, and go through the choices one by one. Is the truck driver in choice **a** "operating a commercial vehicle"? Yes, idling counts as "operating," so he needs to have a commercial driver's license. Likewise, the bus operator in choice **b** is operating a commercial vehicle; the question doesn't say the operator has to be on the street. The limo driver in choice **d** is operating a commercial vehicle, even if it doesn't have passenger in it. However, the cabbie in choice **c** is **not** operating a commercial vehicle, but his own private car.

3. a. You could eliminate choice **b** simply because of the presence of the word *all*. Such absolutes hardly ever appear in correct answer choices. Choice **c** looks attractive until you think a little about what you know—aren't fewer people smoking these days, rather than more? So how could smoking be responsible for a higher mortality rate? (If you didn't know that *mortality rate* means the rate at which people die, you might keep this choice as a possibility, but you'd still be able to eliminate two answers and have only two to choose from.) Choice **d** is plain silly, so you could eliminate that one, too. You're left with the correct choice, **a**.

4. a. How you used the process of elimination here depends on which words you recognized as being spelled incorrectly. If you knew that the correct spellings were *outrageous*, *domesticated*, and *understandable*, then you were home free. You probably knew that at least one of those words was wrong.

Step 6: Know When to Guess

Time to complete: 20 minutes
Activity: Practice guessing on practice test questions.

Armed with the process of elimination, you're ready to take control of one of the big questions in test-taking: Should I guess? The first and main answer is yes. Unless the exam has a so-called "guessing penalty," you have nothing to lose and everything to gain from guessing. The more complicated answer depends both on the exam and on you-your personality and your "guessing intuition."

Most civil service exams don't use a guessing penalty. The number of questions you answer correctly yields your score, and there's no penalty for wrong answers. So most of the time, you don't have to worry—simply go ahead and guess. But if you find that your exam does have a guessing penalty, you should read the section below to find out what that means to you.

How the Guessing Penalty Works

A guessing penalty really only works against random guessing—filling in the little circles to make a nice pattern on your answer sheet. If you can eliminate one or more answer choices, you're better off taking a guess than leaving the answer blank, even on the sections that have a penalty.

Here's how a guessing penalty works: Depending on the number of answer choices in a given exam, some proportion of the number of questions you get wrong is subtracted from the total number of questions you got right. For instance, if there are four answer choices, typically the guessing penalty is $\frac{1}{3}$ of your wrong answers. Suppose you took an exam of 100 questions. You answered 88 of them right and 12 wrong.

If there's no guessing penalty, your score is simply 88. But if there's a $\frac{1}{3}$ point guessing penalty, the scorers take your 12 wrong answers and divide by three to come up with 4. Then they subtract that four from your correct answer score of 88 to leave you with a score of 84. Thus, you would have been better off if you had simply not answered those 12 questions. Then your total score would still be 88 because there wouldn't be anything to subtract.

What You Should Do About the Guessing Penalty

You now know how a guessing penalty works. The first thing this means for you is that marking your answer sheet at random doesn't pay. If you're running out of time on an exam that has a guessing penalty, you should not use your remaining seconds to mark a pretty pattern on your answer sheet. Take those few seconds to try to answer one more question right.

But as soon as you get out of the realm of random guessing, the guessing penalty no longer works against you. If you can use the process of elimination to get rid of even one wrong answer choice, the odds stop being against you and start working in your favor.

Sticking with our example of an exam that has four answer choices, eliminating just one wrong answer makes your odds of choosing the correct answer one in three. That's the same as the one-out-of-three guessing penalty—even odds. If you eliminate two answer choices, your odds are one in two—better than the guessing penalty. In either case, you should go ahead and choose one of the remaining answer choices.

When There Is No Guessing Penalty

As noted, most civil service exams don't have a guessing penalty. That means that, all other things being equal, you should always go ahead and guess, even if you have no idea what the question means. Nothing can happen to you if you're wrong. But all other things aren't necessarily equal. The other factor in deciding whether or not to guess, besides the guessing penalty, is you. There are two things you need to know about yourself before you go into the exam:

- Are you a risk-taker?
- Are you a good guesser?

Your risk-taking temperament matters most on exams with a guessing penalty. Without a guessing penalty, even if you're a play-it-safe person, guessing is perfectly safe. Overcome your anxieties, and go ahead and mark an answer.

But what if you're not much of a risk-taker, and you think of yourself as the world's worst guesser? Complete the Your Guessing Ability worksheet on the next two pages to get an idea of how good your intuition is.

The following are ten really hard questions. You are not supposed to know the answers. Rather, this is an assessment of your ability to guess when you don't have a clue. Read each question carefully, just as if you did expect to answer it. If you have any knowledge at all about the subject of the question, use that knowledge to help you eliminate wrong answer choices. Use this answer grid to fill in your answers to the questions.

ANSWER GRID

1. ⓐ	ⓑ	ⓒ	ⓓ
2. ⓐ	ⓑ	ⓒ	ⓓ
3. ⓐ	ⓑ	ⓒ	ⓓ
4. ⓐ	ⓑ	ⓒ	ⓓ

5. ⓐ	ⓑ	ⓒ	ⓓ
6. ⓐ	ⓑ	ⓒ	ⓓ
7. ⓐ	ⓑ	ⓒ	ⓓ
8. ⓐ	ⓑ	ⓒ	ⓓ

9. ⓐ	ⓑ	ⓒ	ⓓ
10. ⓐ	ⓑ	ⓒ	ⓓ

1. September 7 is Independence Day in
   a. India.
   b. Costa Rica.
   c. Brazil.
   d. Australia.

2. Which of the following is the formula for determining the momentum of an object?
   a. $p = mv$
   b. $F = ma$
   c. $P = IV$
   d. $E = mc^2$

3. Because of the expansion of the universe, the stars and other celestial bodies are all moving away from each other. This phenomenon is known as
   a. Newton's first law.
   b. the big bang.
   c. gravitational collapse.
   d. Hubble flow.

4. American author Gertrude Stein was born in
   a. 1713.
   b. 1830.
   c. 1874.
   d. 1901.

5. Which of the following is NOT one of the Five Classics attributed to Confucius?
   a. *I Ching*
   b. *Book of Holiness*
   c. *Spring and Autumn Annals*
   d. *Book of History*

6. The religious and philosophical doctrine that holds that the universe is constantly in a struggle between good and evil is known as
   a. Pelagianism.
   b. Manichaeanism.
   c. neo-Hegelianism.
   d. Epicureanism.

7. The third Chief Justice of the U.S. Supreme Court was
   a. John Blair.
   b. William Cushing.
   c. James Wilson.
   d. John Jay.

8. Which of the following is the poisonous portion of a daffodil?
   a. the bulb
   b. the leaves
   c. the stem
   d. the flowers

9. The winner of the Masters golf tournament in 1953 was
   a. Sam Snead.
   b. Cary Middlecoff.
   c. Arnold Palmer.
   d. Ben Hogan.

10. The state with the highest per capita personal income in 1980 was
   a. Alaska.
   b. Connecticut.
   c. New York.
   d. Texas.

Answers

Check your answers against the correct answers below.

   1. c.
   2. a.
   3. d.
   4. c.
   5. b.
   6. b.
   7. b.
   8. a.
   9. d.
   10. a.

How Did You Do?

You may have simply gotten lucky and actually known the answer to one or two questions. In addition, your guessing was more successful if you were able to use the process of elimination on any of the questions. Maybe you didn't know who the third Chief Justice was (question 7), but you knew that John Jay was the first. In that case, you would have eliminated choice **d** and therefore improved your odds of guessing correctly from one in four to one in three.

According to probability, you should get $2\frac{1}{2}$ answers correct, so getting either two or three right would be average. If you got four or more right, you may be a really terrific guesser. If you got one or none right, you may be a really bad guesser.

Keep in mind, though, that this is only a small sample. You should continue to keep track of your guessing ability as you work through the sample questions in this book. Circle the numbers of questions you guess on as you make your guess; or, if you don't have time while you take the practice exams, go back afterward and try to remember which questions you guessed at. Remember, on an exam with four answer choices, your chances of getting a right answer is one in four. So keep a separate "guessing" score for each exam. How many questions did you guess on? How many did you get right? If the number you got right is at least one-fourth of the number of questions you guessed on, you are at least an average guesser, maybe better—and you should always go ahead and guess on a real exam. If the number you got right is significantly lower than one-fourth of the number you guessed on, you would, frankly, be safe in guessing anyway, but maybe you would feel more comfortable if you guessed only selectively, when you can eliminate a wrong answer or at least have a good feeling about one of the answer choices.

Step 7: Reach Your Peak Performance Zone

Time to complete: 10 minutes to read; weeks to complete!
Activity: Complete the Physical Preparation Checklist (page 17)

To get ready for a challenge like a big exam, you also have to take control of your physical, as well as your mental, state. Exercise, proper diet, and rest will ensure that your body works with, rather than against, your mind on test day, as well as during your preparation.

Exercise

If you don't already have a regular exercise program going, the time during which you're preparing for an exam is actually an excellent time to start one. And if you're already keeping fit—or trying to get that way—don't let the pressure of preparing for an exam fool you into quitting now. Exercise helps reduce stress by pumping wonderful good-feeling hormones called endorphins into your system. It also increases the oxygen supply throughout your body, including your brain, so you will be at peak performance on exam day.

A half hour of vigorous activity—enough to raise a sweat—every day should be your aim. If you're really pressed for time, every other day is OK. Choose an activity you like and get out there and do it. Jogging with a friend always makes the time go faster, as does running with a radio.

But don't overdo it. You don't want to exhaust yourself. Moderation is the key.

Diet

First of all, cut out the junk. Go easy on caffeine, and try to eliminate alcohol and nicotine from your system at least two weeks before the exam.

What your body needs for peak performance is simply a balanced diet. Eat plenty of fruits and vegetables, along with protein and carbohydrates. Foods that are high in lecithin (an amino acid), such as fish and beans, are especially good "brain foods."

The night before the exam, you might "carbo-load" the way athletes do before a contest. Eat a big plate of spaghetti, rice and beans, or whatever your favorite carbohydrate is.

Rest

You probably know how much sleep you need every night to be at your best, even if you don't always get it. Make sure you do get that much sleep, though, for at least a week before the exam. Moderation is important here, too. Too much sleep will just make you groggy.

If you're not a morning person and your exam will be given in the morning, you should reset your internal clock so that your body doesn't think you're taking an exam at 3 A.M. You have to start this process well before the exam. The way it works is to get up half an hour earlier each morning, and then go to bed half an hour earlier that night. Don't try it the other way around; you will just toss and turn if you go to bed early without having gotten up early. The next morning, get up another half an hour earlier, and so on. How long you will have to do this depends on how late you're used to getting up. Use the Physical Preparation Checklist on the next page to make sure you're in tip-top form.

For the week before the test, write down 1) what physical exercise you engaged in and for how long and 2) what you ate for each meal. Remember, you're trying for at least half an hour of exercise every other day (preferably every day) and a balanced diet that's light on junk food.

Exam minus 7 days

Exercise: _____ for _____ minutes

Breakfast: _____

Lunch: _____

Dinner: _____

Snacks: _____

Exam minus 6 days

Exercise: _____ for _____ minutes

Breakfast: _____

Lunch: _____

Dinner: _____

Snacks: _____

Exam minus 5 days

Exercise: _____ for _____ minutes

Breakfast: _____

Lunch: _____

Dinner: _____

Snacks: _____

Exam minus 4 days

Exercise: _____ for _____ minutes

Breakfast: _____

Lunch: _____

Dinner: _____

Snacks: _____

Exam minus 3 days

Exercise: _____ for _____ minutes

Breakfast: _____

Lunch: _____

Dinner: _____

Snacks: _____

Exam minus 2 days

Exercise: _____ for _____ minutes

Breakfast: _____

Lunch: _____

Dinner: _____

Snacks: _____

Exam minus 1 day

Exercise: _____ for _____ minutes

Breakfast: _____

Lunch: _____

Dinner: _____

Snacks: _____

Step 8: Get Your Act Together

Time to complete: 10 minutes to read; time to complete will vary
Activity: Take control of your test preparation.

You're in control of your mind and body; you're in charge of test anxiety, your preparation, and your test-taking strategies. Now, it's time to take charge of external factors, like the exam site and the materials you need to take the exam.

Find Out Where the Exam Is and Make a Trial Run

The test administer will notify you when and where your exam is being held. Do you know how to get to the exam site? Do you know how long it will take to get there? If not, make a trial run, preferably on the same day of the week at the same time of day. Make note, on the Final Preparations worksheet on the next page, of the amount of time it will take you to get to the exam site. Plan on arriving 10–15 minutes early so you can get the lay of the land, use the bathroom, and calm down. Then, figure out how early you will have to get up that morning, and make sure you get up that early every day for a week before the exam.

Gather Your Materials

The night before the exam, lay out the clothes you will wear and the materials you have to bring with you to the exam. Plan on dressing in layers; you won't have any control over the temperature of the examination room. Have a sweater or jacket you can take off if it's warm.

Don't Skip Breakfast

Even if you don't usually eat breakfast, do so on exam morning. A cup of coffee doesn't count. Don't do doughnuts or other sweet foods, either. A sugar high will leave you with a sugar low in the middle of the exam. A mix of protein and carbohydrates is best. Cereal with milk and just a little sugar or eggs with toast will do your body a world of good.

Step 9: Do It!

Time to complete: 10 minutes, plus test-taking time
Activity: Ace your civil service exam!

Fast forward to exam day. You're ready. You made a study plan and followed through. You practiced your test-taking strategies while working through this book. You're in control of your physical, mental, and emotional state. You know when and where to show up and what to bring with you. In other words, you're better prepared than most of the other people taking the exam with you. You're psyched.

Just one more thing. When you're done with the exam, you will have earned a reward. Plan a celebration. Call up your friends and plan a party, have a nice dinner for two, or pick out a movie to see—whatever your heart desires. Give yourself something to look forward to.

And then do it. Go into the exam, full of confidence, armed with test-taking strategies you've practiced until they're second nature. You're in control of yourself, your environment, and your performance on the exam. You're ready to succeed. So do it. Go in there and ace the exam. And look forward to your future career as a civil servant.

Getting to the Exam Site

Location of exam site: _____

Date: _____

Departure time: _____

Do I know how to get to the exam site?   Yes _____   No _____   (If no, make a trial run.)

Time it will take to get to exam site _____

Things to Lay Out the Night Before

Clothes I will wear   _____

Sweater/jacket   _____

Watch   _____

Photo ID   _____

Four #2 pencils   _____

Other Things to Bring/Remember

_____   _____

_____   _____

_____   _____

_____   _____

2 ▶ CIVIL SERVICE PRACTICE EXAM 1

This is the first of seven practice exams designed to prepare you for your civil service exam. The type of test varies greatly from job to job and from location to location, but most exams include at least some basic reading, writing, and sometimes math skills. The practice exams in this book also test spelling, vocabulary, grammar, civil service skills, memory, and coding.

The test that follows was created not to be identical to one particular civil service exam, but to allow you to practice the kinds of questions you may encounter on your exam. You can hone your skills in commonly tested areas by taking the practice exams and thoroughly reviewing the answers and explanations provided at the end of the chapter.

Civil Service Practice Exam 1

#				
1.	ⓐ	ⓑ	ⓒ	ⓓ
2.	ⓐ	ⓑ	ⓒ	ⓓ
3.	ⓐ	ⓑ	ⓒ	ⓓ
4.	ⓐ	ⓑ	ⓒ	ⓓ
5.	ⓐ	ⓑ	ⓒ	ⓓ
6.	ⓐ	ⓑ	ⓒ	ⓓ
7.	ⓐ	ⓑ	ⓒ	ⓓ
8.	ⓐ	ⓑ	ⓒ	ⓓ
9.	ⓐ	ⓑ	ⓒ	ⓓ
10.	ⓐ	ⓑ	ⓒ	ⓓ
11.	ⓐ	ⓑ	ⓒ	ⓓ
12.	ⓐ	ⓑ	ⓒ	ⓓ
13.	ⓐ	ⓑ	ⓒ	ⓓ
14.	ⓐ	ⓑ	ⓒ	ⓓ
15.	ⓐ	ⓑ	ⓒ	ⓓ
16.	ⓐ	ⓑ	ⓒ	ⓓ
17.	ⓐ	ⓑ	ⓒ	ⓓ
18.	ⓐ	ⓑ	ⓒ	ⓓ
19.	ⓐ	ⓑ	ⓒ	ⓓ
20.	ⓐ	ⓑ	ⓒ	ⓓ
21.	ⓐ	ⓑ	ⓒ	ⓓ
22.	ⓐ	ⓑ	ⓒ	ⓓ
23.	ⓐ	ⓑ	ⓒ	ⓓ
24.	ⓐ	ⓑ	ⓒ	ⓓ
25.	ⓐ	ⓑ	ⓒ	ⓓ
26.	ⓐ	ⓑ	ⓒ	ⓓ
27.	ⓐ	ⓑ	ⓒ	ⓓ
28.	ⓐ	ⓑ	ⓒ	ⓓ
29.	ⓐ	ⓑ	ⓒ	ⓓ
30.	ⓐ	ⓑ	ⓒ	ⓓ
31.	ⓐ	ⓑ	ⓒ	ⓓ
32.	ⓐ	ⓑ	ⓒ	ⓓ
33.	ⓐ	ⓑ	ⓒ	ⓓ
34.	ⓐ	ⓑ	ⓒ	ⓓ
35.	ⓐ	ⓑ	ⓒ	ⓓ
36.	ⓐ	ⓑ	ⓒ	ⓓ
37.	ⓐ	ⓑ	ⓒ	ⓓ
38.	ⓐ	ⓑ	ⓒ	ⓓ
39.	ⓐ	ⓑ	ⓒ	ⓓ
40.	ⓐ	ⓑ	ⓒ	ⓓ
41.	ⓐ	ⓑ	ⓒ	ⓓ
42.	ⓐ	ⓑ	ⓒ	ⓓ
43.	ⓐ	ⓑ	ⓒ	ⓓ
44.	ⓐ	ⓑ	ⓒ	ⓓ
45.	ⓐ	ⓑ	ⓒ	ⓓ
46.	ⓐ	ⓑ	ⓒ	ⓓ
47.	ⓐ	ⓑ	ⓒ	ⓓ
48.	ⓐ	ⓑ	ⓒ	ⓓ
49.	ⓐ	ⓑ	ⓒ	ⓓ
50.	ⓐ	ⓑ	ⓒ	ⓓ
51.	ⓐ	ⓑ	ⓒ	ⓓ
52.	ⓐ	ⓑ	ⓒ	ⓓ
53.	ⓐ	ⓑ	ⓒ	ⓓ
54.	ⓐ	ⓑ	ⓒ	ⓓ
55.	ⓐ	ⓑ	ⓒ	ⓓ
56.	ⓐ	ⓑ	ⓒ	ⓓ
57.	ⓐ	ⓑ	ⓒ	ⓓ
58.	ⓐ	ⓑ	ⓒ	ⓓ
59.	ⓐ	ⓑ	ⓒ	ⓓ
60.	ⓐ	ⓑ	ⓒ	ⓓ
61.	ⓐ	ⓑ	ⓒ	ⓓ
62.	ⓐ	ⓑ	ⓒ	ⓓ
63.	ⓐ	ⓑ	ⓒ	ⓓ
64.	ⓐ	ⓑ	ⓒ	ⓓ
65.	ⓐ	ⓑ	ⓒ	ⓓ
66.	ⓐ	ⓑ	ⓒ	ⓓ
67.	ⓐ	ⓑ	ⓒ	ⓓ
68.	ⓐ	ⓑ	ⓒ	ⓓ
69.	ⓐ	ⓑ	ⓒ	ⓓ
70.	ⓐ	ⓑ	ⓒ	ⓓ
71.	ⓐ	ⓑ	ⓒ	ⓓ
72.	ⓐ	ⓑ	ⓒ	ⓓ
73.	ⓐ	ⓑ	ⓒ	ⓓ
74.	ⓐ	ⓑ	ⓒ	ⓓ
75.	ⓐ	ⓑ	ⓒ	ⓓ
76.	ⓐ	ⓑ	ⓒ	ⓓ
77.	ⓐ	ⓑ	ⓒ	ⓓ
78.	ⓐ	ⓑ	ⓒ	ⓓ
79.	ⓐ	ⓑ	ⓒ	ⓓ
80.	ⓐ	ⓑ	ⓒ	ⓓ
81.	ⓐ	ⓑ	ⓒ	ⓓ
82.	ⓐ	ⓑ	ⓒ	ⓓ
83.	ⓐ	ⓑ	ⓒ	ⓓ
84.	ⓐ	ⓑ	ⓒ	ⓓ
85.	ⓐ	ⓑ	ⓒ	ⓓ
86.	ⓐ	ⓑ	ⓒ	ⓓ
87.	ⓐ	ⓑ	ⓒ	ⓓ
88.	ⓐ	ⓑ	ⓒ	ⓓ
89.	ⓐ	ⓑ	ⓒ	ⓓ
90.	ⓐ	ⓑ	ⓒ	ⓓ
91.	ⓐ	ⓑ	ⓒ	ⓓ
92.	ⓐ	ⓑ	ⓒ	ⓓ
93.	ⓐ	ⓑ	ⓒ	ⓓ
94.	ⓐ	ⓑ	ⓒ	ⓓ
95.	ⓐ	ⓑ	ⓒ	ⓓ
96.	ⓐ	ⓑ	ⓒ	ⓓ
97.	ⓐ	ⓑ	ⓒ	ⓓ
98.	ⓐ	ⓑ	ⓒ	ⓓ
99.	ⓐ	ⓑ	ⓒ	ⓓ
100.	ⓐ	ⓑ	ⓒ	ⓓ

Section 1: Mathematics

Select the best choice for each question.

1. *The Daily Newspaper* asked its 16 salespeople to divide into four sales teams for a competition. Team Dynamo, with Barb, Peter, Boris, and Jason, won the competition by selling 1,500 subscriptions. Barb was responsible for 20% of the subscription sales, Peter sold 325 subscriptions, and Boris sold $\frac{7}{5}$ of what Peter sold. How many subscriptions must Jason have sold?
   a. 275
   b. 420
   c. 455
   d. 1,355

2. If a stock's price has changed from 35\frac{1}{2}$ to 42\frac{3}{4}$, how much is this change in dollars and cents?
   a. $7.75
   b. $7.25
   c. $6.25
   d. $6.50

3. Find the percent equivalent of $\frac{18}{25}$.
   a. 18%
   b. 43%
   c. 7%
   d. 72%

4. Jeanette purchased three items worth $18.42 each. If she had $100.00 to spend, how much does she have left?
   a. $38.42
   b. $44.74
   c. $44.87
   d. $55.26

5. Lynn has a collection of 150 comic books and decides to sell $\frac{3}{5}$ of them. If her friend Justin buys one-third of the comic books for sale, how many comic books does he buy?
   a. 10
   b. 20
   c. 30
   d. 40

6. $\frac{1}{2} + 4\frac{3}{4} + 2\frac{5}{6} =$
   a. $7\frac{3}{4}$
   b. $8\frac{1}{12}$
   c. $1\frac{1}{4}$
   d. $6\frac{3}{4}$

7. Harold wishes to leave a 15% tip for a restaurant meal. If the meal cost $16.80, how much money should Harold leave for the tip?
   a. $2.52
   b. $2.40
   c. $1.68
   d. $1.50

8. $8\frac{1}{5} =$
   a. $\frac{81}{5}$
   b. $\frac{5}{81}$
   c. $\frac{13}{5}$
   d. $\frac{41}{5}$

9. $7\frac{1}{10} - 5\frac{2}{3} =$
   a. $2\frac{1}{3}$
   b. $1\frac{13}{30}$
   c. $1\frac{2}{13}$
   d. $2\frac{2}{7}$

10. A farmer plants 75 rows of cabbage. Each row contains 40 cabbages. How many cabbages does the farmer plant?
 a. 115
 b. 1,150
 c. 1,500
 d. 3,000

Study the following graph, and then use it to answer questions 11 through 13.

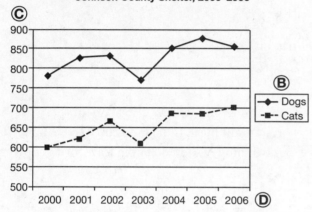

11. Which letter corresponds to the legend of the graph?
 a. A
 b. B
 c. C
 d. D

12. Which letter corresponds to the *y*-axis of the graph?
 a. A
 b. B
 c. C
 d. D

13. In what year were 670 cats and 830 dogs rescued?
 a. 2000
 b. 2002
 c. 2004
 d. 2006

14. A help line receives calls from people with legal questions. The automated voice service can handle simple calls, while challenging calls are directed to a live operator. Challenging calls account for $\frac{3}{5}$ of total calls, and among the challenging calls, 25% require a specialist. How many calls require a specialist on a day when there are 60 total calls?
 a. 9
 b. 15
 c. 21
 d. 27

15. Mr. Stone commutes 15 miles from home to work. After driving $\frac{2}{5}$ of the way from home to work, Mr. Stone stops to buy some breakfast. How far is Mr. Stone from work when he stops for breakfast?
 a. $14\frac{3}{5}$ miles
 b. 6 miles
 c. 4 miles
 d. 9 miles

16. $14 \div \frac{3}{4} =$
 a. $18\frac{2}{3}$
 b. $10\frac{1}{2}$
 c. $13\frac{1}{4}$
 d. $20\frac{1}{4}$

17. What is the decimal equivalent of $\frac{7}{8}$?
  a. 0.75
  b. 0.78
  c. 0.875
  d. 0.888

18. Three teaspoons of water equal 1 tablespoon of water; 2 tablespoons of water equal 1 ounce of water. How many teaspoons of water are there in a pint of water (1 pint = 16 ounces)?
  a. 23 teaspoons
  b. 32 teaspoons
  c. 96 teaspoons
  d. 192 teaspoons

Study the following table, and then use it to answer questions 19 and 20.

BREED	AVERAGE LIFE SPAN IN YEARS	AVERAGE WEIGHT IN POUNDS
Jack Russell Terrier	13.6	15
Chihuahua	13	5
Corgi	11.2	25
Weimaraner	10	75
Rhodesian Ridgeback	9.1	80
Great Dane	8.4	160

AVERAGE LIFE SPAN AND WEIGHT OF DOGS, BY BREED

19. The range of weights shown in the table is
  a. 160 pounds.
  b. 145 pounds.
  c. 80 pounds.
  d. 155 pounds.

20. Which of the following conclusions is best supported by the data in the table?
  a. Small dogs tend to live longer than large dogs.
  b. No dog has ever lived past the age of 15.
  c. A chihuahua is an excellent house pet.
  d. A great dane weighs more than most humans.

21. During a sale, the price of a suit is reduced by 30%. If the suit sold for $350 before the sale, what is the sale price of the suit?
  a. $105
  b. $175
  c. $245
  d. $320

22. Fred burns 60 calories a mile when he walks. How many miles must Fred walk to burn 400 calories?
  a. $1\frac{1}{2}$ miles
  b. 6 miles
  c. $6\frac{1}{3}$ miles
  d. $6\frac{2}{3}$ miles

23. $\frac{12}{9} =$
  a. $1\frac{1}{3}$
  b. $\frac{3}{4}$
  c. $12\frac{1}{3}$
  d. $1\frac{1}{9}$

24. Reduce $\frac{42}{51}$ to lowest terms.
  a. $\frac{4}{5}$
  b. $\frac{14}{17}$
  c. $\frac{21}{25}$
  d. $\frac{1}{9}$

25. A home association is building a new gazebo and wants support from its homeowners. After taking a survey, they discovered that 290 homeowners, or 40%, wanted the gazebo. How many total homeowners are in the neighborhood?

    a. 350

    b. 550

    c. 600

    d. 725

Study the following graph, and then use it to answer questions 26 and 27.

Preferred Lunch Hour at Office X

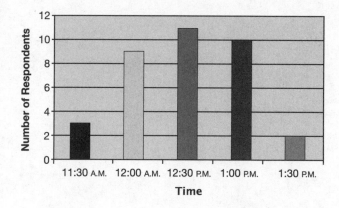

26. The workers at Office X were asked to choose their preferred time to start their lunch hour. The results of the survey are shown in the graph above. How many workers responded to the survey?

    a. 11

    b. 21

    c. 35

    d. 50

27. What is the range of the data shown?

    a. 9

    b. 10

    c. 11

    d. 35

28. Candice works for 9 hours every workday in a childcare center. If she spends 2.5 hours per day changing diapers, how many minutes does she spend per day NOT changing diapers?

    a. 90

    b. 150

    c. 390

    d. 540

29. If Brad can hike 10 miles in $2\frac{1}{4}$ hours, what is his average hiking speed?

    a. 3.5 miles per hour

    b. 4.8 miles per hour

    c. 4.44 miles per hour

    d. 5.33 miles per hour

30. Three of every 25 customers at a grocery store pays for his or her groceries with a check. What percentage of the customers pay for groceries with a check?

    a. 3%

    b. 12%

    c. 28%

    d. 75%

31. A file closet has 5 shelves. If each shelf can hold $7\frac{1}{4}$ boxes and there are 25 files in each box, how many total files can the file closet hold?

    a. 181.25

    b. 262.81

    c. 375.69

    d. 906.25

Study the following graph, and then use it to answer questions 32 and 33.

Percent of Vote Received

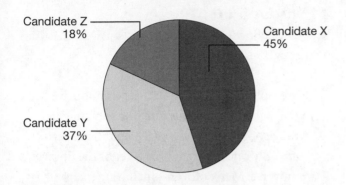

Candidate Z 18%

Candidate X 45%

Candidate Y 37%

32. The pie graph supports which of the following conclusions?
   a. More than 50% of eligible voters partici-pated in the election.
   b. Two candidates each received more than 40% of the vote.
   c. Candidate X received the greatest number of votes.
   d. Voters would have preferred to vote for Candidate W, but she was not running.

33. If 600 voters voted in the election, how many votes did Candidate Z receive?
   a. 60
   b. 108
   c. 222
   d. 260

34. A ream of paper weighs $5\frac{2}{5}$ pounds. Sturdy Paper Company sells reams of paper by the box. If each box contains 8 reams, how much does one of these boxes weigh?
   a. $40\frac{2}{5}$ pounds
   b. $40\frac{8}{5}$ pounds
   c. $43\frac{1}{5}$ pounds
   d. $43\frac{2}{5}$ pounds

35. Of 300 consumers polled, 180 reported that they purchase household cleaning products at least once per week. Based on these results, approximately how many consumers out of 1,000 could be expected to buy household cleaning products at least once per week?
   a. 480
   b. 600
   c. 720
   d. 880

36. $\frac{5}{6} \times 2\frac{1}{4} =$
   a. $\frac{46}{25}$
   b. $1\frac{2}{5}$
   c. $1\frac{7}{8}$
   d. $\frac{51}{24}$

37. A computer firm employs 2,032 people in the Southeast and 3,000 in the West. If, during an economic slowdown, the West loses 15% of its workers, how many total workers remain at the company nationwide?
   a. 2,032
   b. 2,550
   c. 3,000
   d. 4,582

38. An airplane flight takes exactly 4 hours to complete. If the airplane travels at an average speed of 480 miles per hour, how many miles long is the flight?
   a. 1,920 miles
   b. 2,000 miles
   c. 2,080 miles
   d. 2,400 miles

Study the following table, and then use it to answer questions 39 and 40.

PRICE OF LEADING DVD PLAYERS	
Ultrabo4000	$89.00
Vizzione MR-1	$74.50
Clara 718	$95.00
Abomino 1	$61.50

39. What is the average (arithmetic mean) price of the leading DVD players?
   a. $61.50
   b. $76.00
   c. $80.00
   d. $95.00

40. What is the range of prices shown in the table?
   a. $28.50
   b. $27.50
   c. $32.50
   d. $33.50

Section 2: Written Communication

Reading Comprehension—Questions 41 through 60

Read the following passage. Then, answer questions 41 through 44.

We generally think of libraries as publicly managed facilities offering books on a wide range of subjects, but, in fact, public libraries are only one highly visible facet of the library universe. Many offices—including many government offices—maintain large collections of reference materials, historical documents, and other relevant resources. In other words, such offices maintain libraries.

Any sizeable library collection must be organized in order to be useful. Librarians may organize a collection in any way they choose, but they generally choose between two options: the Dewey decimal classification system, which assigns a number between 000 and 999 to books based on their subject matter; and the Library of Congress classification system, which assigns an initial letter to books based on subject matter.

What are the differences between the two systems? The Dewey decimal system contains fewer subject classifications, with only ten general subject categories, as opposed to the Library of Congress's 21. The latter system not only uses more general subject categories, but also subdivides each category into more, and more specific, subcategories. In the area of specificity, it is generally agreed that the Library of Congress system is more efficient.

When it comes to ease of use, however, the Dewey decimal system is typically the favorite. Users searching for books about dogs, for example, almost always find it easier to remember the Dewey code for such books

(636) than the Library of Congress code (SF427). Furthermore, there is an internal logic to the entire Dewey system; the principles of code assignment are consistent throughout all ten subjects. Each Library of Congress subject category, on the other hand, was developed independently of the others, so each follows its own unique set of rules.

The differences between the two systems means that they are suited to <u>diverse</u> purposes. Ease of use makes the Dewey decimal system the system of choice for general public-use libraries. Research institutions, archives, and government agencies cataloging a great deal of highly specific or technical material, on the other hand, tend to prefer the Library of Congress system.

41. Which sentence best summarizes the main idea of the passage?
- **a.** The Library of Congress classification system is better than the Dewey decimal classification system.
- **b.** The differences between two cataloging systems makes each more appropriate for a particular purpose.
- **c.** More libraries should consider cataloging their collections alphabetically by the authors' last names, without regard to subject matter.
- **d.** There is an urgent need for librarians to develop a new classification system because the two most common systems are deeply flawed.

42. In the passage, the word *diverse* is closest in meaning to
- **a.** unlike.
- **b.** unimportant.
- **c.** scientific.
- **d.** illogical.

43. The passage supports which of the following conclusions?
- **a.** Libraries that use the Dewey system typically contain more books about dogs than libraries that use the Library of Congress system do.
- **b.** Libraries must pay a licensing fee to use either the Dewey or the Library of Congress system, so they typically choose whichever system is cheaper.
- **c.** The Library of Congress system is more difficult to memorize than is the Dewey system.
- **d.** Books with certain subjects cannot be classified within the Dewey system because the system makes no place for them.

44. According to the passage, in comparison to the Dewey decimal system, the Library of Congress system is
- **a.** appropriate only to collections owned by the U.S. Congress.
- **b.** more likely to be used by public libraries.
- **c.** easier for casual library users to master.
- **d.** more specific in its categorization of books.

Read the following passage. Then, answer questions 45 through 48.

Throughout the years, many professions have realized the importance of a college education as a prerequisite to employment, but this has not necessarily been true of U.S. police departments. For police, an educational requirement as a prerequisite for employment or promotion has been a topic of considerable controversy, dating back to the 1900s. One hundred years later, there still does not appear to be an agreement among police professionals as to whether the benefits of requiring higher educational standards outweigh the costs. Previous research findings have pointed to the beneficial effects of higher education on policing. Education correlates with a <u>myriad</u> of favorable factors including less authoritarian attitudes, fewer citizen complaints, more mature candidates, a greater understanding of constitutional rights, greater empathy for minorities and the effects of racial discrimination, greater understanding of diverse cultural values, and better communication skills. Police officers are often required to make difficult decisions, and they face ethical challenges throughout their careers. Research shows that higher education is positively related to sound ethical and moral decision making. College requires a commitment of time, effort, money, and motivation, but it often results in many positive outcomes. If police departments do not recognize this, they risk losing potentially valuable college-educated officers. Based on extant research, it appears that a college-educated officer is a more effective officer.

45. Which of the following would be the best title for this passage?
a. *Professionalizing the Police: Is Effectiveness Achieved Through Education?*
b. *Losing College-Educated Officers: A Tragedy for U.S. Police Departments*
c. *Strained Relationships: How to Improve Community and Police Relations*
d. *College and the Preservation of Constitutional Rights*

46. According to this passage, education benefits police in all of the following ways EXCEPT
a. fewer citizen complaints.
b. better ethical decision making.
c. better understanding of diverse values.
d. more authoritarian attitudes.

47. According to this passage, what topic remains controversial?
a. teaching officers to respect the rights of minority citizens
b. ensuring that officers make sound moral decisions
c. requiring college credits for police applicants
d. helping officers to communicate more effectively

48. As used in the passage, the word *myriad* is closest in meaning to
a. a bad decision.
b. a rare condition.
c. almost none.
d. a great number.

Read the following passage. Then, answer questions 49 through 52.

Some scholars believe that all roads in American criminology eventually lead to issues of race. Some available statistics show that African-Americans are disproportionately represented at every point in the criminal justice system. Considering the impact of the criminal justice system on minorities, the issue of race and crime is clearly integral to the study of criminal justice. Surprisingly, given the importance of race and ethnicity, criminal justice educators have often been reluctant to confront the issue directly. Some go so far as to declare that race has been virtually ignored in the area of criminal justice education. It would appear then that it is the responsibility of criminal justice educators to build a foundation of knowledge that integrates diverse multicultural perspectives.

Previous research examining race and crime education focused on undergraduate teaching. One survey of introductory criminal justice textbooks found that issues of race and ethnicity received inadequate coverage. Moreover, when African-American doctoral students were asked, 50% said that they regarded their professors as insensitive to issues of race; at the same time, 25% of white students described their professors as insensitive to issues of race. Furthermore, while it is widely recognized that race and ethnicity must be incorporated into any effective criminal justice or criminology program, there is no consensus on the best method to do so. Some scholars suggest that a segment of the core knowledge must involve a multicultural perspective, while others emphasize the importance of recognizing the work of African-American scholars, and note how their work has been historically ignored by the mainstream.

49. What is the primary purpose of this passage?
   a. to review how race is presented in criminal justice textbooks
   b. to establish the extent to which race and ethnicity are taught to students
   c. to argue that the work of African-American scholars should be studied by students
   d. to teach students about how race and ethnicity should be taught

50. According to the passage, who believes that teaching race and ethnicity to criminal justice students is important?
   a. the police
   b. students
   c. some scholars
   d. doctoral students

51. According to the passage, why is race and ethnicity ignored by criminal justice scholars?
   a. The topic is omitted from textbooks.
   b. Some teachers are reluctant to discuss the topic.
   c. Some students are not interested in the topic.
   d. Doctoral students do not believe the topic is important to their teachers.

52. According to the passage, why is it important to study issues of race and ethnicity?
   a. Racial differences appear at each stage of the criminal justice system.
   b. African-American scholars believe the topic has been ignored.
   c. Undergraduate students have asked for it to be taught.
   d. Criminal justice educators believe it may be important.

Read the following passage. Then, answer questions 53 through 56.

The political activity of federal employees presents policy makers with a double-edged sword of a problem. On one hand, the integrity of the federal government requires that employees not pursue personal political goals through their offices; therefore, some restrictions on the political activities of federal employees seem <u>prudent</u> and even necessary. On the other hand, individual liberty and the right to participate in the political process are two bedrock principles of American government. Surely we cannot deny our government's employees rights so fundamental to the nation's identity.

Government leaders have been visiting and revisiting this question since the beginning of the republic. Thomas Jefferson issued an executive circular in 1801 advising federal employees to abstain from campaigning and electioneering. The Pendleton Act of 1883, which created a merit-based system for awarding civil service jobs, further codified proscribed political behavior.

These measures were deemed inadequate to check political coercion and patronage in the 1930s, when the massive expansion of the federal government created many new opportunities for the abuse of power. In response, Congress passed the Hatch Act of 1939, which prohibited a wide range of political activities by federal employees. The law made it illegal for federal civil servants to endorse candidates, seek political contributions, or run for office with the endorsement of a political party. Not all political activity was forbidden; Hatch allowed federal employees to vote, discuss politics privately, and contribute money to political parties.

The constitutionality of the Hatch Act has been challenged several times, with two such cases reaching the Supreme Court; in both instances,

the court ruled that the Hatch Act was indeed constitutional. Nonetheless, discontent ultimately led to a 1993 amendment that allowed federal employees to participate in elections so long as their activity occurred outside their place of work. At the same time, the amendment increased penalties for those who abused the powers of their offices for political gain. At the signing ceremony, President Bill Clinton observed that "People who devote their lives to public service should not be denied the right to participate more fully in the democratic process. This law moves us in a more sensible direction."

53. As used in the passage, the word *prudent* is closest in meaning to
a. optional.
b. ill-advised.
c. sensible.
d. counterproductive.

54. The author's main purpose in writing this passage is to
a. report the historical developments of a particular issue in American government.
b. argue that the 1993 amendment to the Hatch Act had a destructive impact on good governance in the United States.
c. describe the conditions under which the Hatch Act of 1939 was passed.
d. propose the repeal of both the Pendleton Act of 1883 and the Hatch Act of 1939.

55. According to the passage, Thomas Jefferson did which of the following?
a. oversaw the massive expansion of the federal government
b. suggested to federal employees that they refrain from public politics
c. signed an amendment to the Hatch Act
d. endorsed the Pendleton Act

56. The passage supports which of the following conclusions?

   a. Under the Hatch Act, federal employees were prohibited from engaging in all political activity, including voting.

   b. Thomas Jefferson believed that there was no conflict in holding a federal office and engaging in such political activity as campaigning for candidates.

   c. The amendment to the Hatch Act aimed to preserve integrity in government while freeing federal employees to become more politically active as private citizens.

   d. Under the Hatch Act, federal employees could actively promote political parties but not individual candidates.

Read the following passage. Then, answer questions 57 through 60.

Community policing has frequently been touted as the best way to reform urban law enforcement. The idea of putting more officers on foot patrol in high crime areas, where relations with the police have frequently been strained, was most famously implemented in Houston in 1983 under then-Commissioner Lee Brown. Brown believed that officers should be accessible to the community at the street level. If officers were assigned to the same area over a period of time, those officers would eventually build a network of trust with neighborhood residents. As a result, merchants and residents in the community would be more likely to inform officers about criminal activities in the area and support police intervention.

Since Brown's <u>initiative</u>, many large cities have experimented with community-oriented policing services (COPS), with somewhat mixed results. Some have found that police and citizens are grateful for the opportunity to work together. Others have found that unrealistic expectations by citizens and resistance from officers have combined to hinder the effectiveness of COPS.

Overall, however, the verdict on community policing is positive, as the concept has evidently yielded notable successes. Since the federal government began funding COPS programs, national crime rates have declined measurably. Although this drop in crime rates has occurred nationwide (including areas that receive no federal assistance), the drops have been more pronounced in those locations that receive substantial COPS funding.

Unfortunately, stress on the federal budget in the post–9/11 era has resulted in a sharp decrease in federal assistance to local police. This decrease comes at a time when the federal government is expecting local law enforcement to contribute more to the national fight against terror, further increasing the strain on state and city government law enforcement budgets. As a result, many have had to reduce or even eliminate their COPS programs. The debate over the effectiveness of COPS programs might once and for all be settled as a result; if crime rates increase as COPS programs disappear, that would certainly provide a strong indicator that the programs are effective in reducing crime.

57. Which of the following best summarizes the main idea of the passage?

   a. Opponents of community policing correctly argue that such programs cause more problems than they solve.

   b. Community policing is a promising concept, but implementation of effective community policing programs faces several problems.

   c. Many local police forces lack the funding necessary to support community policing programs.

   d. Lee Brown is an innovative law enforcement leader whose talents should be utilized by the federal government.

58. As used in the passage, the word *initiative* most nearly means
 a. misfortune.
 b. blunder.
 c. victory.
 d. decision.

59. In paragraph 3, the author suggests that
 a. community policing programs have helped to reduce crime rates.
 b. community policing programs have had no effect on crime rates.
 c. community policing programs have resulted in an increase in crime rates.
 d. the government does not accurately track crime rates, making it impossible to determine the effectiveness of community policing programs.

60. According to Commissioner Brown, community policing is effective because
 a. criminals are less likely to commit crimes if they are familiar with their local police officers.
 b. community policing emphasizes the need for street patrols late at night, the time at which most crimes occur.
 c. community policing deputizes members of the community, allowing them to make arrests without an actual police officer present.
 d. citizens are more likely to cooperate with police if they have a closer relationship with local officers.

Spelling—Questions 61 through 65
Select the choice that is spelled correctly.

61. The shopkeeper was known for selling the best _____ in town.
 a. merchandise
 b. merchendise
 c. merchindise

62. The carpenter tied a red _____ around her forehead to keep the sweat out of her eyes.
 a. bandanner
 b. banndana
 c. bandanna

63. Jim's outburst was not planned; on the contrary, it was entirely _____.
 a. spontaneous
 b. spontainious
 c. spontaineus

64. Which of the following words is spelled incorrectly?
 a. frivolous
 b. embelish
 c. confound

65. Which of the following words is spelled incorrectly?
 a. lunar
 b. scapegoat
 c. retalliate

Vocabulary—Questions 66 through 70

Select the best answer for each question.

66. Find the word that is closest in meaning to the underlined word.
<u>attest</u> to the truth
   a. contradict
   b. verify
   c. inquire

67. Find the word that is closest in meaning to the underlined word.
a <u>consumate</u> performer
   a. expert
   b. novice
   c. strange

68. Find the word that is most nearly the opposite of the underlined word.
the <u>virtuoso</u> musician
   a. amateur
   b. experimental
   c. unpopular

69. Find the word that best completes the sentence.
The _____ window shades kept the hotel room nice and dark well into the late morning.
   a. malfunctioning
   b. flimsy
   c. opaque

70. Find the word that best completes the sentence.
Minimum wage is poor _____ for a fry cook's hard work.
   a. reprisal
   b. retribution
   c. remuneration

Grammar—Questions 71 through 80

Select the best answer for each question.

71. Which of the following is a complete sentence?
   a. The onset of the Cold War, having been brought on by natural tensions between the communist and free worlds and the end of World War II.
   b. Natural tensions between the communist and free worlds, the end of World War II, bringing on the onset of the Cold War.
   c. The onset of the Cold War was brought on by natural tensions between the communist and free worlds and the end of World War II.

72. Select the sentence that is written most correctly.
   a. Genetically modified to increase yield and reduce disease, many consumers do not trust crops developed recently by agricultural scientists.
   b. Genetically modified to increase yield and reduce disease, crops developed recently by agricultural scientists are distrusted by many consumers.
   c. Crops developed recently by agricultural scientists have been genetically modified to increase yield and reduce disease that consumers do not trust.

73. Select the sentence that is written most correctly.
   a. Last Thursday, my Mother, my Aunt Barbara, and I went to the museum to see an exhibit of African art.
   b. Last Thursday, my mother, my Aunt Barbara, and I went to the museum to see an exhibit of African art.
   c. Last Thursday, my mother, my aunt Barbara, and I went to the Museum to see an exhibit of african art.

74. Select the sentence that is written most correctly.
   a. The Band we saw last night consisted of two guitarists, a bass player, a drummer a keyboardist and two percussionists.
   b. The band we saw last night consisted of two, guitarists, a bass player, a drummer, a keyboardist, and, two percussionists.
   c. The band we saw last night consisted of two guitarists, a bass player, a drummer, a keyboardist, and two percussionists.

75. Select the sentence that is written most correctly.
   a. The perpetrator was stopped by the police officer, and he struck him with a stick.
   b. The perpetrator, striking him with a stick, was stopped by the police officer.
   c. The police officer stopped the perpetrator, who then struck the officer with a stick.

76. Select the sentence that is written most correctly.
   a. Billy wasn't going to join us at the park, but he couldn't refuse the invitation after I told him there is a basketball court there.
   b. Billy was'nt going to join us at the park, but he could'nt refuse the invitation after I told him there is a basketball court there.
   c. Billy wasnt going to join us at the park, but he couldnt refuse the invitation after I told him there is a basketball court there.

77. Select the sentence that is written most correctly.
   a. Make sure that everyone in the office have turned off their desk lights before leaving for the day.
   b. Make sure that everyone in the office has turned off his or her desk light before leaving for the day.
   c. Make sure that everyone in the office has turned off their desk lights before leaving for the day.

78. Select the sentence that is written most correctly.
   a. The benefits of this therapy far outweigh its potential drawbacks.
   b. The positive benefits of this therapy far outweigh its potentially negative drawbacks.
   c. The benefits of this therapy far outweigh their potentially negative drawbacks.

79. Select the sentence that is written most correctly.
- **a.** After completing the obstacle course Renee proceeded to the shooting range.
- **b.** After completing the obstacle course, Renee proceeded to the shooting range.
- **c.** After completing the obstacle course, Renee proceeded, to the shooting range.

80. Select the sentence that is written most correctly.
- **a.** David asked me "whether I wanted to attend the baseball game with him tonight?"
- **b.** David asked me "whether I wanted to attend the baseball game with him tonight."
- **c.** David asked me whether I wanted to attend the baseball game with him tonight.

Section 3: Civil Service Skills

Customer Service— Questions 81 through 85
Select the best answer for each question.

81. Records of an office's prior contacts with a customer should be maintained in order to
- **a.** document the amount of work done by the office so that staffing will not be reduced.
- **b.** make sure that no one customer overuses the office's facilities and services.
- **c.** minimize the need for the customer to provide the same basic information (e.g., address, Social Security number) repeatedly.
- **d.** prevent customers from asking for and receiving services that have already been provided.

82. When one is creating a recorded message to be heard by customers calling a government agency after hours of operation, which of the following pieces of information is least important?
- **a.** the agency's hours of operation
- **b.** the street address of the agency
- **c.** instructions on how to access the agency's website
- **d.** instructions on how to leave a message

83. An agency's phone system offers the capacity for audio during a customer's hold time. The agency would be best served to use this capacity to provide
  a. music to entertain customers while they are waiting.
  b. live programming from a local talk-radio station.
  c. live audio, transmitted via speaker phone, of the office with which they are waiting to speak.
  d. a recorded message providing choices to commonly asked questions.

84. The term *abandonment rate* refers to the
  a. frequency with which customers calling an office hang up before reaching a representative.
  b. number of times a customer must contact an office before receiving final resolution to an inquiry.
  c. average amount of time a customer visiting an office must wait on a service line before speaking with a representative.
  d. speed at which a government agent can redirect a telephone inquiry to the appropriate recipient.

85. An agency serving walk-in customers should consider offering appointments whenever
  a. customers cannot begin resolving their inquiry upon arrival.
  b. average wait times for customers exceed one hour.
  c. average wait times for customers exceed 15 minutes.
  d. such a policy would result in fewer visitors to the agency's office.

Memory—Questions 86 through 90

Take five minutes to study the following picture. Then, answer questions 86 and 87 without looking back at the picture.

86. The number of destinations other than Broadway Station that are shown in the photo is
   a. one.
   b. two.
   c. three.
   d. zero; no other destinations are shown in the photo.

87. Based on the directional arrows on the signage at Broadway Station, a rail rider could correctly assume that the train will be heading _____ from Broadway Station to Union Station.
   a. south
   b. north
   c. east
   d. west

Take five minutes to study the following text. Then, answer questions 88 through 90 without looking back at the text.

A city is divided into five sectors. In each sector, garbage is collected twice a week and recycling is scheduled once a week, according to the schedule that follows:

SECTOR	GARBAGE	RECYCLING
1	Monday, Thursday	Friday
2	Tuesday, Saturday	Wednesday
3	Wednesday, Saturday	Thursday
4	Tuesday, Friday	Saturday
5	Monday, Friday	Tuesday

88. Recycling is collected in sector 2 on
   a. Monday.
   b. Tuesday.
   c. Wednesday.
   d. Saturday.

89. Garbage is collected Monday through Saturday. On which day is recycling NOT collected?
   a. Monday
   b. Wednesday
   c. Friday
   d. Saturday

90. In three of five sectors, the second garbage collection of the week occurs exactly three days after the first. In which two sectors is this NOT the case?
   a. 1 and 2
   b. 1 and 4
   c. 2 and 5
   d. 3 and 4

Coding—Questions 91 through 100

To answer questions 91 through 95, refer to the following scenario.

A municipal agency uses a code to log each visitor to its office. Each code is five characters long and is assigned according to the rules that follow. Each code is preceded by the time of the visit (format: 10:00 A.M.).

Gender
M = Male
F = Female

Citizenship
C = Citizen
N = Noncitizen

Age
1 = under age 18
2 = age 18 to 30
3 = age 31 to 65
4 = over age 65

Residence
V = northeast quadrant of city
W = southeast quadrant of city
X = northwest quadrant of city
Y = southwest quadrant of city
Z = outside the city

Purpose of Visit
5 = responding to summons
6 = filing complaint
7 = applying for employment
8 = other

91. A male citizen, age 38, who resides in the northwest quadrant of the city visits the office at 11:46 A.M. to file a complaint. How should this visit be coded?
a. MC3X6
b. MC38 11:46 A.M. X6
c. 11:46 A.M. MC3X6
d. MC 11:46 A.M. V6

92. A female citizen, age 67, who resides outside the city visits the office at 4:00 P.M. to solicit charitable contributions from employees. How should this visit be coded?
a. FC67Z 4:00 P.M.8
b. FC67X8 4:00 P.M.
c. 4:00 P.M. FC67Z8
d. 4:00 P.M. FC4Z8

93. A male noncitizen who resides in the southeast quadrant of the city visits the office at 10:45 A.M. to respond to a summons. He is 16 years old. How should the visit be coded?
a. 10:45 A.M. MN1W5
b. 10:45 A.M. MC1Z8
c. MNW 11:45 A.M. 168
d. MNW168 11:45 A.M.

94. Which of the following describes the visitor whose visit was coded 12:00 P.M. FC3Y6?
a. The visitor was a noncitizen residing in the southwest quadrant of the city.
b. The visitor was a female who filed a complaint.
c. The visitor was a male citizen over the age of 65.
d. The visitor was a female under the age of 18.

95. The visitor whose visit was coded 9:10 A.M. MC2Z7 visited the office in order to
a. respond to a summons.
b. file a complaint.
c. apply for employment.
d. none of the above

To answer questions 96 through 100, refer to the following scenario.

A state assigns numbers to the fishing licenses it issues using the following code:
2 letters = first two letters of county of residence
8 digits = license recipient's date of birth (e.g., September 30, 1957 = 09301957)
2 letters = license recipient's initials (e.g., Robert Sims = RS)
2 digits = license recipient's height in inches (rounded to nearest whole number)
3 letters = randomly assigned

96. Danielle Valenzuela receives a fishing license. She resides in Ardmore County and is 62 inches tall. Her date of birth is May 11, 1973. Which of the following could be her fishing license number?
a. AR05111973DV62
b. DV05111973AR62MPY
c. DV051173AR62
d. AR05111973DV62XLE

97. Milton Mazur, a resident of Hazelton County, receives a fishing license. His date of birth is December 7, 1948. He is 70.4 inches tall. Which of the following could be his fishing license number?
a. HA12071948MM70EEE
b. HA12071948MM70.4WQA
c. MM12071948HA70LBD
d. MMHC120714870.4

98. Jerome Fielding, a resident of Buncomb County, is 75 inches tall. His date of birth is August 26, 1980. The number assigned to his license, BU26081980JF75RBC, is incorrectly assigned. What error does his license number contain?
   a. His height was incorrectly recorded.
   b. His height and date of birth have been transposed.
   c. The three randomly assigned letters have been omitted.
   d. His date of birth is incorrectly recorded.

99. A fishing license with the number TR11151938WE72DVA could belong to an individual named
   a. Toni Rouse.
   b. Warren Evers.
   c. David Van Allen.
   d. Victoria Andrews.

100. A fishing license with the number LA08081967MU66ABO belongs to someone
   a. born in 1967.
   b. born in 1966.
   c. who lives in Munroe County.
   d. named Linda Almonte.

Answers

Section 1: Mathematics

1. b. To answer this question, you must first determine how many subscriptions were sold by Barb, Peter, and Boris, and then take the sum of those subscriptions and subtract it from the total of 1,500 to determine how many Jason sold. Barb sold 20% of the total (1,500), which equals $1,500 \times .20 = 300$. It is given that Peter sold 325 subscriptions. Boris sold $\frac{7}{5}$ of what Peter sold. To determine this multiply 325 by the numerator (7), and divide the product by the denominator (5). So, $325 \times 7 = 2,275$; $2,275 \div 5 = 455$. Thus, $1,500 - 300$ (Barb) $- 325$ (Peter) 455 (Boris) $= 420$. Therefore, Jason sold 420 newspaper subscriptions.

2. b. Find the difference between $35\frac{1}{2}$ and $42\frac{3}{4}$. First, subtract $\frac{3}{4}$ and $\frac{1}{2}$ to get $\frac{1}{4}$. Then, subtract $42 - 35$ to get 7. So, the difference is $7 - \frac{1}{4}$, which is the same as $7 and 0.25, or choice **b**.

3. d. To rewrite a fraction as a percent, create an equation that allows you to rewrite the fraction with a denominator of 100. Here's the equation you should write: $\frac{18}{25} = \frac{x}{100}$. Next, cross multiply to create the equation $1,800 = 25x$. Finally, divide both sides of the equation by 25 to produce the result $72 = x$. So, $\frac{72}{100} = 72\%$, which is the correct choice.

4. b. There are 3 items at $18.42 *each*. Multiply 3 times 18.42 to get $55.26. Then, subtract $100.00 - 55.26$ to get $44.74.

5. c. Multiply 150 times $\frac{3}{5}$ to get comic books. Justin buys $\frac{1}{3}$ of the 90 comic books. So, multiply 90 times $\frac{1}{3}$ to get 30 comic books.

6. b. To answer this question, you must rewrite the fractions over a common denominator; 12 is a good common denominator because it is divisible by 2, 4, and 6, the denominators in the problem. Rewrite the problem as $\frac{6}{12} + 4\frac{9}{12} + 2\frac{10}{12}$. Next, add the fractions; $\frac{6}{12} + \frac{9}{12} + \frac{10}{12} = \frac{25}{12}$, which can be rewritten as the mixed number $2\frac{1}{12}$. Add $4 + 2 + 2\frac{1}{2}$ to get $8\frac{1}{12}$.

7. a. To calculate 15% of \$16.80, multiply \$16.80 by 0.15. The product, \$2.52, is your correct answer. You might also try this shortcut: Find 10% of \$16.80 by moving the decimal point one place to the left. Thus, 10% of \$16.80 is \$1.68. Immediately eliminate choices **c** and **d**, because 15% of \$16.80 must be greater than 10% of \$16.80. Next, find 5% of \$16.80 by dividing \$1.68 (10% of \$16.80) in half. Half of \$1.68 is \$0.84. Therefore, 15% of \$16.80 equals \$1.68 + \$0.84 = \$2.52.

8. d. Write the mixed number $8\frac{1}{5}$ as an improper fraction. To do this, multiply the whole number 8 by the denominator 5 to get the product 40. Add 40 to the numerator 1 and rewrite the fraction $\frac{41}{5}$. Choices **a**, **b**, and **c** all represent results achieved by incorrect procedures; if you chose one of these, review the correct procedure for rewriting mixed numbers as improper fractions.

9. b. To answer this question. One way is to rewrite each mixed number as an improper fraction, and then find a common denominator for the two fractions and subtract. By this method, you would rewrite $7\frac{1}{10}$ as $\frac{71}{10}$ and $5\frac{2}{3}$ as $\frac{17}{3}$. You would then rewrite the improper fractions over the common denominator of 30 as $\frac{213}{30}$ and $\frac{170}{30}$. Finally, you would subtract $\frac{213}{30} - \frac{170}{30}$ to get $\frac{43}{30}$, which equals the mixed number $1\frac{13}{30}$.

10. d. The farmer plants 40 cabbages in each of 75 rows; therefore, he plants 40 × 75 cabbages, which equals 3,000 cabbages.

11. b. The legend of a graph shows which line represents which set of data. In this graph, the legend tells you which line represents the number of dogs and which line represents the number of cats.

12. c. The y-axis is the vertical axis of a graph.

13. b. The dashed line represents cats. Find the point for 670 along the y-axis (vertical). Circle this point. Then, find the point for 830 on the solid line for dogs. Circle this point. Read the years along the x-axis (horizontal) to see the points line up over the year 2002.

14. a. To answer this question, convert the percentage of challenging calls (25%) to a fraction, which is $\frac{1}{4}$. Next, multiply the fraction of challenging calls ($\frac{3}{5}$) by the fraction representing challenging calls that require a specialist ($\frac{1}{4}$): $\frac{3}{5} \times \frac{1}{4} = \frac{3}{20}$. Lastly, multiply the total number of calls (60) by the numerator (3) and divide by the denominator (20) to determine the number of calls that required a specialist: $60 \times 3 = 180; 180 \div 20 = 9$.

15. d. First find $\frac{2}{5}$ of 15, the distance from Mr. Stone's home to his work, by multiplying $\frac{2}{5}$ and 15. $\frac{2}{5}$ of 15 equals 6, meaning that Mr. Stone has driven 6 miles when he stops for breakfast. The question asks how far Mr. Stone is from work, however, so you must subtract 6 (the distance traveled so far) from 15 (the entire distance of the trip) to determine how much distance remains in his trip. Thus, the correct answer to the question is 9.

16. a. To divide fractions, multiply 14 by the reciprocal of $\frac{3}{4}$. To find the reciprocal of $\frac{3}{4}$, invert it. Thus, $14 \div \frac{3}{4}$ should be rewritten as $14 \times \frac{4}{3}$, which equals $\frac{56}{3}$. Rewrite $\frac{56}{3}$ as $18\frac{2}{3}$ to identify the correct answer.

17. c. To find the decimal equivalent of a fraction, divide the numerator by the denominator: $7 \div 8 = 0.875$.

18. c. Because 3 teaspoons of water equal 1 tablespoon of water and 2 tablespoons of water equal 1 ounce of water, 3×2 teaspoons of water equal 1 ounce of water. Therefore, there are 6 teaspoons of water in 1 ounce of water, and there are 6×16 teaspoons of water in a pint of water; $6 \times 16 = 96$, so 96 is the correct answer to this question.

19. d. The range of a data set is the difference between the greatest and least values in the set. The greatest value in this set is 160 and the least value is 5, so the range of the data is $160 - 5$, which equals 155.

20. a. The data in the table show a correlation between weight and expected life span. In general, smaller dogs tend to live longer than larger dogs. Choice **b** cannot be correct because the table tells us about the average age for an entire breed of dogs only, not the lifespan of any individual member of that breed. Choice **c** cannot be correct because the table does not contain any information about how good or bad a house pet each breed makes. Choice **d** cannot be correct because the table does not include any information about the weight of an average human.

21. c. You can solve this problem by finding 30% of $350 and subtracting the result from $350, the original price of the suit. Or, you can find 70% of the price of the suit, because a suit discounted by 30% will sell for 70% of its original price. Calculate 70% of $350 by finding 10% of $350 and multiplying the result by 7; 10% of $350 is $35, and 35×7 = $245.

22. d. You can solve this problem by dividing the goal of 400 calories burnt by the rate of 60 calories a mile. $400 \div 60 = \frac{20}{3}$, which equals $6\frac{2}{3}$.

23. a. The question asks you to rewrite the improper fraction $\frac{12}{9}$ as a mixed number. To do this, divide the numerator 12 by the denominator 9. The result is $1\frac{3}{9}$, which reduces to $1\frac{1}{3}$.

24. b. To reduce $\frac{42}{51}$, you must find a number that divides evenly into both 42 and 51. Both numbers are divisible by 3, so you can reduce $\frac{42}{51}$ to $\frac{14}{17}$.

25. d. Since the total is unknown, let variable x represent the total. Write 40% as the decimal 0.40, and find x in the equation $0.40x = 290$. To solve, divide both sides by 0.40 to get $x = \frac{290}{0.40} = 725$. The correct answer is choice **d**.

26. c. To determine the number of workers who responded to the survey, add the number of workers who gave each response. Three workers chose 11:30 A.M., nine workers chose 12 P.M., 11 chose 12:30 P.M., ten chose 1 P.M., and two chose 1:30 P.M.; $3 + 9 + 11 + 10 + 2 = 35$, the correct answer to this question.

27. a. The range of a data set is the difference between the greatest and least values in the set. The greatest value in this set is 11 and the least value is 2, so the range of the data is $11 - 2$, which equals 9.

28. c. There are 60 minutes in 1 hour. To find the minutes she spends changing diapers, multiply 2.5×60 to get 150 minutes. Multiply 9×60 to get 540 total minutes in her workday. Candice does not change diapers for $540 - 150$ minutes, which is 390 minutes.

29. c. The average speed is the total miles divided by the number of hours. So, Brad's speed is 10 miles divided by $2\frac{1}{4}$ hours. First change $2\frac{1}{4}$ to the decimal 2.25. Then, divide 10 by 2.25 to get 4.44.

30. b. To rewrite a proportion as a percent, create an equation that allows you to rewrite the fraction with a denominator of 100. Here's the equation you should write: $\frac{3}{25} = \frac{x}{100}$. Next, cross multiply to create the equation $300 = 25x$. Finally, divide both sides of the equation by 25 to produce the result $12 = x$. Because a percent is the numerator of a fraction when it is written with a denominator of 100, this is the correct answer.

31. d. Change $7\frac{1}{4}$ to the decimal 7.25. Since the closet can hold 5 shelves with 7.25 boxes each, multiply 5 shelves times 7.25 to find the closet can hold a total of 36.25 boxes. Each box has 25 files. So, multiply 36.25 boxes by 25 to get 906.25 files.

32. c. The pie chart shows that Candidate X received 45% of the votes, more than any other single candidate received. Thus, the graph supports the conclusion that Candidate X received the greatest number of votes. The graph does not mention what percent of eligible voters participated in the election, so choice **a** cannot be correct. Only one candidate received more than 40% of the vote, so choice **b** is incorrect. The graph does not mention whether voters would have chosen Candidate W if she were running, so choice **d** cannot be correct.

33. b. A total of 600 votes were cast in the election. Candidate Z received 18% of the votes; therefore, Candidate Z received 18% of 600 votes; $\frac{18}{100} \times 600 = 108$, the correct answer.

34. c. One way to solve this problem is to convert the mixed number $5\frac{2}{5}$ into an improper fraction. To do this, multiply the whole number (5) by the denominator (5) to get 25. Add 25 to the numerator (2) and set above the denominator: $\frac{27}{5}$. Next, multiply the numerator by 8 and divide by the denominator: $27 \times 8 = 216$; $216 \div 5$ is equivalent to the mixed number $43\frac{1}{5}$.

35. b. 180 of 300 consumers polled purchase household cleaning products once per week. To find out how many of 1,000 consumers would be likely to purchase household cleaning products once per week, write the proportion $\frac{180}{300} = \frac{x}{1,000}$ and solve by cross multiplying to get $300 = 18,000$. Divide both sides by 300 to get $\frac{x}{600} = 600$, the solution to the problem.

36. c. First write the mixed number $2\frac{1}{4}$ as an improper fraction $\frac{9}{4}$. To multiply two fractions $\frac{5}{6}$ and $\frac{9}{4}$, multiply the numerators and then multiply denominators. So, $\frac{5}{6} \times \frac{9}{4} = \frac{45}{24}$; $\frac{45}{24}$ reduces to $\frac{15}{8}$, so the correct answer is $1\frac{7}{8}$.

37. d. Change 15% to the decimal 0.15 and multiply 3,000 times 0.15 to get 450. So, the adjusted number of workers in the West is $3,000 - 450$ which is 2,550. The total number of workers in the companies is now 2,032 in the Southeast and 2,550 in the West for a total of $2,032 + 2,550$, which is 4,582 workers.

38. a. To solve rate problems, apply the equation $rt = d$, where r equals rate, t equals time, and d equals distance. This problem provides the time (4 hours) and the rate (480 miles per hour), allowing you to write the equation $4(480) = d$; 4×480 equals 1,920, the correct answer to the problem.

39. c. To find the mean price of the DVD players shown in the table, add all the prices together and divide by the number of DVD players shown. The sum of the four prices is $320.00 $320.00 divided by 4, the number of DVD players shown, is $80.00, so $80.00 is the average price.

40. d. The range of a data set is the difference between the greatest and least values in the set. The greatest value in this set is $95.00 and the least value is $61.50, so the range of the data is $95.00 – $61.50, which equals $33.50.

Section 2: Written Communication

41. b. The main idea of the passage is that there are significant differences between the Library of Congress classification system and the Dewey decimal classification system. The details of the passage enumerate those differences. An expression of the main idea of the passage should focus on the fact that there are important differences between the two systems; of the choices, choice **b** does that best. Choices **a**, **c**, and **d** express opinions that the author never states, so neither can be the correct answer.

42. a. Reread the sentence, substituting each choice for the word *diverse*. Of the four choices, only choice **a** makes sense in context.

43. c. The passage points out that "Users searching for books about dogs, for example, almost always find it easier to remember the Dewey code for such books (636) than the Library of Congress code (SF427)" and also that "there is an internal logic to the entire Dewey system" while "[e]ach Library of Congress subject category . . . was developed independently of the others, so each follows its own unique set of rules." These statements all support the conclusion in choice **c**.

44. d. The passage states this clearly in paragraph 2. Of the incorrect choices, choice **a** covers information not mentioned in the passage, while choices **b** and **c** are directly contradicted by information in the passage.

45. a. The purpose of this passage is to describe how education can improve police effectiveness. It begins by telling the reader that many professions have recognized the importance of requiring college as a prerequisite to employment. It then informs the reader about the benefits associated with obtaining a college education.

46. d. The fourth sentence lists many of the benefits associated with a college education, but this list does not include a more authoritarian attitude among police officers. In fact, the author states that higher education produces less authoritarian attitudes.

47. c. The second sentence tells the reader that requiring a college education for police officers has been controversial for over 100 years. The other choices contain the benefits associated with education, but are not the main source of controversy.

48. d. Reread the sentence, substituting each choice for the word *myriad*. Choices **a** and **b** make no sense in context; choice **c** has the opposite meaning of *myriad*. *A great number* makes the most sense in context, so choice **d** is the best answer.

49. b. The overall subject of the passage concerns the extent to which race and ethnicity are taught to criminal justice students. Choices **a**, **c**, and **d**, are not even mentioned in the passage, so they should be eliminated.

50. c. This is a slightly tricky one because the passage acknowledges that many students feel that their professors need to be more sensitive to issues of race. However, the passage does not suggest that students believe teaching race and ethnicity in criminal justice courses is directly important, which means choice **b** is incorrect. The first sentence of the passage states "Some scholars believe all roads in American criminology eventually lead to issues of race," so choice **c** is the best answer.

51. b. The answer is clearly stated in the first sentence of the second paragraph: "even given the importance of race and ethnicity, criminal justice educators have been reluctant to confront the issue directly."

52. a. The first paragraph establishes that race statistics show disproportionate representation of people of color at each stage of the criminal justice system. The other answer choices are not supported by the passage.

53. c. Use context clues here; the sentence tells us that the *prudent* restrictions are perhaps necessary. Could they be *optional*? No, they can't be optional and necessary, so choice **a** cannot be correct. Can they be *ill-advised* or *counterproductive* and also be necessary? No, so choices **b** and **d** must also be incorrect. The answer must be choice **c**, *sensible*.

54. a. The passage provides a summary of regulations on the political activity of federal employees. Both choices **b** and **d** suggest that the author has written a persuasive passage that argues a particular point of view; in fact, the author has written an informational passage that does not expound any opinion. Thus, choices **b** and **d** must both be incorrect. Choice **c** refers to a detail in the passage; the answer to a main idea question, however, must address the entire passage, not just one detail in it.

55. b. In paragraph 2, the passage states that "Thomas Jefferson issued an executive circular in 1801 advising federal employees to abstain from campaigning and electioneering." Choice **b** is a good paraphrase of this sentence.

56. c. This statement is supported in the final paragraph, which states that "discontent ultimately led to a 1993 amendment that allowed federal employees to participate in elections so long as their activity occurred outside their place of work. At the same time, the amendment increased penalties for those who abused the powers of their offices for political gain." Thus, the passage supports the conclusion drawn in choice **c**.

57. b. The passage discusses both the potential strengths and some of the possible problems with community policing programs; thus, choice **b** is a good summary of the entire passage. Choices **a** and **c** address specific details in the passage; the answer to a main idea question, however, must address the entire passage, not just one detail in it. Choice **d** offers an opinion that the author never states or implies.

58. d. Consider the context; *initiative* clearly connotes something positive, so choices **a** and **b** cannot be correct. Although Brown's *initiative* may have represented a victory, that is not the clear sense of the word here; therefore, choice **c** is not the best answer. Clearly Brown made a *decision* to implement the COPS program in Houston. Thus, the word closest in meaning to *initiative* is choice **d**, *decision*.

59. a. Paragraph 3 states that "Although this drop in crime rates has occurred nationwide (including areas that receive no federal assistance), the drops have been more pronounced in those locations that receive substantial COPS funding." The fact that the drops have been greater in areas that receive COPS funding suggests that COPS programs have contributed to the drop in crime rates.

60. d. The passage points out that "Brown believed that officers should be accessible to the community at the street level. If officers were assigned to the same area over a period of time, those officers would eventually build a network of trust with neighborhood residents. As a result, merchants and residents in the community would be more likely to inform officers about criminal activities in the area and support police intervention." These sentences best support choice **d**. None of the other choices is supported by information in the passage.

61. a. The correct spelling is *merchandise*.

62. c. The correct spelling is *bandanna*.

63. a. The correct spelling is *spontaneous*.

64. b. The correct spelling of choice **b** is *embellish*.

65. c. The correct spelling of choice **c** is *retaliate*.

66. b. Another word for *attest* is *verify*.

67. a. Another word for *consummate* is *expert*.

68. a. A *virtuoso* musician is a musician with great expertise. An *amateur* musician is one who plays music for the love of playing, but who lacks the experience and/or skill to be considered a *virtuoso*.

69. c. The sentence provides necessary context clues. What sort of shade could keep a hotel room nice and dark? An *opaque* shade is one that does not let light through. Therefore, *opaque* is the best choice.

70. c. *Remuneration* means *payment*. *Reprisal* and *retribution* (choices **a** and **b**) both mean *revenge*.

71. c. Choice **a** has a subject (*the onset of the cold war*) but no predicate. Likewise, choice **b** has a compound subject that is never completed with a predicate.

72. b. Choice **a** begins with a misplaced modifier, thereby incorrectly indicating that *many consumers* have been genetically modified. Choice **c** also misplaces a modifying phrase (*that consumers do not trust*), thereby inaccurately indicating that the consumers do not trust *disease*.

73. b. Every proper noun and adjective in this sentence is correctly capitalized.

74. c. The series commas in this sentence are in the correct places.

75. c. In choices **a** and **b**, it is unclear whether the pronouns refer to the *perpetrator* or the *police officer*. Only choice **c** clearly identifies the antecedents to the pronouns.

76. a. Choice **a** uses apostrophes correctly. In choice **b**, the apostrophes are misplaced in the words *wasn't* and *couldn't*, and they are missing completely in choice **c**.

77. b. Choice **a** contains a subject-verb agreement error; *everyone* is a collective pronoun that should take the singular verb *has*, not the plural verb *have*. Also, *everyone* should take a singular pronoun such as *his* or *her*, not the plural pronoun *their*. The latter error appears in choice **c** as well.

78. a. Choice **b** contains a pronoun error; the singular pronoun *its* does not agree with its plural antecedent *benefits*. Choice **c** also contains a pronoun error; the pronoun *their* refers to *therapy*, not *benefits*, and, therefore, should be singular rather than plural.

79. b. Choices **a** and **c** both contain punctuation errors. In choice **a**, there should be a comma between *course* and *Renee*. In choice **c**, the comma after *proceeded* is confusing and ungrammatical.

80. c. Choices **a** and **b** are incorrectly punctuated; because the sentence includes no direct quotes, the quotation marks are incorrectly used. The question mark in choice **a** is also grammatically incorrect because the sentence is a statement of fact, not a question.

Section 3: Civil Service Skills

81. c. The primary governing principle of customer service is to make things as easy and pleasant for the customer as possible. Thus, the primary reason for maintaining customer records is to minimize the need for the customer to provide redundant information. Choice **a** has nothing to do with customer service and, therefore, cannot be the correct answer to a question in this section of the test. Choice **b** falsely suggests that there is a limit to the amount of government service a citizen may receive. Choice **d** falsely suggests that citizens are not entitled to a government service if they have previously received it.

82. b. Callers should be able to find the street address of the agency via numerous accessible means (e.g., telephone book, Internet). The information mentioned in choices **a**, **c**, and **d** is not as easy to find. Furthermore, it is more immediately relevant to the needs of a person who calls an agency outside of business hours.

83. d. A recorded message providing choices to frequently asked questions should allow some callers to resolve their queries without speaking to a representative, which is beneficial for both the caller and the agency. Music, choice **a**, is a good second choice but is not as advantageous as the recorded message. Choices **b** and **c** represent options likely to annoy callers.

84. a. Some customers left on hold for a long time will hang up before they get to speak with a representative. The number of total calls divided by the number of hang-ups is used to calculate the *abandonment rate*. If 5 out of every 100 calls results in a hang-up, then the abandonment rate is 1 in $\frac{100}{5}$, or 1 in 20.

85. c. This is a common-sense question. It would not be economically feasible or practical to give appointments simply because customers cannot see a representative immediately (choice **a**); a short wait is reasonable. A one-hour wait (choice **b**), however, is far beyond reasonable. Fifteen minutes (choice **c**, the correct choice) is a reasonable amount of time to expect people to wait. Choice **d** falsely suggests that it is a good idea to implement policies that discourage citizens from using government services.

86. c. Three other station names are shown, 18th and California, 30th and Downing, and Union Station.

87. b. The arrow in the photograph indicates the train will be traveling north from the Broadway Station to Union Station.

88. c. Recycling is never collected on the same day as garbage, so if you remembered that Sector 2's garbage was collected on Tuesday and Saturday, you would have been able to eliminate choices **b** and **d**.

89. a. Recycling is collected Tuesday through Saturday; Monday is not a recycling-collection day.

90. c. In Sector 2, garbage is collected on Tuesday and on Saturday, creating a four-day break between the first and second collection. Garbage in Sector 5 is collected on Monday and Friday, which also leaves a four-day break between the first and second collection.

91. c. The instructions indicate that each code is preceded by the time of the visit it represents. Eliminate choices **a**, **b**, and **d**, none of which begins with the time. The correct answer, by process of elimination, must be choice **c**.

92. d. The instructions indicate that each code is preceded by the time of the visit it represents. Eliminate choices **a** and **b**, neither of which begins with the time. Choice **c** records the visitor's actual age of 67 rather than the code for her age (4 = over age 65). Therefore, choice **d** must be the correct answer.

93. a. Eliminate choices **c** and **d**, neither of which begins with the time. Choice **b** incorrectly includes the code Z, indicating that the visitor lives outside the city. In fact, the visitor lives in the southwest quadrant of the city, as choice **a** correctly indicates.

94. b. The F in the code indicates that the visitor was female. The 6 in the code indicates that she filed a complaint. The code indicates that the visitor arrived at 12:00 P.M., was a female (F) citizen (C) between the ages of 31 and 65 (3) from the southwest quadrant of the city (W) who filed a complaint (6).

95. c. The question asks for the purpose of the visit, which is represented by the final digit of the code. That digit, 7, indicates "applying for employment," meaning that choice **c** is the correct answer.

96. d. The first two letters of the code correspond to the first two letters of the recipient's county of residence. The recipient lives in Ardmore County, so her license will begin with the letters AR. This eliminates choices **b** and **c**, which begin with the letters DV (the recipient's initials). The final three characters in the license must be randomly generated letters; choice **a** omits these characters and so cannot be correct.

97. a. The first two letters of the code correspond to the first two letters of the recipient's county of residence. The recipient lives in Hazelton County, so his license will begin with the letters HA. This eliminates choices **c** and **d**, which do not begin with these letters. Choice **b** does not round the recipient's height to the nearest whole inch as required by the rules; therefore, choice **a** must be the correct answer.

98. d. The rules state that the birth date should be recorded as month-date-year. Thus, the correct coding of the recipient's birth date would be 08261980, not 26081980 as it erroneously appears on the license.

99. b. The code indicates that the recipient's initials are WE. Therefore, the license could belong to someone named Warren Evers.

100. a. The recipient of this license lives in a county that begins with the letters LA; was born on August 8, 1967; has the initials MU; and is 66 inches tall.

3 ▶ CIVIL SERVICE PRACTICE EXAM 2

L ike the first practice exam, this test was designed to prepare you for the kinds of questions you will encounter on your civil service exam. The 100 multiple-choice questions that follow will test your knowledge of math, reading, spelling, vocabulary, grammar, civil service skills, memory, and coding.

Make sure you take the time to score your test, and then read all the answer explanations, regardless of whether you answered the question correctly. Compare your score on this test with your score on the first test. Are there areas in which you need more improvement?

Civil Service Practice Exam 2

1.	ⓐ ⓑ ⓒ ⓓ	36.	ⓐ ⓑ ⓒ ⓓ	71.	ⓐ ⓑ ⓒ ⓓ
2.	ⓐ ⓑ ⓒ ⓓ	37.	ⓐ ⓑ ⓒ ⓓ	72.	ⓐ ⓑ ⓒ ⓓ
3.	ⓐ ⓑ ⓒ ⓓ	38.	ⓐ ⓑ ⓒ ⓓ	73.	ⓐ ⓑ ⓒ ⓓ
4.	ⓐ ⓑ ⓒ ⓓ	39.	ⓐ ⓑ ⓒ ⓓ	74.	ⓐ ⓑ ⓒ ⓓ
5.	ⓐ ⓑ ⓒ ⓓ	40.	ⓐ ⓑ ⓒ ⓓ	75.	ⓐ ⓑ ⓒ ⓓ
6.	ⓐ ⓑ ⓒ ⓓ	41.	ⓐ ⓑ ⓒ ⓓ	76.	ⓐ ⓑ ⓒ ⓓ
7.	ⓐ ⓑ ⓒ ⓓ	42.	ⓐ ⓑ ⓒ ⓓ	77.	ⓐ ⓑ ⓒ ⓓ
8.	ⓐ ⓑ ⓒ ⓓ	43.	ⓐ ⓑ ⓒ ⓓ	78.	ⓐ ⓑ ⓒ ⓓ
9.	ⓐ ⓑ ⓒ ⓓ	44.	ⓐ ⓑ ⓒ ⓓ	79.	ⓐ ⓑ ⓒ ⓓ
10.	ⓐ ⓑ ⓒ ⓓ	45.	ⓐ ⓑ ⓒ ⓓ	80.	ⓐ ⓑ ⓒ ⓓ
11.	ⓐ ⓑ ⓒ ⓓ	46.	ⓐ ⓑ ⓒ ⓓ	81.	ⓐ ⓑ ⓒ ⓓ
12.	ⓐ ⓑ ⓒ ⓓ	47.	ⓐ ⓑ ⓒ ⓓ	82.	ⓐ ⓑ ⓒ ⓓ
13.	ⓐ ⓑ ⓒ ⓓ	48.	ⓐ ⓑ ⓒ ⓓ	83.	ⓐ ⓑ ⓒ ⓓ
14.	ⓐ ⓑ ⓒ ⓓ	49.	ⓐ ⓑ ⓒ ⓓ	84.	ⓐ ⓑ ⓒ ⓓ
15.	ⓐ ⓑ ⓒ ⓓ	50.	ⓐ ⓑ ⓒ ⓓ	85.	ⓐ ⓑ ⓒ ⓓ
16.	ⓐ ⓑ ⓒ ⓓ	51.	ⓐ ⓑ ⓒ ⓓ	86.	ⓐ ⓑ ⓒ ⓓ
17.	ⓐ ⓑ ⓒ ⓓ	52.	ⓐ ⓑ ⓒ ⓓ	87.	ⓐ ⓑ ⓒ ⓓ
18.	ⓐ ⓑ ⓒ ⓓ	53.	ⓐ ⓑ ⓒ ⓓ	88.	ⓐ ⓑ ⓒ ⓓ
19.	ⓐ ⓑ ⓒ ⓓ	54.	ⓐ ⓑ ⓒ ⓓ	89.	ⓐ ⓑ ⓒ ⓓ
20.	ⓐ ⓑ ⓒ ⓓ	55.	ⓐ ⓑ ⓒ ⓓ	90.	ⓐ ⓑ ⓒ ⓓ
21.	ⓐ ⓑ ⓒ ⓓ	56.	ⓐ ⓑ ⓒ ⓓ	91.	ⓐ ⓑ ⓒ ⓓ
22.	ⓐ ⓑ ⓒ ⓓ	57.	ⓐ ⓑ ⓒ ⓓ	92.	ⓐ ⓑ ⓒ ⓓ
23.	ⓐ ⓑ ⓒ ⓓ	58.	ⓐ ⓑ ⓒ ⓓ	93.	ⓐ ⓑ ⓒ ⓓ
24.	ⓐ ⓑ ⓒ ⓓ	59.	ⓐ ⓑ ⓒ ⓓ	94.	ⓐ ⓑ ⓒ ⓓ
25.	ⓐ ⓑ ⓒ ⓓ	60.	ⓐ ⓑ ⓒ ⓓ	95.	ⓐ ⓑ ⓒ ⓓ
26.	ⓐ ⓑ ⓒ ⓓ	61.	ⓐ ⓑ ⓒ ⓓ	96.	ⓐ ⓑ ⓒ ⓓ
27.	ⓐ ⓑ ⓒ ⓓ	62.	ⓐ ⓑ ⓒ ⓓ	97.	ⓐ ⓑ ⓒ ⓓ
28.	ⓐ ⓑ ⓒ ⓓ	63.	ⓐ ⓑ ⓒ ⓓ	98.	ⓐ ⓑ ⓒ ⓓ
29.	ⓐ ⓑ ⓒ ⓓ	64.	ⓐ ⓑ ⓒ ⓓ	99.	ⓐ ⓑ ⓒ ⓓ
30.	ⓐ ⓑ ⓒ ⓓ	65.	ⓐ ⓑ ⓒ ⓓ	100.	ⓐ ⓑ ⓒ ⓓ
31.	ⓐ ⓑ ⓒ ⓓ	66.	ⓐ ⓑ ⓒ ⓓ		
32.	ⓐ ⓑ ⓒ ⓓ	67.	ⓐ ⓑ ⓒ ⓓ		
33.	ⓐ ⓑ ⓒ ⓓ	68.	ⓐ ⓑ ⓒ ⓓ		
34.	ⓐ ⓑ ⓒ ⓓ	69.	ⓐ ⓑ ⓒ ⓓ		
35.	ⓐ ⓑ ⓒ ⓓ	70.	ⓐ ⓑ ⓒ ⓓ		

Section 1: Mathematics

Select the best choice for each question.

1. What fraction in lowest terms is equal to 82%?
  a. $\frac{8}{100}$
  b. $\frac{24}{50}$
  c. $\frac{41}{50}$
  d. $\frac{82}{100}$

2. $\frac{16}{5} =$
  a. $2\frac{1}{5}$
  b. $16\frac{1}{5}$
  c. $3\frac{1}{5}$
  d. $1\frac{5}{6}$

3. A tortoise crawls 3 feet per minute. How far does the tortoise crawl in 1 hour?
  a. 3 feet
  b. 30 feet
  c. 60 feet
  d. 180 feet

4. Almonds are sold in bulk for $5.60 per pound (16 ounces) or in a 12-ounce package for $3.60. If Pierre only needs 12 ounces for a recipe, how much would he save by purchasing the 12-ounce package instead of 12 ounces of almonds sold in bulk?
  a. $0.60
  b. $0.65
  c. $0.80
  d. $0.85

Study the following graph, and then use it to answer questions 5 through 7.

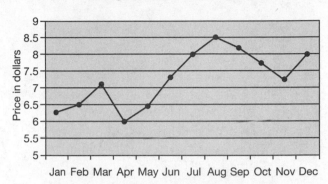

Price of Amalgamated Stock 2009 (per share)

5. The graph shows the price of amalgamated stock throughout 2009. Across what two consecutive months did the largest change in price occur in 2009?
  a. February to March
  b. March to April
  c. May to June
  d. July to August

6. A person who bought one share of stock in January and sold it in December would have realized a
  a. profit of $2.25.
  b. profit of $1.75.
  c. loss of $0.50.
  d. loss of $1.25.

7. What information is displayed on the *y*-axis of the graph?
  a. the months of the year
  b. the price of the stock in dollars
  c. the number of shares sold
  d. the title of the graph

8. $10\frac{2}{3} - 3\frac{1}{8} =$

   a. $7\frac{1}{5}$

   b. $7\frac{11}{24}$

   c. $7\frac{13}{24}$

   d. $7\frac{3}{11}$

9. Jamal invests $2,000 in a certificate of deposit that yields 6% simple interest compounded annually. How much is the certificate of deposit worth 2 years after Jamal's initial investment?

   a. $2,247.20

   b. $2,240.00

   c. $2,120.00

   d. $2,060.00

10. Reduce $\frac{28}{45}$ to lowest terms.

   a. $\frac{2}{3}$

   b. $\frac{4}{7}$

   c. $\frac{3}{5}$

   d. The fraction cannot be reduced.

11. Belinda walked a total of 18.6 miles in 4 days. On average, how many miles did Belinda walk each day?

   a. 14.6 miles

   b. 4.65 miles

   c. 4.6 miles

   d. 4.15 miles

12. A piece of ribbon 3 feet 4 inches long was divided into 5 equal parts. How long was each part?

   a. 1 foot 2 inches

   b. 8 inches

   c. 10 inches

   d. 6 inches

13. $2\frac{2}{5} + 3\frac{1}{3} + 1\frac{1}{2} =$

   a. $7\frac{7}{30}$

   b. $7\frac{4}{17}$

   c. $6\frac{2}{5}$

   d. $6\frac{1}{15}$

14. A bulk store is offering a sale of 25% on all electronics. A 72" inch television has been reduced by $500. How much was the original television before the sale?

   a. $1,050

   b. $1,500

   c. $2,000

   d. $5,000

15. In Mr. Cortez's swim class, $\frac{1}{5}$ of the students are nine years old, and the remaining students are eight years old. One-eighth of the students at the "guppy" level can tread water for two minutes. What fraction of students at the guppy level are eight-year-old guppies?

   a. $\frac{1}{20}$

   b. $\frac{2}{13}$

   c. $\frac{1}{10}$

   d. $\frac{5}{8}$

16. A bread recipe calls for $3\frac{1}{2}$ cups of flour during the initial mixing process and an additional $\frac{1}{4}$ cup of flour during the kneading process. How much flour is used to produce the bread?

   a. $3\frac{1}{8}$ cups

   b. $3\frac{3}{4}$ cups

   c. $\frac{7}{8}$ cup

   d. $7\frac{1}{4}$ cups

Study the following graph, and then use it to answer questions 17 through 19.

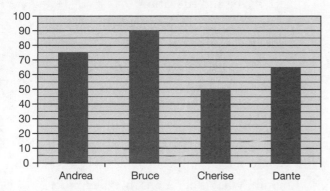

Automobiles Sold in Autumn 2009

17. Andrea, Bruce, Cherise, and Dante sell automobiles for a living. The graph shows the number of cars sold during the autumn of 2009. Determine the average number of automobiles sold by each salesperson. Find the difference between this average and each salesperson's individual total. What is the sum of the absolute differences between the group average and the salespeople's actual totals?
a. 40
b. 45
c. 50
d. 70

18. What is the range of the data shown in the graph?
a. 15
b. 25
c. 40
d. 90

19. What information is displayed on the *x*-axis of the graph?
a. the number of automobiles sold
b. the names of the salespeople
c. the title of the graph
d. the months of autumn

20. What is $\frac{1}{2} - (\frac{3}{4} - \frac{2}{5})$?
a. $\frac{1}{10}$
b. $\frac{2}{5}$
c. $\frac{3}{20}$
d. $\frac{7}{15}$

21. Find the decimal equivalent of 4%.
a. 0.4
b. 4.0
c. 0.04
d. 0.004

22. What is $\frac{2}{5}$ divided by 10, represented as a decimal?
a. 0.01
b. 0.04
c. 0.05
d. 0.10

23. The ratio of men to women attending a university is 5:4. If there are 7,650 students at the school, how many are men?
a. 4,250
b. 3,400
c. 1,530
d. 850

24. Steven earns $70,200 as a network engineer. If he receives a 2% raise, what is his new salary?
a. $70,200
b. $71,604
c. $72,040
d. $74,060

25. One day Sam spent $\frac{1}{8}$ of his workday in a meeting and $\frac{5}{6}$ of his workday doing research. The rest of the workday was spent making calls. What fraction of Sam's workday was spent not making calls?

   a. $\frac{3}{7}$

   b. $\frac{6}{13}$

   c. $\frac{3}{4}$

   d. $\frac{23}{24}$

Study the following graph, and then use it to answer questions 26 through 28.

Wendy's Monthly Budget

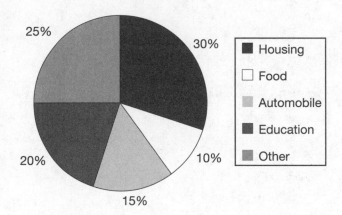

26. The legend of the graph tells you
   a. how much money Wendy has to spend each month.
   b. which categories correspond to which sections of the graph.
   c. what type of food Wendy buys each month.
   d. why type of expenses are classified under the category "other."

27. Which of the following conclusions is supported by the graph?
   a. Wendy spends half her monthly budget on housing and education.
   b. Automobile expenses are Wendy's single biggest monthly expense.
   c. Wendy does not spend any money on entertainment.
   d. If Wendy earned more money, she would spend more money on food.

28. Wendy budgets for $3,000 in expenditures each month. What is her monthly expenditure on education?
   a. $300
   b. $450
   c. $600
   d. $900

29. If a runner averages $5\frac{1}{2}$ miles per hour during a 26-mile marathon, how many hours will it take the runner to complete the marathon?
   a. 3.2
   b. 4.7
   c. 5.5
   d. 20.5

30. A warbler that weighs 9 grams eats 80% of its body weight each day. How much food, in grams, does a warbler eat daily?
   a. 7.2 grams
   b. 8.0 grams
   c. 8.9 grams
   d. 9.8 grams

31. There are 5,280 feet in a mile. If David biked a distance of 19,800 feet how many miles did he travel?
   a. $2\frac{2}{3}$ miles
   b. $3\frac{1}{2}$ miles
   c. $3\frac{5}{8}$ miles
   d. $3\frac{3}{4}$ miles

32. $8\frac{1}{2} \times 3\frac{1}{4} =$
   a. $27\frac{5}{8}$
   b. $24\frac{1}{8}$
   c. $24\frac{3}{4}$
   d. $11\frac{3}{4}$

33. While Nicole checked tickets at a concert she would rip the tickets in half when a patron presented them, keep one half of each, and return the other half to the purchaser. If Nicole ripped 38 tickets, how many half tickets (counting portions kept by both her and the patron) would she have created?
   a. 17
   b. $38\frac{1}{2}$
   c. 76
   d. 78

34. Last Monday, 20% of the 140-member nursing staff was absent. How many nurses were absent on Monday?
   a. 14
   b. 20
   c. 28
   d. 112

35. Derek jogs for 2 hours 15 minutes at an average rate of 8 kilometers per hour. How far does Derek jog?
   a. 19 kilometers
   b. 18 kilometers
   c. 17 kilometers
   d. 16 kilometers

Study the following table, and then use it to answer questions 36 and 37.

CITY OF HULE 911 CALL FREQUENCY		
MONTH	911 CALLS	TEST SCORE
May	213	66
June	196	70
July	257	61
August	267	78
September	279	70
October	308	68

36. What was the average (arithmetic mean) of 911 calls for the six months in the table?
   a. $248\frac{2}{5}$
   b. $253\frac{1}{3}$
   c. 257
   d. 279

37. The data in the table supports which of the following conclusions?
   a. The city of Hule has a high crime rate.
   b. October is always a high crime month.
   c. 911 call frequency tended to increase over the period range shown.
   d. The number of 911 calls can be used to predict how many times police will be dispatched.

38. Reduce $\frac{14}{35}$ to lowest terms.

   a. $\frac{7}{17}$

   b. $\frac{2}{5}$

   c. $\frac{1}{21}$

   d. $\frac{2}{3}$

39. Of the 840 crimes committed last month, 42 involved petty theft. What percent of crimes committed last month involved petty theft?

   a. 5%

   b. 0.5%

   c. 0.05%

   d. 2%

40. A recipe calls for $5\frac{1}{4}$ cups of apples for six servings. How many cups of apples would be required to make nine servings?

   a. $7\frac{3}{4}$ cups

   b. $7\frac{7}{8}$ cups

   c. $8\frac{1}{4}$ cups

   d. 9 cups

Section 2: Written Communication

Reading Comprehension—Questions 41 through 60

Read the following passage. Then, answer questions 41 through 44.

Today, bicycles are elegant and simple machines that are common all over the globe. Many people ride bicycles for recreation, while others use them as a means of transportation. The first bicycle, called a draisienne, was invented in Germany in 1818 by Baron Karl de Draid de Sauerbrun. Because it was made of wood, the draisienne was not very durable,

nor did it have pedals. Riders moved it by pushing their feet against the ground.

In 1839, Kirkpatrick Macmillan, a Scottish blacksmith, invented a much better bicycle. Macmillan's machine had tires with iron rims to keep them from getting worn down. He also used foot-operated cranks—similar to pedals—so that his bicycle could be ridden at a quick pace. It did not look much like a modern bicycle because its back wheel was substantially larger than its front wheel. Although Macmillan's bicycle could be ridden easily, it was never produced in large numbers. In 1861, Frenchman Pierre Michaux and his brother Ernest invented a bicycle with an improved crank mechanism. They called their bicycle a velocipede, but many people called it a bone shaker because of the jarring effect that the wood and iron frame had on the rider. Despite the unflattering nickname, the velocipede was a hit and the Michaux family made hundreds of the machines annually. Most of them were sold to fun-seeking young people.

Ten years later, James Starley, an English inventor, made several innovations that <u>revolutionized</u> bicycle design. He made the front wheel many times larger than the back wheel, put a gear on the pedals to make the bicycle more efficient, and lightened the wheels by using wire spokes. Although this bicycle was much lighter and less tiring to ride, it was still clumsy, extremely top-heavy, and ridden mostly for entertainment.

It was not until 1874 that the first truly modern bicycle appeared on the scene. Invented by another Englishman, H. J. Lawson, this safety bicycle would look familiar to today's cyclists. The safety bicycle had equalized wheels, which made it much less prone to toppling over. Lawson also attached a chain to the pedals to drive the rear wheel. By 1893, the safety bicycle had been further improved with air-filled rubber tires, a diamond-shaped frame, and an improved brake system. With the improvements made by Lawson, bicycles became extremely popular and useful for transportation. Today, bicycles are built and enjoyed all over the world.

41. There is enough information in this passage to show that
   a. several people contributed to the development of the modern bicycle.
   b. only a few velocipedes built by the Michaux family are still in existence.
   c. for most of the nineteenth century, few people rode bicycles just for fun.
   d. bicycles with wheels of different sizes cannot be ridden by today's riders.

42. The first person to use a gear system on bicycles was
   a. H. J. Lawson.
   b. Kirkpatrick Macmillan.
   c. Pierre Michaux.
   d. James Starley.

43. This passage was most likely written to
   a. persuade readers to use bicycles for transportation.
   b. describe the problems that bicycle manufacturers encounter.
   c. compare bicycles used for fun with bicycles used for transportation.
   d. tell readers a little about the history of the bicycle.

44. As used in the passage, the word *revolutionized* most nearly means
   a. canceled.
   b. transformed.
   c. maintained.
   d. preserved.

Read the following passage. Then answer questions 45 through 48.

Our fire department has always been a leader in creating positive community initiatives and providing new services to the community as they are needed. Our newest service is the Fire Assistance and Support Team (FAST). In the past, we would arrive on the scene of a residential fire, put out the fire as <u>expeditiously</u> as possible, and then leave—the homeowners would be left to deal with the aftermath on their own. With this new program, the families affected are not left alone to deal with everything that needs to be done. The FAST will stay with the victims and assist them in a variety of ways. The services provided by FAST personnel include:

- explaining what is going on at the fire scene.
- keeping the family informed as to when they will be able to re-enter their home.
- making phone calls on the family's behalf (insurance company, family members, schools, etc.).
- assisting the family with finding a place to stay for the night.
- accompanying the family as the investigator goes through their home.
- assisting with the removal of any items the family may wish to retrieve.
- providing the family with transportation.

The team works with the Red Cross, Salvation Army, and other service organizations. The team will remain in contact with the victims until their assistance is no longer required.

45. What is this passage about?
a. cooperating with the Red Cross and similar private agencies
b. getting insurance companies to deliver on their contracts
c. explaining fire department operations to the general public
d. assisting victims in dealing with the aftermath of a fire

46. The description of FAST in this passage includes all the following duties listed EXCEPT
a. explaining fire department actions at the fire scene.
b. boarding up the home after the fire.
c. finding the family a place to stay for the night.
d. transporting the victims to a shelter.

47. What would be the best possible title for this passage?
a. A FAST Way to Happiness
b. A New Way to Assist and Support Fire Victims
c. Standing Up for All Victims
d. Providing Help for Those Without Hope

48. As used in the passage, the word *expeditiously* most nearly means
a. furiously.
b. intensely.
c. quickly.
d. cleanly.

Read the following passage. Then, answer questions 49 through 52.

This information sheet is provided courtesy of the Centers for Disease Control and Prevention (CDC). It is intended to help citizens make informed choices when deciding whether to consume raw oysters.

Nearly all oysters carry the *Vibrio vulnificus* bacteria, although in the vast majority of cases it is present in concentrations too low to affect humans adversely. The bacteria tends to be more active during the warmer months, making oysters harvested during this period substantially more dangerous. There is an old saying: "Never eat an oyster in a month that does not have an 'r' in it." The saying is grounded in fact, as there is a markedly increased danger of *Vibrio vulnificus* infection during these months.

In healthy adults, a *Vibrio vulnificus* infection usually manifests itself in symptoms commonly associated with food poisoning. These symptoms typically include stomach pain, diarrhea, and vomiting. The infection is much more dangerous to people with weakened immune systems, especially those who suffer from chronic liver disease. In such individuals, *Vibrio vulnificus* can infect the bloodstream, resulting in decreased blood pressure, fever, chills, and skin lesions. Such infections are fatal approximately half the time. Such individuals should avoid not only eating oysters, but also swimming in oyster-inhabited waters during the summer months, as infection can be transmitted in the water through open wounds.

People infected with *Vibrio vulnificus* should seek immediate help; antibiotics can be effective in reducing mortality. In the case of infection through an open wound on a limb, amputation may be necessary.

Fortunately, the incidence of *Vibrio vulnificus* is low, with only about 40 cases reported annually. Most cases occur in the Gulf Coast region. Researchers suspect that many low-grade cases of *Vibrio vulnificus*—those that result in food-poisoning-like symptoms—go unreported, making the actual incidence of infection difficult to calculate accurately. The CDC strongly urges patients and medical professionals to report such incidents, as it allows the agency to identify potentially risky oyster beds and thus to prevent <u>subsequent</u> infections. To reduce the risk of *Vibrio vulnificus* infection, eat only shellfish that has been fully cooked and wear gloves and other protective clothing when handling raw shellfish.

49. The author's main purpose is to
a. convince readers to avoid all seafood.
b. warn readers about a specific danger.
c. refute an erroneous report.
d. describe the life cycle of an oyster.

50. According to the passage, a *Vibrio vulnificus* infection is especially dangerous to
a. children and the elderly.
b. people who do not live on the Gulf Coast.
c. those with compromised immune systems.
d. amputees.

51. It can be inferred from the passage that
a. one does not have to eat an oyster to contract a *Vibrio vulnificus* infection.
b. it is safer to eat oysters in the summertime than in the wintertime.
c. a *Vibrio vulnificus* infection is usually fatal to everyone who contracts it.
d. there is currently no effective treatment for a *Vibrio vulnificus* infection.

52. As used in the passage, the word *subsequent* most nearly means
a. vigilant.
b. unnecessary.
c. more dangerous.
d. future.

Read the following passage. Then, answer questions 53 through 56.

The "broken window" theory was originally developed to explain how minor acts of vandalism or disrespect can quickly escalate to crimes and attitudes that break down the entire social fabric of an area. This theory can easily be applied to any situation in society. The theory contends that if a broken window in an abandoned building is not replaced quickly, soon all the windows will be broken. In other words, a small violation, if condoned, leads to other similar or greater violations. Thus, after all the windows have been broken, the building is more likely to be looted and perhaps even burned down.

According to the theory, violations increase exponentially. Thus, if disrespect to a superior is tolerated, others will be tempted to be disrespectful as well. A management crisis could erupt literally overnight. For example, if one firefighter begins to disregard proper housewatch procedure by neglecting to keep up the housewatch administrative journal, and if this firefighter is not <u>reproved</u>, others will follow suit by committing similar violations of procedure. The theory is that group members begin to reason, "If he can get away with it, why can't I?" Thus, what starts out as a minor problem, such as a violation that may not seem to warrant disciplinary action, may ultimately undermine efficiency throughout the entire firehouse, putting the people the firehouse serves at risk.

There are, of course, dangers inherent to implementing the broken window theory. Many conclude that the theory mandates a zero tolerance policy toward malfeasance and even toward legal but disrespectful behavior. In practice, such a policy can quickly result in the abuse of power by authority figures, whether they be police officers patrolling a community, firefighters maintaining a firehouse, or managers supervising a team of employees. Excessive exertion of authority typically gives rise to its own set of problems, such as resentment of authority and disobedience as an act of defiance.

53. Which of the following best expresses the main idea of the passage?

- **a.** A theory explains how disorder can escalate under certain conditions.
- **b.** If order is not maintained in a firehouse, public safety can be compromised.
- **c.** Some bosses are too demanding, which results in employee insubordination.
- **d.** The housewatch administrative journal is the most important document in a firehouse.

54. As used in the passage, the word *reproved* most nearly means

- **a.** condoned.
- **b.** ostracized.
- **c.** fired.
- **d.** scolded.

55. With which of the following statements would the author most likely agree?

- **a.** The broken window theory is a fatally flawed concept.
- **b.** The broken window theory may help explain certain behavior.
- **c.** The broken window theory should be applied to all situations.
- **d.** The broken window theory really pertains to firehouses only.

56. According to the passage, the broken window theory helps explain

- **a.** how disciplinary problems can arise quickly seemingly from nowhere.
- **b.** why cities today are more successful in combating vandalism than they have been in the past.
- **c.** which organizations the broken window phenomenon is mostly likely to affect adversely.
- **d.** what personality traits drive a citizen to disrespect authority.

Read the following passage. Then, answer questions 57 through 60.

If you are looking for a new pet in your life, please consider adopting one from the county animal shelter. Every year the county takes custody of thousands of stray cats and dogs. Those pets that the county cannot find homes for, sadly, must be euthanized. By adopting a pet from the county, you'll be saving the life of an innocent animal and adding a new and wonderful member to your family.

As an <u>inducement</u> to adopt, the county provides a number of valuable services for your pet. Your dog will receive his or her first round of bordatella, parvo, parainfluenza, distemper, and hepatitis vaccinations; if your pet is old enough, he or she will also receive the first rabies shot and implantation of an identifying microchip. Your dog will also be wormed and given a full physical examination by our in-house veterinarian. Cats receive their first round of vaccinations for calici virus, chlamydia, panleukopenia, and rhinotracheitis. If he or she is old enough, your cat will also receive the first rabies shot and implantation of an identifying microchip.

The county charges a uniform adoption fee of $60 for all pets. Please note that you are required to have your pet spayed or neutered. The county does not perform these operations;

however, it will provide you with a certificate that pays for the entire cost of the operation, redeemable at a number of local veterinarian hospitals. Failure to have your pet spayed or neutered will result in a $100-per-month fine, so please fulfill your obligation.

Keep in mind that owning a pet is a big responsibility. We hope that you will decide to adopt one of our animals, but only if you make the commitment to care for your pet correctly. The shelter offers regular evening seminars in pet care. You may wish to enroll in one before you adopt an animal to learn more about a pet owner's responsibilities so you can decide whether a pet is right for you.

57. The author's main purpose in this passage is to
   a. persuade all citizens to adopt at least one pet.
   b. warn citizens of fines they may face.
   c. inform citizens of the details regarding pet adoption.
   d. explain why the county shelter must put down so many animals each year.

58. It can be inferred from the passage that
   a. most people are not responsible enough to take care of a pet.
   b. the author believes the adoption fee charged by the county is too high.
   c. cats and dogs must reach a certain age before they can be implanted with a microchip.
   d. it is less expensive to care for a cat than to care for a dog.

59. According to the passage, dogs adopted from the county shelter receive vaccinations for all of the following EXCEPT
   a. parvo.
   b. distemper.
   c. bordatella.
   d. panleukopenia.

60. As used in the passage, the word *inducement* most nearly means
   a. imperative.
   b. encouragement.
   c. evasion.
   d. ultimatum.

Spelling—Questions 61 through 65

Select the choices that are spelled correctly in questions 61 and 62.

61. We will be able to move forward after the planning office _____ _____ a policy.
   a. formalates
   b. formulates
   c. formulaits

62. The _____ inspected the corpse and found no evidence of foul play.
   a. coroner
   b. corroner
   c. coronor

63. Which of the following words is spelled incorrectly?
   a. congeal
   b. sirmount
   c. personnel

64. Which of the following words is spelled incorrectly?
   a. demeanor
   b. cuncoct
   c. whimsical

65. Which of the following words is spelled incorrectly?
   a. mischievous
   b. exhilarate
   c. negoshiate

Vocabulary—Questions 66 through 70
Select the best choice for each question.

66. Find the word that is closest in meaning to the underlined word.
an <u>excruciating</u> experience
a. enlightening
b. boring
c. painful

67. Find the word that is closest in meaning to the underlined word.
a <u>trite</u> saying
a. biblical
b. nonsensical
c. overused

68. Find the word that is most nearly the opposite of the underlined word.
a <u>monotonous</u> speech
a. annoying
b. interesting
c. short

69. Find the word that best completes the sentence.
Smoking can have a _____ effect on ones health.
a. zealous
b. detrimental
c. benevolent

70. Find the word that best completes the sentence.
The spies arranged a secret _____ to exchange secrets.
a. liaison
b. confection
c. premonition

Grammar—Questions 71 through 80
Select the best choice for each question.

71. Which of the following sentences is NOT a complete sentence?
a. Hearing the thunder, the lifeguard ordered us out of the water.
b. Turn off the lights.
c. Sunday afternoon spent reading and playing computer games.

72. Select the sentence that is written most correctly.
a. A program to reduce homelessness in community is worked on by the council.
b. The council is working on a program to reduce homelessness in the community.
c. The counsil is working on program to reduce homelessness in the community.

73. Select the sentence that is written most correctly.
a. While visiting the zoo, Chelsea could not believe how large in size a elephant was.
b. While visiting the zoo, Chelsea could not believe how large the elephant was.
c. While visiting the zoo, Chelsea could not believe how large the elephant was at the zoo.

74. Select the sentence that is written most correctly.
a. Police commissioner jarrett will be retiring from the department on October 23rd.
b. Police Commissioner Jarrett will be retiring from the Department on October 23rd.
c. Police Commissioner Jarrett will be retiring from the department on October 23rd.

75. Select the sentence that is written most correctly.
   a. Please make sure that Mr and Mrs Anderson receive an invitation to the meeting.
   b. Please make sure that Mr. and Mrs. Anderson receive an invitation to the meeting.
   c. Please make sure that Mr. and Mrs Anderson receive an invitation to The Meeting.

76. Select the sentence that is written most correctly.
   a. Unlike other pianists, Thelonious Monk played in a style that is difficult to trace to that of an earlier musician.
   b. Unlike other pianists, the style of Thelonious Monk is difficult to trace to an earlier musician.
   c. Unlike other pianists, whose styles can be traced to an earlier musician, Thelonious Monk's cannot.

77. Select the sentence that is written most correctly.
   a. William Morrison the president of the local Chamber of Commerce will address the class next Thursday.
   b. William Morrison, the president of the local Chamber of Commerce will address the class next Thursday.
   c. William Morrison, the president of the local Chamber of Commerce, will address the class next Thursday.

78. Select the sentence that is written most correctly.
   a. The use of electronic devices, including cellular phones, are prohibited on airplanes when the aircraft is in flight.
   b. The use of electronic devices, including a cellular phone, are prohibited on airplanes when the aircraft are in flight.
   c. The use of electronic devices, including cellular phones, is prohibited on airplanes when the aircraft are in flight.

79. Select the sentence that is written most correctly.
   a. Miguel has been assigned to work on the project with Leticia and I.
   b. Miguel has been assigned to work on the project with Leticia and me.
   c. Miguel, he has been assigned to work on the project with Leticia and I.

80. Select the sentence that is written most correctly.
   a. Roberta went to the store to pick up some butter, sugar, milk, and flour.
   b. Roberta went to the store to pick up some butter sugar milk and flour.
   c. Roberta went to the store to pick up some butter, sugar, milk and, flour.

Section 3: Civil Service Skills

Customer Service—
Questions 81 through 85
Select the best choice for each question.

81. Customers who complain about government service should
   a. receive a response even if they request that no response be provided.
   b. be offered a variety of outlets through which to complain (e.g., complaint desk, e-mail, website).
   c. register their complaints in person so they can receive an immediate response.
   d. be allowed to complain only if they can register the complaint in English.

82. Quality-assurance agents focus primarily on
   a. citizens' level of satisfaction in their government interactions.
   b. government employees' level of satisfaction with their pay and benefits.
   c. the speed and frequency at which agencies update their websites.
   d. the punctuality of government employees.

83. An office that offers language translation services should have as its highest priority
   a. offering the greatest number of languages possible.
   b. providing accurate translation of those languages it offers.
   c. requiring non-English-speaking users to enroll in English courses.
   d. making sure that all forms are available in multiple languages.

84. When transferring a call, which of the following pieces of information is least important to provide the customer?
   a. the number of the extension to which they are being transferred
   b. the reason they are being transferred
   c. the number to call in case they are disconnected
   d. the name of your supervisor

85. The term *web chat* refers to
   a. a list of frequently asked questions and choices posted on a website.
   b. a telephone line dedicated to customer queries about how to navigate a website.
   c. a training program designed to teach government employees how to use the Internet.
   d. live interactive online help from an agency representative.

Memory—Questions 86 through 90

Take five minutes to study the following picture. Then, answer questions 86 and 87 without looking back at the picture.

© Corbis

86. The automobile on the right-hand side of the photograph is a
   a. two-door sedan.
   b. station wagon.
   c. sport-utility vehicle.
   d. motorcycle.

87. The skateboarder is wearing
   a. a large hat.
   b. a jacket.
   c. Bermuda shorts.
   d. a cape.

Take five minutes to study the following text. Then, answer questions 88 through 90 without looking back at the text.

You are about to begin a meeting with six professional peers you have never met before. Their images and names follow.

Sylvia Martinez

Victor Dinapoli

Janet Barnes

Arthur Jones

Maureen Cho

Carlos Domingo

88. Sylvia Martinez's hair
  a. is worn in an afro style.
  b. is blonde.
  c. is shoulder-length.
  d. covers her ears.

89. Arthur Jones is distinguished from all the other people by all of the following details EXCEPT for which?
  a. He is the only one with dark hair.
  b. He is the only one wearing a hat.
  c. He is the only one with a beard and moustache.
  d. He is the only one wearing sunglasses.

90. Which is a complete list of all the people who are wearing glasses?
  a. Sylvia Martinez, Victor Dinapoli
  b. Victor Dinapoli, Arthur Jones, Maureen Cho
  c. Victor Dinapoli, Janet Barnes, Carlos Domingo
  d. Arthur Jones, Carlos Domingo

Coding—Questions 91 through 100

To answer questions 91 through 95, refer to the following scenario.

A record of all correspondences sent from a particular government office must be entered into a log. The following code is used to record the information.

letters = first four letters of the recipient's last name and the first letter of the recipient's first name

2 digits = first two digits of the recipient's street address; if the address is one digit long, precede that digit with a zero (0)

1 letter = I if the correspondence represents an inquiry originating in the government office;

R if the correspondence represents a response to an inquiry from the recipient

1 digit = 0 if the letter is high priority; 1 if the letter is medium priority; 2 if the letter is low priority

3 letters and 2 digits = First three letters of the month and date correspondence was sent (e.g., July 6 = JUL06)

91. In response to an inquiry from Denise Fong of 3724 Haywood Boulevard, the office sends a letter graded medium priority on November 15. How should this correspondence be entered into the log?
  a. RFONGD37241NOV15
  b. FONGD37R1NOV15
  c. FONG3724RNOV15
  d. 37R1NOV15FONG

92. The office originated an inquiry to Martin Ramirez of 8 Elm Court on June 2. The office graded the letter high priority. How should this correspondence be entered into the log?
  a. MARTR8I0JUN2
  b. MARTR08I0JUN02
  c. RAMIM8I0JUN2
  d. RAMIM08I0JUN02

93. In response to a letter from John Davis of 1277 Highland Road on October 15, the office sent a low priority letter on October 23. How should the office's response be entered into the log?
  a. JOHND12R2OCT15
  b. DAVIJ12R2OCT15
  c. JOHND12R2OCT23
  d. DAVIJ12R2OCT23

94. A log entry reading BERNM35I0FEB05 could represent
- **a.** a reply sent to Martin Bernstein of 3 Fifth Avenue on February 5.
- **b.** an inquiry sent to Bernard Moskowitz of 3 Fifth Avenue on February 5.
- **c.** an inquiry sent to Martin Bernstein of 35 Michigan Drive on February 5.
- **d.** a reply sent to Bernard Moskowitz of 35 Michigan Drive on February 5.

95. The following log entry for a response to Harold McCarthy of 5 Stevenson Road, sent high priority on March 6, was coded MCCAH5R0MAR06. It contains which of the following errors?
- **a.** It omits a zero (0) that should appear between H and 5.
- **b.** It incorrectly codes the recipient's name.
- **c.** The date on which the letter was sent is recorded incorrectly.
- **d.** The priority level of the letter is miscoded.

To answer questions 96 through 100, refer to the following scenario.

A city health department inspects salad bars in grocery stores as well as the areas in which foods for the salad bars are prepared. It logs violations of the health code according to the following rules:

Major Infraction (subtract 5 points for each incident; infraction must be remedied immediately)
A—Cooked foods not cooked through
B—Cooked foods stored under 140° F
C—Cold food stored above 41° F
D—Raw and cooked foods stored together, allowing for cross-contamination
E—Improper cleaning of knives and other utensils

F—Employee with contagious condition (e.g., flu) preparing food
G—Employee fails to wash hands thoroughly
H—Presence of animal droppings detected

Minor infraction (subtract 3 points for each incident; infraction must be remedied within two business days)
j—Hand-washing facilities not immediately accessible to food preparers
k—Lack of soap or towels at hand-washing facility
m—Improper temperature or water pressure in automatic dishwasher or washing machine
n—Inaccurate labeling of food items
p—Inaccurate labeling or improper storage of toxic cleaning materials
r—Consumer advisories (e.g., notices about safety of shellfish) improperly displayed
s—Smoking in the food preparation area

Multiple infractions are logged multiple times (e.g., an inspector who observes three incidents of undercooked food would log the code AAA). A health code score is tabulated by adding the value of all infractions and subtracting the sum from 100.

96. An inspector visits Wilson's Supermarket to observe its salad bar and preparation areas. During her visit, she notes one incident of cold food stored at too high a temperature. She also finds animal droppings in two separate areas of the store. Finally, she notes that one food item is improperly labeled. What code does the inspector record for this visit?
- **a.** CCHp
- **b.** CHp
- **c.** CHHp
- **d.** CHHppp

97. An inspector visits Hungry Bob's Mini-Mart to inspect its salad bar and preparation areas. The inspector observes three incidents of improper storage of toxic cleaning materials. He also notes that a consumer advisory that should be posted clearly is not posted. What code should he assign for his visit?

a. pppr
b. EEEn
c. En
d. pr

98. An inspector visits Hungry Bob's Mini-Mart to inspect its salad bar and preparation areas. The inspector observes three incidents of improper storage of toxic cleaning materials. He also notes that a consumer advisory that should be posted clearly is not posted. What score should the inspector assign for this visit?

a. 88
b. 80
c. 90
d. 94

99. An inspector visits Mega-Mart and logs the following code:
EGkss
The inspector observed more than one incident of

a. poor cleaning of utensils.
b. poor hand-washing technique.
c. insufficient amount of soap or towels.
d. smoking where food is prepared.

100. An inspector visits Mega-Mart and logs the following code:
EGkss
What score should the inspector assign for the report?

a. 75
b. 81
c. 79
d. 85

Answers

Section 1: Mathematics

1. c. To find the fraction for 82%, write 82 over 100 to get $\frac{82}{100}$. Reduce this to $\frac{41}{50}$.

2. c. The question asks you to rewrite the improper fraction $\frac{16}{5}$ as a mixed number. To do this, divide the numerator 16 by the denominator 5. The result is $3\frac{1}{5}$.

3. d. Use a proportion to solve this problem with a proportion. Write a proportion with *feet* in the numerator and *minutes* in the denominator. Convert 1 hour to 60 minutes so that your time units remain constant throughout your calculations. Write the following proportion: $\frac{3}{1} = \frac{x}{60}$. Now cross multiply to solve; $x = 180$, so 180 feet is the answer to the question.

4. a. Begin to solve this problem by finding the price per ounce of both options. Do this by dividing the price by the number of ounces gotten for that price. For bulk, it is $5.60 ÷ 16 = $0.35; for the package it is $3.60 ÷ 12 = $0.30. Therefore, bulk almonds cost $0.05 more per ounce. Since Pierre buys 12 ounces of almonds in a package he saves 12 × $0.05 = $0.60 by purchasing the package instead of in bulk.

5. b. The question asks for the greatest change seen in consecutive months. This change is in absolute terms and could be either negative or positive. The change from February to March was +.5, from March to April was −1.0, from May to June was about +.80, and from July to August was +.5. Therefore, among the four options given, the change from March to April (−1.0) was the greatest.

6. b. To answer this question, first determine whether the stock price in December was higher or lower than it was in January. Because it was higher, you know that the stock showed a profit for 2009. Eliminate choices **c** and **d** because they say the stock took a loss. Next, subtract the December price from the January price. $8.00 − $6.25 equals $1.75, so the stock showed a $1.75 per share profit between January and December.

7. b. The *y*-axis is the vertical axis of a graph.

8. c. To solve this problem, rewrite each mixed number as a fraction. Rewrite $10\frac{2}{3}$ as $\frac{32}{3}$ and $3\frac{1}{8}$ as $\frac{25}{8}$. Next, find a common denominator by multiplying the two denominators. 3 × 8 equals 24, so rewrite each fraction with 24 in its denominator. $\frac{32}{3} \times \frac{8}{8}$ equals $\frac{256}{24}$; $\frac{25}{8} \times \frac{3}{3} = \frac{75}{24}$. Now you can subtract. $\frac{256}{24} - \frac{75}{24} = \frac{181}{24}$. Divide 181 by 24 to get the result $7\frac{13}{24}$.

9. a. To solve this problem, first determine the value of Jamal's certificate of deposit after one year. The certificate of deposit is worth $2,000 and it earns 6% interest, so it increases in value by 6% of $2,000, which is $120. After one year, then, the certificate of deposit is worth $2,120. In the second year, the certificate of deposit earns 6% interest on its entire value of $2,120. Therefore, it earns another $127.20, meaning that after two years, its value is $2,247.20.

10. d. In order to reduce a fraction, the numerator and the denominator must be divisible by a common factor. 28 and 45 have no common factors; therefore, $\frac{28}{45}$ cannot be reduced.

11. d. To solve rate problems, apply the equation $rt = d$, where r equals rate, t equals time, and d equals distance. This question provides the time (4 days) and the distance (18.6) miles, so you can write the equation $4r = 18.6$. Next, divide both sides by 4 to get $r = 4.15$. Therefore, Belinda walked 4.15 miles per day on average.

12. b. When solving problems that include two different units, convert to one of the units. In this problem, both feet and inches are included. Convert 3 feet 4 inches to 40 inches by converting 3 feet to 36 inches. Next, divide 40 inches by 5 to determine that each of the five pieces of ribbon is 8 inches long.

13. a. To add mixed numbers with uncommon denominators, first convert all mixed numbers to improper fractions. Convert $2\frac{2}{5}$ to $\frac{12}{5}$, $3\frac{1}{3}$ to $\frac{10}{3}$, and $1\frac{1}{2}$ to $\frac{3}{2}$. Next, multiply the denominators 2, 3, and 5 to find a common denominator of 30. Now, rewrite all three fractions so that 30 is in the denominator of each: $\frac{12}{5} \times \frac{6}{6} = \frac{72}{30}$; $\frac{10}{3} \times \frac{10}{10} = \frac{100}{30}$; $\frac{3}{2} \times \frac{15}{15} = \frac{45}{30}$. Now you can add the fractions: $\frac{72}{30} + \frac{100}{30} + \frac{45}{30} = \frac{217}{30}$. Finally, divide 217 by 30 to produce the result $7\frac{7}{30}$.

14. c. Since the original price of the television is unknown, write variable x for this amount. Then, write an equation for this problem. Given 25% of the original price of the television (x) is $500, translate the equation for this problem as $0.25x = 500$. Divide both sides by .25 to get $x = \$2,000$.

15. c. Because the class is exclusively populated by eight- and nine-year-olds, and nine-year-olds represent $\frac{1}{5}$ of the class, it can be determined that eight-year-olds represent the remaining $\frac{4}{5}$ of the class. To estimate the fraction of guppies that are eight-year-olds, you must multiply $\frac{4}{5}$ by the fraction of students that are guppies ($\frac{1}{8}$). To multiply fractions, multiply numerators and then denominators, and reduce if necessary. $\frac{4}{5} \times \frac{1}{8} = \frac{4}{40}$, which reduces to $\frac{1}{10}$.

16. b. This question asks you to add $3\frac{1}{2}$ and $\frac{1}{4}$. Fractions can be added together only if they have a common denominator, so rewrite $\frac{1}{2}$ as $\frac{2}{4}$. Now you can add $3\frac{2}{4}$ and $\frac{1}{4}$ to get $3\frac{3}{4}$, the correct answer. If you chose choice **a**, you probably tried to add the fractions without first finding a common denominator. If you chose choice **c**, you probably multiplied the two numbers.

17. c. To find the average number of cars sold by each salesperson, add up all the cars sold by each and then divide by the total number of salespeople. The total number of cars sold was $75 + 90 + 50 + 65 = 280$. Now divide: $280 \div 4 = 70$, which is the mean for each salesperson. Next, find the absolute difference between the mean (70) and each salesperson's total and add them together. $75 - 70 = 5$; $90 - 70 = 20$; $50 - 70 = -20$, and $65 - 70 = -5$. We are looking for absolute numbers so we can disregard the signs and add these numbers to arrive at the correct answer: $5 + 20 + 20 + 5 = 50$.

18. c. The range of a data set is the difference between the greatest and least values in the set. The greatest value in this set is 90 and the least value is 50, so the range of the data is $90 - 50$, which equals 40.

19. b. The x-axis is the horizontal axis of a graph.

20. c. First, subtract $\frac{3}{4} - \frac{2}{5}$. To subtract, first rewrite each fraction over the common denominator 20 to get $\frac{15}{20} - \frac{8}{20}$, which equals $\frac{7}{20}$. Next, subtract $\frac{1}{2} - \frac{7}{20}$. Rewrite each fraction over a common denominator 20 to get $\frac{10}{20} - \frac{7}{20} = \frac{3}{20}$.

21. c. One way to find the decimal equivalent of a percent is to rewrite the percent as a fraction: 4% equals $\frac{4}{100}$. Now, write $\frac{4}{100}$ as a decimal. If seeing the fraction "four hundredths" isn't enough to help you write the correct decimal, simply divide the numerator by the denominator to get the correct answer, 0.04.

22. b. To divide $\frac{2}{5}$ by 10, first write 10 as the fraction $\frac{10}{1}$. To divide two fractions, flip the second fraction and multiply. So, $\frac{2}{5} \times \frac{1}{10} = \frac{2}{50}$. Then, $\frac{2}{50}$ reduces to $\frac{1}{25}$. The decimal equivalent of $\frac{1}{25}$ is 0.04.

23. a. To solve this problem, deduce a fraction from the ratio provided. The ratio of men to women at the school is 5:4, which means that 5 out of every 9, or $\frac{5}{9}$, of all students are men. Next, calculate $\frac{5}{9}$ of 7,650 by multiplying to get 4,250.

24. b. First write 2% raise as the decimal 0.02. A 2% raise on $70,200 is $70,200 × 0.02 = $1,404. To find the new salary, add $70,200 + $1,404 = $71,604.

25. d. To determine the fraction of Sam's time spent not making calls you must add together the portions of Sam's day spent not making telephone calls. Fractions can only be added together if they have a common denominator, so rewrite $\frac{1}{8}$ and $\frac{5}{6}$ using the common denominator 24; $\frac{1}{8} = \frac{3}{24}$ and $\frac{5}{6} = \frac{20}{24}$; $\frac{3}{24} + \frac{20}{24} = \frac{23}{24}$.

26. b. The legend of a circle graph shows which sections represents which set of data.

27. a. Add the sections of the pie that represent housing and education. Wendy spends 30% of her budget on housing and 20% on education; therefore, she spends 50%, or half, her monthly budget on housing and education. Because housing is Wendy's biggest single expense, choice **b** is incorrect. Because entertainment spending could be included in the "other" category, choice **c** is not necessarily true. The graph includes no information about what Wendy would do if she had more money, so choice **d** cannot be correct.

28. c. Wendy spends 20% of her budget on education, so if her total monthly budget is $3,000, then her education spending is 20% of $3,000. First, rewrite 20% as $\frac{20}{100}$. Then, calculate 20% of $3,000 by translating the question into the equation $\frac{20}{100} \times 3,000$ and solving to get $600.

29. b. First, write $5\frac{1}{2}$ as the decimal 5.5. Set up the following proportion: $\frac{1 \text{ hour}}{5.5 \text{ miles}} = \frac{x \text{ hours}}{26 \text{ miles}}$. To solve the proportion, cross-multiply to get the equation, $5.5x = 26$. Solve the equation by dividing both sides by 5.5 to get $x = 4.727$ hours. So, the correct choice is 4.7.

30. a. Use the percent equation translation technique to write an equation for this question. The problem states that a warbler weighs 9 grams and eats an amount equal to 80% of its body weight. This means that the warbler eats $\frac{80}{100} \times 9$, which equals $\frac{720}{100}$. In decimal form, $\frac{720}{100}$ equals 7.2.

31. d. To solve this problem, divide the distance (19,800 feet) by the amount of feet in a mile (5,280). $19,800 \div 5,280 = 3.75$ or $3\frac{3}{4}$ miles.

32. a. To multiply mixed numbers, first rewrite them as improper fractions; $8\frac{1}{2}$ should be rewritten as $\frac{17}{2}$, and $3\frac{1}{4}$ should be rewritten as $\frac{13}{4}$. Next, multiply numerator by numerator and denominator by denominator; $\frac{17 \times 13}{2 \times 4} = \frac{221}{8}$. Next, rewrite the product as a mixed number by dividing the numerator by the denominator. The result is 27 with a remainder of 5, so $27\frac{5}{8}$.

33. c. There are several ways to answer this problem. One way is to multiply the number of tickets by 2; $38 \times 2 = 76$. Another way would be to divide the number of tickets by $\frac{1}{2}$; $38 \div \frac{1}{2}$ can be rewritten $38 \times \frac{1}{2} = 76$.

34. c. 20% of 140 equals 28.

35. b. To solve rate problems, apply the equation $rt = d$, where r equals rate, t equals time, and d equals distance. This question provides the time (2 hours 15 minutes) and the rate (8 kilometers per hour). Before plugging these numbers into the equation, rewrite the time as a mixed number. 2 hours 15 minutes equals $2\frac{1}{4}$ hours, so use the mixed number $2\frac{1}{4}$; $8 \times 2\frac{1}{4} = d$; $8 \times 2\frac{1}{4}$ equals $8 \times \frac{9}{4}$, which equals $\frac{72}{4}$, which reduces to 18.

36. b. To find the average number of 911 calls placed each month, add up the 911 calls for every month, and then divide by the total number of months. The total number of calls was $213 + 196 + 257 + 267 + 279 + 308 = 1,520$; $1,520 \div 6 = 253.33$ or $253\frac{1}{3}$.

37. c. The number of 911 calls per month in chronological order was 213, 196, 257, 267, 279, and 308. With the exception of the second month, the frequency of calls had increased with every month in question. Thus, the data supports the conclusion that the frequency of 911 calls tended to increase during the period range shown.

38. b. Reduce fractions by dividing numerator and denominator by a common factor. 14 and 35 are both divisible by 7, so $\frac{14}{35}$ can be reduced to $\frac{2}{5}$.

39. a. According to the problem, last month 42 out of 840 crimes involved petty theft. You can convert this proportion to a percent using the equation $\frac{42}{840} = \frac{x}{100}$. Cross multiply to get $4,200 = 840x$, and then divide both sides of the equation by 840 to get $x = 5$. The correct answer is 5%.

40. d. One way to solve this problem is to convert the mixed number $5\frac{1}{4}$ into an improper fraction. To do this, multiply the whole number (5) by the denominator (4); $5 \times 4 = 20$. Add 20 to the numerator (1) to get $\frac{21}{4}$. Notice we are increasing the size from 6 to 9—this is $\frac{9}{6}$ the size we needed before, which can be reduced to $\frac{3}{2}$. Next, multiply the numerator of $\frac{21}{4}$ by $\frac{3}{2}$ and divide by the denominator; $21 \times \frac{3}{2} = 31\frac{1}{2}$; $31\frac{1}{2} \div 4$ is equivalent to the mixed number $7\frac{7}{8}$.

Section 2: Written Communication

41. a. Each paragraph of the passage describes an inventor whose innovations improved upon the bicycle. There is no evidence to support choice **b**. Choices **c** and **d** are incorrect because they both make statements that, according to the passage, are untrue.

42. d. The fourth paragraph states that James Starley added a gear to the pedals.

43. d. The passage gives a brief history of the bicycle. Choice **a** is incorrect because few opinions are included in the passage. There is no support for choices **b** and **c** within the passage.

44. b. Based on the passage, this is the only possible choice. Starley *revolutionized—transformed—* the bicycle.

45. d. The passage does mention the Red Cross and other agencies, and aiding victims when contacting their insurance companies, but the main focus of the passage is the role FAST plays in assisting victims dealing with the aftermath of a fire.

46. b. The team may help a victim to arrange for boarding up the fire-damaged home, but they do not do it themselves.

47. b. Among all the possible titles, choice **b** is the one that best captures the passage's main point.

48. c. Try replacing the word *expeditiously* with each answer choice. The choice that makes the most sense is **c**, *quickly*.

49. b. The passage is an information sheet about a particular food-borne illness. The main purpose of the passage is to warn readers about the dangers of contracting *Vibrio vulnificus* bacteria from oysters. Of the incorrect choices, choice **a** is too strongly worded; the passage suggests cooking all seafood but does not advise readers to avoid all seafood. No erroneous report is referenced in the passage, so choice **c** cannot be correct. Similarly, the life cycle of oysters is not discussed, so choice **d** cannot be correct.

50. c. In paragraph 2, the passage states: "The infection is much more dangerous to people with weakened immune systems, especially those who suffer from chronic liver disease."

51. a. Choice **a** is supported by the following statement from the passage: "Such individuals should avoid not only eating oysters, but also swimming in oyster-inhabited waters during the summer months, as infection can be transmitted in the water through open wounds." Choices **b**, **c**, and **d** are all contradicted by information in the passage.

52. d. Reread the sentence, substituting each choice for the word *subsequent*. In the context, only choice **d** makes sense.

53. a. The main purpose of the passage is to describe the "broken window" theory, which explains how disorder escalates if it is not checked early. Choices **b** and **d** refer to conditions in a firehouse; the example of the firehouse, however, is offered as a detail in support of the main idea. The answer to a main idea question must summarize the entire passage, not just one part of the passage. Choice **c** summarizes an idea presented in the final paragraph; however, this idea is not the main idea of the entire passage, so this cannot be the correct answer.

54. d. This is a tricky question because several of the choices are potentially challenging vocabulary words. *Condoned* (choice **a**) means *approved*, making it the opposite of *reproved*. *Ostracized* (choice **b**) means *to be outcast*, which like *reproved* has a negative connotation but is not the right word for the context; the passage suggests that the firefighter should be disciplined, not that he or she should be dismissed from the fire department. For this reason, choice **c** is also incorrect.

55. b. Use the process of elimination to get rid of answers that cannot be correct. The author discusses the merits of the broken window theory throughout the first two paragraphs of the passage; therefore, it is inaccurate to say that the author finds the theory "fatally flawed," so choice **a** cannot be correct. The author devotes paragraph 3 to situations in which the broken window theory causes as many problems as it addresses; therefore, choice **c** cannot be correct. Because the author describes the broken window theory as one "that can easily be applied to any situation in society," choice **d** cannot be correct.

56. a. The author makes this point most clearly at the beginning of paragraph 2: ". . . if disrespect to a superior is tolerated, others will be tempted to be disrespectful as well. A management crisis could erupt literally overnight."

57. c. The main purpose of the passage is to outline the procedure for adopting a pet. Because the passage warns that not all citizens make good pet owners, choice **a** cannot be correct. Choices **b** and **d** refer to details in the passage; neither of these details, though important, can be described as the main idea of the passage.

58. c. The passage states that adopted dogs and cats receive implantation of an identifying microchip if they are old enough. Therefore, it can be assumed that some animals are too young to be implanted with a microchip; thus, the passage supports the statement in choice **c**.

59. d. According to the passage, cats receive vaccination for panleukopenia. Dogs do not receive that vaccination.

60. b. This is a tricky question because several of the choices are potentially challenging vocabulary words. The word *imperative* (choice **a**) means *order* or *command*. Neither makes sense in the context of the sentence, so choice **a** cannot be correct. *Evasion* (choice **c**) means *the act of trying to avoid*. This also makes no sense in the context of the sentence. The word *ultimatum* (choice **d**) means *challenge*, which again does not fit the context of the sentence. An *inducement* is a type of *encouragement* (choice **b**).

61. b. The correct spelling is *formulates*.

62. a. The correct spelling is *coroner*.

63. b. The correct spelling is *surmount*.

64. b. The correct spelling is *concoct*.

65. c. The correct spelling is *negotiate*.

66. c. *Painful* is the word that is closest in meaning to *excruciating*.

67. c. *Overused* is the word that is closest in meaning to *trite*.

68. b. The word *monotonous* means *boring*, so the word most nearly its opposite is *interesting*.

69. b. Choices **a** and **c** can be eliminated because neither makes sense in the context of this sentence. The word *zealous* means *passionate* and *benevolent* means *charitable*. Smoking can have a damaging effect on ones health, and *detrimental* and *damaging* are synonyms.

70. a. The word *liaison* means *meeting*; a *liaison* is usually held in secret. Choice **b**, *confection*, means *candy*. Choice **c**, *premonition*, means *hunch* or *suspicion*.

71. c. This is a sentence fragment and is missing the helping verb *was* that would make it a complete sentence.

72. b. Choice **a** uses the passive voice when a better alternative written in the active voice— choice **b**—is available. Choice **c** uses the incorrect spelling of the word *council*.

73. b. Sentences **a** contains the redundant phrase *in size*, and choice **c** does not need the words *at the zoo*.

74. c. Choices **a** and **b** contain capitalization errors. In choice **a**, the words *Commissioner* and *Jarrett* should be capitalized. In choice **b**, the word *department* should not be capitalized.

75. b. Choice **a** is incorrectly punctuated; there should be periods after *Mr.* and *Mrs.* Choice **c** incorrectly capitalizes the words *the meeting*.

76. a. Choice **b** contains an apples and oranges error, comparing *other pianists* to *the style of Thelonious Monk*. A properly formulated sentence must either compare one pianist to another or one pianist's style to another's style. Choice **c** is awkwardly and confusingly worded; choice **a** is a much better formulation of the same idea, so it is the better answer.

77. c. In choice **a**, the phrase *the president of the local Chamber of Commerce* is an appositive that should be set apart with commas. Choice **b** makes a similar error, failing to conclude the appositive phrase *the president of the local Chamber of Commerce* with a comma.

78. c. Choices **a** and **b** contain a subject-verb agreement error; the subject *use* requires a singular verb, not the plural verb *are*.

79. b. Choices **a** and **c** incorrectly use *I* where they should use *me*. Omit *Leticia* from the sentence to see why; would you say *Miguel has been assigned to work on the project with me* or *Miguel has been assigned to work on the project with I*? Because the sentence calls for an indirect object, the word *me* should be used, not *I*.

80. a. When you write a list of items, separate each item on the list with a comma, including the item preceding the word *and*. There should be no comma after the word *and*, as there is in the incorrect choice **c**.

Section 3: Civil Service Skills

81. b. The primary governing principle of customer service is to make things as easy and pleasant for the customer as possible. Choice **b** makes things easier for customers by offering them a variety of means by which to register their complaints. Choice **a** incorrectly suggests that it is good to offer services customers do not want. Choices **c** and **d** make it more difficult and inconvenient for customers to register complaints.

82. a. Once again, the focus of this exam is customer service, so choose the answer that indicates that customer service is the primary priority. Of the choices, only choice **a** focuses on customer satisfaction, so it is the best answer.

83. b. Inaccurate translation creates unnecessary problems and can, in certain circumstances, be even less desirable than no translation service at all (because inaccurate translation typically results in the transmission of incorrect information). Offering the greatest number of languages possible (choice **a**) would be extremely desirable in large diverse communities like New York City, but in most areas the availability of many languages is not that important; translating the most common foreign languages accurately would certainly be more important. Choice **c** would discourage non-English speakers from using government services. Choice **d** represents an important priority but not as important as the one presented in choice **b** because many forms have extremely limited applicability and because all forms, regardless of the language in which they are written, can be filled out with the assistance of an able and accurate translator.

84. d. Choices **a**, **b**, and **c** all provide information that will help the customer resume his or her query should he or she be disconnected during the transfer. Knowing the name of your supervisor will not help the customer continue his or her query, so it is the least important of the four.

85. d. The term *web chat* is used to describe live help provided via the Internet. Web chat is delivered via text in a chat window.

86. a. The only automobile visible in its entirety is a two-door sedan.

87. b. The skateboarder is wearing a jacket. He is hatless and is wearing long trousers. He is not wearing a cape.

88. c. Sylvia Martinez has dark shoulder-length hair. Janet Barnes is the only person whose hair is in an afro style (choice **a**).

89. a. Arthur Jones is the only person wearing a hat, the only one with a beard and moustache, and the only one wearing sunglasses. Sylvia Martinez and Janet Barnes also have dark hair.

90. b. Victor Dinapoli, Arthur Jones, and Maureen Cho all wear glasses. Carlos Domingo wears an eye patch but does not wear glasses.

91. b. The first four letters of the code must be the first four letters of the recipient's last name; therefore, the code for this entry should begin with the letters FONG. Choices **a** and **d** do not start with the letters FONG and, therefore, can be eliminated. The fifth letter in the code must be the recipient's first initial; therefore, the fifth letter of the code should be D. Only choice **b** has D as its fifth letter, so it must be the correct answer.

92. d. The first four letters of the code must be the first four letters of the recipient's last name; therefore, the code for this entry should begin with the letters RAMI. This information allows you to eliminate choices **a** and **b**. Study choices **c** and **d** to detect differences. You should see that choice **c** records the date of the correspondence JUN2, while choice **d** records the date JUN02. Check the rules to see that JUN02 is the proper format; the correct answer is choice **d**.

93. d. The code for this response should be: the first four letters of the recipient's last name (DAVI); the recipient's first initial (J); the first two digits of the recipient's street address (12); response (R); low priority (2); on October 23 (OCT23). The correct code is DAVIJ12R2OCT23.

94. c. This letter was sent to a recipient whose last name begins with the letters BERN; therefore, only choices **a** and **c** can be correct. Eliminate choices **b** and **d**. The first two digits of the recipient's address are 35; therefore, choice **a** cannot be correct. By process of elimination, the answer must be choice **c**.

95. a. The code states that two digits are to be used to indicate the recipient's street address; if the address is only one digit long, that digit should be preceded by a zero (0).

96. c. One incident of cold food stored at too high a temperature should be coded C. Two incidents of animal droppings should be coded HH. One incident of improperly labeled food should be coded p. The correct code for this set of violations is CHHp.

97. a. Three incidents of improper storage of toxic cleaning materials should be coded ppp. One incident of a misplaced consumer advisory should be coded r. The correct code for this set of violations is pppr.

98. a. All four of the incidents described earn a three-point deduction from 100, a perfect score: 4 × 3 equals 12; 100 − 12 equals 88.

99. d. The inspector observed multiple incidents of the violation coded s. The letter s is the code for smoking in the food preparation area.

100. b. Each of the violations coded with a capital letter results in a five-point deduction; each of the violations coded with a lower-case letter results in a three-point deduction: 2 × 5 equals 10 and 3 × 3 equals 9; 10 + 9 equals 19, and 100 − 19 equals 81.

CIVIL SERVICE PRACTICE EXAM 3

For this exam, pull together all the tips you've been practicing since the first practice exam. Give yourself the time and space to work. Because you won't be taking the real test in your living room, you might want to take this one in an unfamiliar location, such as a library. Make sure you have plenty of time to complete the exam in one sitting. In addition, use what you have learned from reading the answer explanations on the previous practice exams. Remember the types of questions that have caused problems for you in the past, and when you are unsure, try to consider how those answers were explained.

Once again, use the answer explanations at the end of the exam to understand questions you may have missed.

Civil Service Practice Exam 3

1.	ⓐ	ⓑ	ⓒ	ⓓ
2.	ⓐ	ⓑ	ⓒ	ⓓ
3.	ⓐ	ⓑ	ⓒ	ⓓ
4.	ⓐ	ⓑ	ⓒ	ⓓ
5.	ⓐ	ⓑ	ⓒ	ⓓ
6.	ⓐ	ⓑ	ⓒ	ⓓ
7.	ⓐ	ⓑ	ⓒ	ⓓ
8.	ⓐ	ⓑ	ⓒ	ⓓ
9.	ⓐ	ⓑ	ⓒ	ⓓ
10.	ⓐ	ⓑ	ⓒ	ⓓ
11.	ⓐ	ⓑ	ⓒ	ⓓ
12.	ⓐ	ⓑ	ⓒ	ⓓ
13.	ⓐ	ⓑ	ⓒ	ⓓ
14.	ⓐ	ⓑ	ⓒ	ⓓ
15.	ⓐ	ⓑ	ⓒ	ⓓ
16.	ⓐ	ⓑ	ⓒ	ⓓ
17.	ⓐ	ⓑ	ⓒ	ⓓ
18.	ⓐ	ⓑ	ⓒ	ⓓ
19.	ⓐ	ⓑ	ⓒ	ⓓ
20.	ⓐ	ⓑ	ⓒ	ⓓ
21.	ⓐ	ⓑ	ⓒ	ⓓ
22.	ⓐ	ⓑ	ⓒ	ⓓ
23.	ⓐ	ⓑ	ⓒ	ⓓ
24.	ⓐ	ⓑ	ⓒ	ⓓ
25.	ⓐ	ⓑ	ⓒ	ⓓ
26.	ⓐ	ⓑ	ⓒ	ⓓ
27.	ⓐ	ⓑ	ⓒ	ⓓ
28.	ⓐ	ⓑ	ⓒ	ⓓ
29.	ⓐ	ⓑ	ⓒ	ⓓ
30.	ⓐ	ⓑ	ⓒ	ⓓ
31.	ⓐ	ⓑ	ⓒ	ⓓ
32.	ⓐ	ⓑ	ⓒ	ⓓ
33.	ⓐ	ⓑ	ⓒ	ⓓ
34.	ⓐ	ⓑ	ⓒ	ⓓ
35.	ⓐ	ⓑ	ⓒ	ⓓ

36.	ⓐ	ⓑ	ⓒ	ⓓ
37.	ⓐ	ⓑ	ⓒ	ⓓ
38.	ⓐ	ⓑ	ⓒ	ⓓ
39.	ⓐ	ⓑ	ⓒ	ⓓ
40.	ⓐ	ⓑ	ⓒ	ⓓ
41.	ⓐ	ⓑ	ⓒ	ⓓ
42.	ⓐ	ⓑ	ⓒ	ⓓ
43.	ⓐ	ⓑ	ⓒ	ⓓ
44.	ⓐ	ⓑ	ⓒ	ⓓ
45.	ⓐ	ⓑ	ⓒ	ⓓ
46.	ⓐ	ⓑ	ⓒ	ⓓ
47.	ⓐ	ⓑ	ⓒ	ⓓ
48.	ⓐ	ⓑ	ⓒ	ⓓ
49.	ⓐ	ⓑ	ⓒ	ⓓ
50.	ⓐ	ⓑ	ⓒ	ⓓ
51.	ⓐ	ⓑ	ⓒ	ⓓ
52.	ⓐ	ⓑ	ⓒ	ⓓ
53.	ⓐ	ⓑ	ⓒ	ⓓ
54.	ⓐ	ⓑ	ⓒ	ⓓ
55.	ⓐ	ⓑ	ⓒ	ⓓ
56.	ⓐ	ⓑ	ⓒ	ⓓ
57.	ⓐ	ⓑ	ⓒ	ⓓ
58.	ⓐ	ⓑ	ⓒ	ⓓ
59.	ⓐ	ⓑ	ⓒ	ⓓ
60.	ⓐ	ⓑ	ⓒ	ⓓ
61.	ⓐ	ⓑ	ⓒ	ⓓ
62.	ⓐ	ⓑ	ⓒ	ⓓ
63.	ⓐ	ⓑ	ⓒ	ⓓ
64.	ⓐ	ⓑ	ⓒ	ⓓ
65.	ⓐ	ⓑ	ⓒ	ⓓ
66.	ⓐ	ⓑ	ⓒ	ⓓ
67.	ⓐ	ⓑ	ⓒ	ⓓ
68.	ⓐ	ⓑ	ⓒ	ⓓ
69.	ⓐ	ⓑ	ⓒ	ⓓ
70.	ⓐ	ⓑ	ⓒ	ⓓ

71.	ⓐ	ⓑ	ⓒ	ⓓ
72.	ⓐ	ⓑ	ⓒ	ⓓ
73.	ⓐ	ⓑ	ⓒ	ⓓ
74.	ⓐ	ⓑ	ⓒ	ⓓ
75.	ⓐ	ⓑ	ⓒ	ⓓ
76.	ⓐ	ⓑ	ⓒ	ⓓ
77.	ⓐ	ⓑ	ⓒ	ⓓ
78.	ⓐ	ⓑ	ⓒ	ⓓ
79.	ⓐ	ⓑ	ⓒ	ⓓ
80.	ⓐ	ⓑ	ⓒ	ⓓ
81.	ⓐ	ⓑ	ⓒ	ⓓ
82.	ⓐ	ⓑ	ⓒ	ⓓ
83.	ⓐ	ⓑ	ⓒ	ⓓ
84.	ⓐ	ⓑ	ⓒ	ⓓ
85.	ⓐ	ⓑ	ⓒ	ⓓ
86.	ⓐ	ⓑ	ⓒ	ⓓ
87.	ⓐ	ⓑ	ⓒ	ⓓ
88.	ⓐ	ⓑ	ⓒ	ⓓ
89.	ⓐ	ⓑ	ⓒ	ⓓ
90.	ⓐ	ⓑ	ⓒ	ⓓ
91.	ⓐ	ⓑ	ⓒ	ⓓ
92.	ⓐ	ⓑ	ⓒ	ⓓ
93.	ⓐ	ⓑ	ⓒ	ⓓ
94.	ⓐ	ⓑ	ⓒ	ⓓ
95.	ⓐ	ⓑ	ⓒ	ⓓ
96.	ⓐ	ⓑ	ⓒ	ⓓ
97.	ⓐ	ⓑ	ⓒ	ⓓ
98.	ⓐ	ⓑ	ⓒ	ⓓ
99.	ⓐ	ⓑ	ⓒ	ⓓ
100.	ⓐ	ⓑ	ⓒ	ⓓ

Section 1: Mathematics

Select the best answer for each question.

1. Patrolman Peterson drove $3\frac{1}{2}$ miles to the police station. Then he drove $4\frac{3}{4}$ miles to his first assignment. Next, he drove $3\frac{2}{3}$ miles back to the police station for a meeting. Finally, he drove $3\frac{1}{2}$ miles home. How many miles did Patrolman Peterson drive?
   a. $15\frac{5}{12}$
   b. $14\frac{5}{12}$
   c. $14\frac{1}{4}$
   d. $13\frac{11}{12}$

2. Martine made a pie and cut it into eight equal slices. He kept two slices for himself and gave the rest of the pie to April. April gave Mae $\frac{1}{3}$ of her share of the pie and ate the rest of what she had gotten from Martine. How many slices of pie did April eat?
   a. 2
   b. $2\frac{1}{3}$
   c. 3
   d. 4

3. $\frac{3}{5} - \frac{2}{10}$
   a. $\frac{1}{5}$
   b. $\frac{2}{5}$
   c. $\frac{3}{10}$
   d. $\frac{7}{10}$

4. A bus travels along a highway at a constant rate of 55 miles per hour. How far does the bus travel in 3 hours 24 minutes?
   a. 165 miles
   b. 178.2 miles
   c. 187 miles
   d. 192.5 miles

5. A local municipality charges 5.5% tax on all liquor purchases. What is the decimal equivalent of this tax?
   a. 0.50
   b. 0.055
   c. 0.05
   d. 0.005

Study the following graph, and then use it to answer questions 6 through 8.

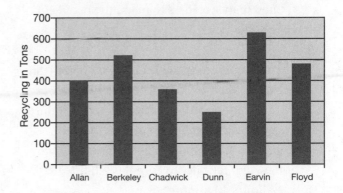

Tons of Recycling Collected Annually by County

6. The data on the *x*-axis represents the
   a. amount of recycling collected, in tons.
   b. names of the counties.
   c. time period during which the data was collected.
   d. names of the companies hired to collect recycling.

7. The data on the *y*-axis represents the
   a. amount of recycling collected in tons.
   b. names of the counties.
   c. time period during which the data was collected.
   d. names of the companies hired to collect recycling.

8. The graph best supports which of the following conclusions?

   a. The population of Berkeley County is greater than the population of Floyd County.

   b. Of all the state's residents, the people of Berkeley County are most enthusiastic about recycling.

   c. Dunn County does not need to collect its recycling as frequently as does Earvin County.

   d. The people of Floyd County are more avid newspaper readers than are the people of Chadwick County.

9. Joanne must complete three tasks at work. She estimates that the first two tasks will each take her 45 minutes to complete and that the third task will take her 2 hours 10 minutes to complete. If Joanne's estimate is correct, how long will it take her to complete all three tasks?

   a. 2 hours 40 minutes

   b. 3 hours

   c. 3 hours 20 minutes

   d. 3 hours 40 minutes

10. The Gleason Theater seats 296 people and was sold out for the premier of a new play, *Captain Coffee*. Friends and family of the cast accounted for $\frac{5}{8}$ of all the seats. VIP tickets were given away on the radio and winners accounted for 37 of the seats. The general public bought the remaining tickets. What portion of the total seats was taken by the general public?

   a. $\frac{1}{4}$

   b. $\frac{3}{8}$

   c. $\frac{2}{5}$

   d. $\frac{1}{2}$

11. $\frac{2}{3} + \frac{1}{5} =$

   a. $\frac{3}{15}$

   b. $\frac{7}{15}$

   c. $\frac{10}{15}$

   d. $\frac{13}{15}$

12. Reduce $\frac{55}{120}$ to lowest terms.

   a. $\frac{10}{12}$

   b. $\frac{25}{60}$

   c. $\frac{2}{7}$

   d. $\frac{11}{24}$

13. Ken earns a bonus when he works on Saturdays. The bonus is $1\frac{1}{2}$ times his standard hourly pay for the first four hours, and 2 times his standard pay on any additional hours he works. If his standard hourly pay is $12.50, how much bonus pay does Ken earn when he works six hours on a Saturday?

   a. $75

   b. $100

   c. $112.50

   d. $125

14. $\frac{72}{10} =$

   a. $7\frac{1}{10}$

   b. $\frac{10}{72}$

   c. $\frac{5}{36}$

   d. $7\frac{1}{5}$

Study the following graph, and then use it to answer questions 15 through 17.

	RETAIL PRICE (STICKER)	MILES PER GALLON (CITY)	MILES PER GALLON (HIGHWAY)
PRICE AND MILES PER GALLON BY MAKE OF AUTOMOBILE			
MAKE			
Voltero	$16,600	31	38
Accellator	$22,100	22	28
Montannic	$27,800	16	20
GXC 501	$31,500	27	32

15. Which conclusion is best supported by the data in the table?
   a. There is no correlation between the price of a car and its gas mileage.
   b. The more an automobile costs, the poorer its gas mileage.
   c. The chief factors in determining the price of an automobile are its size and weight.
   d. Most people pay considerably less than retail price for a new car.

16. What is the range of highway mileage shown in the table?
   a. 38
   b. 15
   c. 10
   d. 18

17. Compare the price of the different automobiles as a function of miles per gallon each is able to drive in the city. Which is the most expensive in this comparison?
   a. Voltero
   b. Accellator
   c. Montannic
   d. GXC 501

18. An investment banker earns $1.2 million in salary in a year. If his firm gives him a 4.5% raise, how much is his new salary?
   a. $54,000
   b. $1,054,000
   c. $1,254,000
   d. $15,240,000

19. $7\frac{1}{5} - 4\frac{4}{5} =$
   a. $2\frac{2}{5}$
   b. $3\frac{2}{5}$
   c. $1\frac{3}{5}$
   d. 0

20. Find the percent equivalent of 0.7.
   a. 7%
   b. 70%
   c. 0.7%
   d. 700%

21. Mr. Wallace is writing a budget request to upgrade his personal computer system. He wants to purchase 256 mb of SDRAM, which costs $80; two new software programs that cost $350 each; a 2 GB flash memory card for $65; and a new scanner for $165. What is the total amount Mr. Wallace should write on his budget request?
  a. $660
  b. $1,010
  c. $1,356
  d. $1,366

22. A migrating bird flies 12 hours per day. If the bird flies at an average speed of 20 miles per hour, how far does the bird fly in one day?
  a. 400 miles
  b. 240 miles
  c. 200 miles
  d. 32 miles

23. $\frac{2}{5} \div \frac{4}{7} =$
  a. $\frac{8}{35}$
  b. 1
  c. $\frac{1}{2}$
  d. $\frac{7}{10}$

24. Frank wants a pair of jeans that are priced at $86.00. He has a coupon for 20% off that price. What price would Frank pay if he used his coupon to buy this pair of jeans?
  a. $64.50
  b. $66.00
  c. $68.00
  d. $68.80

25. $5\frac{1}{7} =$
  a. $\frac{5}{7}$
  b. $\frac{13}{7}$
  c. $\frac{34}{7}$
  d. $\frac{36}{7}$

26. Find the fraction equivalent of 0.0034.
  a. $\frac{34}{100}$
  b. $\frac{34}{1,000}$
  c. $\frac{34}{10,000}$
  d. $\frac{34}{100,000}$

Study the following graph, and then use it to answer questions 27 and 28.

Causes of Household Fires in Percentages

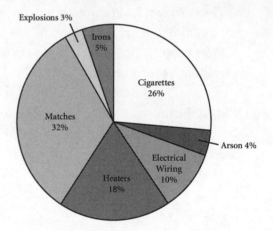

27. According to the circle graph, the most common cause of household fires is
  a. matches.
  b. cigarettes.
  c. heaters.
  d. arson.

28. The city of Grandee had 500 household fires last year. Based on the information in the graph, how many of those fires were most likely caused by explosions?
- **a.** 3
- **b.** 5
- **c.** 15
- **d.** 30

29. A community service organization has a staff of 40 people. At any given time, six members of the staff are on duty. What percentage of the staff is on duty at the organization?
- **a.** 6%
- **b.** 8%
- **c.** 12%
- **d.** 15%

30. A lottery jackpot of $30,000 was split between four co-workers. Will and David each received 20% of the jackpot and the rest was split between June and Karen. If Karen is given a portion of the jackpot that is 3 times the size of the portion given to June, how much was given to Karen?
- **a.** $4,500
- **b.** $6,000
- **c.** $12,000
- **d.** $13,000

31. Bill leaves his house and walks directly toward Melissa's house at a rate of 110 yards per minute. Melissa leaves her house at the same time and walks directly toward Bill's house at a rate of 95 yards per minute. Bill and Melissa's houses are exactly 2,870 yards apart. In how many minutes will Bill and Melissa meet?
- **a.** 11 minutes
- **b.** 14 minutes
- **c.** 26 minutes
- **d.** 30 minutes

32. Thirty percent of The Parking Authority's employees are over the age of 50. If The Parking Authority has 150 employees, how many are over the age of 50?
- **a.** 45
- **b.** 50
- **c.** 105
- **d.** 120

33. At her local supermarket, Eva purchases eggs for $4.99, crackers for $2.69, and two yogurts for $0.60 each. If she has $20.00, how much change does she receive?
- **a.** $7.68
- **b.** $8.88
- **c.** $11.12
- **d.** $20.00

34. $5\frac{1}{3} \div 1\frac{5}{9} =$
- **a.** $3\frac{3}{7}$
- **b.** $3\frac{7}{9}$
- **c.** $6\frac{8}{9}$
- **d.** $4\frac{289}{42}$

35. An empty swimming pool is filled by two inlet pipes. One pipe can fill $\frac{1}{10}$ of the swimming pool in one hour. The other can fill $\frac{1}{8}$ of the swimming pool in one hour. If both inlet pipes are used to fill the pool, how many hours will it take to fill the empty pool?
- **a.** 8 hours
- **b.** 6 hours
- **c.** 4 hours 6 minutes
- **d.** 2 hours 45 minutes

36. A jar with 200 marbles weighs 5 pounds. If 5% of the marbles are red, how much do just the red marbles weigh?

a. $\frac{1}{40}$ pound

b. $\frac{1}{20}$ pound

c. $\frac{1}{4}$ pound

d. $\frac{2}{5}$ pound

37. $6\frac{1}{5} \times 75 =$

a. 450

b. $71\frac{1}{5}$

c. 465

d. $522\frac{3}{5}$

Study the following graph, and then use it to answer questions 38 through 40.

Automobile Accidents by Time Period

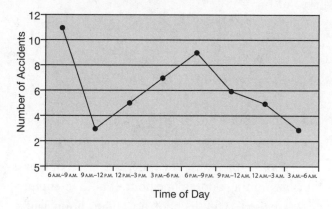

38. What is the range of the data shown in the graph?

a. 3

b. 8

c. 11

d. 14

39. The average (arithmetic mean) number of accidents per three-hour time period is

a. between 3 and 4.

b. between 4 and 5.

c. between 5 and 6.

d. between 6 and 7.

40. The number of accidents per time period is represented by the

a. scale.

b. *x*-axis.

c. *y*-axis.

d. legend.

Section 2: Written Communication

Reading Comprehension—Questions 41 through 60

Read the following passage. Then, answer questions 41 through 44.

Federal, state, and local courts produce a mountain of documents every day. Those documents need to be recorded and stored accurately in order for the various legal systems to function. The person who maintains these records is called the clerk of the court.

The parameters of the clerk of the court's job is defined by statute and so varies somewhat from <u>jurisdiction</u> to jurisdiction, but most clerks share a number of responsibilities in common. First and foremost, the clerk maintains the court's clerical records. Everything from the court's seal to the contracts and the orders it approves, to the judgments it issues to the verdicts it hands down must be accurately recorded and filed. The clerk also maintains official records of all marriages, leases, mortgages, deeds, and other property transfers.

Most localities assign additional responsibilities to the clerk of the court. In many jurisdictions, the clerk is empowered to perform marriages; the clerk of the court in St. Mary's County, Maryland, for example, conducts more than 3,000 marriages per year. Many clerks are responsible for issuing passports and jury summons, distributing jurors' pay, and overseeing the collection and distribution of court fines and court-ordered child support and alimony. As if those jobs weren't enough to keep a clerk busy, in some jurisdictions the clerk is also the chief financial officer of the court, responsible for making sure that budgets are met, that paychecks are issued, and that court expenditures all conform with the law.

With such a formidable list of tasks, it's no wonder that most clerks' offices are busy places. The operation of the clerk's duties requires a well-trained, dedicated, and efficient staff. Organizational skill is obviously required of anyone working for the clerk, but people skills are also important; the clerk's office deals with the public on a regular basis, often under stressful circumstances. Although demanding, work in a clerk's office brings with it the satisfaction of knowing that one has performed an essential role in allowing our court system to function properly.

41. The author's primary purpose in writing this passage is to
   a. argue that most clerks of the court deserve salary increases.
   b. inform people of the number of marriages performed annually in the United States.
   c. describe the many functions of the clerk of the court.
   d. define the term *clerical records*.

42. The final paragraph of the passage suggests that
   a. very few people are qualified to work in the clerk of the court's office.
   b. the clerk of the court's office is a satisfying place to work.
   c. all one needs to succeed in the clerk of the court's office is good people skills.
   d. the court's seal is an extremely important document.

43. As used in the passage, the word *jurisdiction* most nearly means
   a. domain.
   b. nation.
   c. individual.
   d. political party.

44. According to the passage, the clerk of courts
   a. decides verdicts in criminal cases.
   b. determines alimony levels in divorce cases.
   c. exists only in the state of Maryland.
   d. maintains the court's records.

Read the following passage. Then, answer questions 45 through 48.

State and local governments are almost always underfunded, a situation that compels them to constantly seek new ways to cut costs. Of course, the same governments are run by elected officials who, as a consequence of the conditions of their employment, must concern themselves with their constituents' satisfaction with government services. Thus, government leaders face a near-impossible challenge: reduce costs while improving—or at least, not diminishing—the quality of service.

In recent years, governments have increasingly turned to outsourcing as a solution to their problems. Working on the belief that the private sector operates more efficiently than does the government, state and local governments have started contracting private companies to perform jobs previously managed publicly. The results have been mixed.

One of the great success stories of government outsourcing is found in New York City. The city owns 13 public golf courses, which, under city management, fell into disrepair. The courses were not only poorly kept, they were dangerous; one course in the Bronx became a notorious dumping ground for garbage and the occasional corpse. Making matters worse, the city lost an average of $2 million per year on the golf courses. Since contracting out operations, the city has reversed that $2 million loss, instead realizing an annual profit of $2 million; best of all, they've done it without significantly increasing course income. Furthermore, conditions on the courses have greatly improved, as the private operators have invested substantially in material upgrades.

Texas has not been quite as fortunate, however, in its effort to privatize management of welfare benefits. With its caseload increasing and federal funding shrinking, the state naturally looked for a way to reduce costs. Privatization seemed the best choice: Contract bids suggested that the states could save hundreds of millions of dollars by shifting benefits administration services to a private company. The relationship started promisingly: The company replaced the state's <u>antiquated</u> computer program with a modern database, and then opened four new call centers to handle client queries. Unfortunately, the quality of service was initially poor, with many clients complaining that the call centers were difficult to reach and that the information they provided was often inaccurate. As a result, clients quickly grew to distrust the new system. The state and

its contractor are now attempting to address the problems; it is too early to know whether they will succeed.

Outsourcing offers some benefits to governments eyeing the bottom line. It is by no means a guaranteed panacea, however, and public officials must consider each situation closely before deciding whether outsourcing is an appropriate solution.

45. The author's main idea is best summarized by which of the following?
   a. The municipal golf courses of New York have both grown more profitable and improved in quality since their management was outsourced.
   b. The state of Texas may never be able to undo the damage caused by its experiment in outsourcing social services.
   c. State and local governments always save money and improve services when they outsource.
   d. Outsourcing of government services can be successful, but by no means is it guaranteed to solve more problems than it causes.

46. As used in the passage, the word *antiquated* most nearly means
   a. outdated.
   b. broken.
   c. slow.
   d. uncertain.

47. According to the passage, clients of Texas's outsourced social service programs complained that
   a. call center operators did not speak Spanish.
   b. benefits checks were slow in arriving.
   c. clients were often given incorrect information.
   d. user fees discouraged them from taking advantage of the programs.

48. The passage suggests that the contractors who took control of New York City's golf courses
- **a.** had little previous experience in golf course management.
- **b.** used course income more efficiently than did the city.
- **c.** charged golfers much higher user fees than did the city.
- **d.** were difficult to reach by telephone.

Read the following passage. Then, answer questions 49 through 52.

Most criminals do not suffer from antisocial personality disorder; however, nearly all persons with this disorder have been in trouble with the law at some point in their lives. Sometimes labeled sociopaths, they are often a grim problem for society. Their crimes often range from con games to murder, and they are set apart by what appears to be a complete lack of conscience. Often attractive and charming, and always inordinately self-confident, they nevertheless demonstrate a disturbing emotional shallowness, as if they had been born without a faculty as vital as sight or hearing. These individuals are not legally insane, nor do they suffer from the distortions of thought associated with mental illness; however, some experts believe they are mentally ill. If so, it is an illness that is exceptionally resistant to treatment, particularly since these individuals have a marked inability to learn from their past actions. It is this latter trait that makes them a special problem for law enforcement officials. Their ability to mimic true emotion enables them to convince prison officials, judges, and psychiatrists that they feel remorse. However, when released from incarceration they go back to their old tricks, impulsive destructiveness, and sometimes lethal deceptions.

49. Based on the passage, which of the following is likely not a characteristic of a person with antisocial personality disorder?
- **a.** delusions of persecution
- **b.** feelings of superiority
- **c.** inability to suffer deeply
- **d.** inability to feel joy

50. Which of the following careers would probably best suit a person with antisocial personality disorder?
- **a.** soldier with ambition to make officer
- **b.** warden of a large penitentiary
- **c.** loan officer in a bank
- **d.** salesperson dealing in nonexistent real estate

51. Based on the passage, which of the following words best sums up the inner emotional life of a person with antisocial personality?
- **a.** angry
- **b.** empty
- **c.** anxious
- **d.** repressed

52. According to the passage, which of the following characteristics is most helpful to a person with an antisocial personality in terms of getting out of trouble with the law?
- **a.** inability to learn from the past
- **b.** ability to mimic the emotions of others
- **c.** attractiveness and charm
- **d.** indifference to the suffering of others

Read the following passage. Then, answer questions 53 through 56.

Did you ever wonder how the U.S. Postal Service chooses the images that appear on postage stamps? Nearly all the subjects of stamps originate with a suggestion from the public. The Citizens' Stamp Advisory Committee (CSAC), a 15-member board appointed by the Postmaster General, is charged with reviewing suggestions and selecting approximately 25 <u>commemorative</u> stamps each year.

Upon receiving a suggestion, the CSAC first determines whether the stamp meets the 12 major criteria for selection. Among the qualifying characteristics: The subject must be American or related to America; the subject must be of national, rather than regional or local, interest; if human, the subject must been deceased for at least ten years (except for former presidents, who can be honored immediately after their deaths); and, if commemorating an historic event, the stamp must be released on an anniversary that is a multiple of 50. Prohibited subjects include individual towns, cities, elementary and secondary schools, hospitals, and libraries; fraternal, political, sectarian, and service organizations; and religious groups.

If a nominee meets all the qualifications, it is added to the roster for consideration at the upcoming meeting of the CSAC, which meets four times each year. The committee may decide to reject the nominee, or it may set it aside for consideration of future issuance. All stamps in the latter category must undergo a second round of review before they can be scheduled for design and their subsequent release.

If you've submitted a suggestion to the CSAC, don't expect to be notified of the committee's decision; the committee has no staff, and announcements of upcoming stamp subjects are made by press release only. In other words, if you want to see whether your stamp has been chosen, you'll have to read the newspaper or check the U.S. Postal Service website. You should also be aware that the entire selection process typically takes three years. If you're the impatient type, suggesting subjects for stamps is probably not the right hobby for you!

53. As used in the passage, the word *commemorative* most nearly means
   a. funereal.
   b. mnemonic.
   c. celebratory.
   d. exclusive.

54. The author's purpose in writing this passage is to
   a. explain a process.
   b. define terms.
   c. persuade an audience.
   d. propose a new idea.

55. According to the passage, the Citizens' Stamp Advisory Committee
   a. determines the rules for selecting stamps.
   b. meets four times each year.
   c. is made up of former Postmasters General of the United States.
   d. contacts everyone who suggests a subject for a stamp.

56. Based on information in the passage, which of the following is the subject most likely to be honored with a U.S. postage stamp?
   a. the city of Chicago
   b. the current president of the United States
   c. the Republican Party
   d. Yellowstone National Park

Read the following passage. Then, answer questions 57 through 60.

Although many companies offer tuition reimbursement, most reimburse employees only for classes that are relevant to their position. This is a very limiting policy. A company that reimburses employees for all college courses—whether job related or not—offers a service not only to the employees, but to the entire company and greater community as well.

One good reason for giving employees unconditional tuition reimbursement is that it shows the company's dedication to its employees. In today's economy, where job security is a thing of the past and employees feel more and more expendable, it is important for a company to demonstrate to its employees that it cares. The best way to do this is with concrete investments in its employees and their futures.

In turn, this dedication will create greater employee loyalty. A company that releases funds to pay for the education of its employees will get its money back by having employees stay with the company longer. Employee turnover will be reduced because even the employees who do not take advantage of the tuition reimbursement program will be more loyal—just knowing that their company cares enough to pay for their education invokes loyalty. Most importantly, the company that has an unrestricted tuition reimbursement program will have higher quality employees.

Although these companies do indeed run the risk of losing money on an employee who goes on to another job at a different company as soon as he or she gets a degree, more often than not the employee will stay with the company. And even if employees do leave after graduation, it generally takes several years to complete any degree program. If the employee leaves upon graduation, the employer will have had a more sophisticated, more intelligent, and therefore more valuable and productive employee during that employee's tenure. If the employee stays, that education will doubly benefit the company. Not only is the employee more educated, but now that employee is in a better position to be promoted, and the company does not have the challenge of filling a high-level vacancy from the outside. Though unconditional tuition reimbursement requires a significant investment on the employer's part, it is perhaps one of the wisest investments a company can make.

57. According to the passage, unconditional tuition reimbursement is good for which of the following reasons?
   a. employees get a cheaper education
   b. employees become more valuable
   c. employees can find better jobs
   d. employers lose a great deal of money

58. The author's reason for writing this passage was to
   a. entertain the reader.
   b. narrate a story.
   c. explain tuition reimbursement.
   d. persuade the reader.

59. The writer most likely uses the word *wisest* in the last sentence, rather than words such as *profitable*, *practical*, or *beneficial*, because
   a. wisdom is associated with education, the subject of the passage.
   b. the writer is trying to appeal to people who are already highly educated.
   c. education could not be considered practical.
   d. the word *beneficial* is too abstract for readers to comprehend.

60. In paragraph two, the word *expendable* most nearly means
   a. expensive.
   b. flexible.
   c. replaceable.
   d. extraneous.

Spelling—Questions 61 through 65

Select the choice that is spelled correctly.

61. Mrs. Ramirez agrees that the effectiveness of her new hiring policy is _____
   a. debatible
   b. debateable
   c. debatable

62. The archaeologist strained the sand through a _____ to see if it contained any small artifacts.
   a. sieve
   b. sive
   c. seive

63. Which of the following words is spelled incorrectly?
   a. subside
   b. feesable
   c. impersonal

64. Which of the following words is spelled incorrectly?
   a. recktify
   b. narrate
   c. transcribe

65. Which of the following words is spelled incorrectly?
   a. atrocious
   b. infernal
   c. detearierating

Vocabulary—Questions 66 through 70

Select the best choice for each question.

66. Find the word that is closest in meaning to the underlined word.
   an <u>opulent</u> home
   a. luxurious
   b. shabby
   c. occasional

67. Find the word that is closest in meaning to the underlined word.
   a <u>laborious</u> task
   a. profitable
   b. simple
   c. difficult

68. Find the word that is most nearly the opposite of the underlined word.
   the <u>pompous</u> professor
   a. uneducated
   b. humble
   c. strict

69. Find the word that best completes the sentence.
   If you collect my mail while I am on vacation, I will _____ by mowing your lawn when I return.
   a. renege
   b. reciprocate
   c. rejuvenate

70. Find the word that best completes the sentence.
   The defendant's fingerprints on the murder weapon provided the most _____ evidence against her.
   a. incriminating
   b. exonerating
   c. dubious

Grammar—Questions 71 through 80

Select the best choice for each question.

71. Which of the following is a complete sentence?
a. Because of the worsening weather conditions, the cancellation of tonight's event.
b. The worsening of weather conditions has caused the cancellation of tonight's event.
c. The cancellation of tonight's event on account of there being worsening weather conditions.

72. Select the sentence that is written most correctly.
a. "Would you prefer sugar or artificial sweetener with your coffee?" Humphrey inquired.
b. Would you prefer sugar or artificial sweetener with your coffee, Humphrey inquired?
c. "Would you prefer sugar or artificial sweetener with your coffee?" Humphrey inquired?

73. Select the sentence that is written most correctly.
a. Located along the railroad tracks, the noise of passing trains disrupted performances at the community theater.
b. Located along the railroad tracks, the community theater had, by the noise of passing trains, its performances disrupted.
c. Because it was located along the railroad tracks, the community theater had its performances disrupted by the noise of passing trains.

74. Select the sentence that is written most correctly.
a. Mr. and Mrs. Harrison decided to have a picnic to celebrate Labor Day.
b. Mr. and mrs. Harrison decided to have a picnic to celebrate Labor day.
c. Mr. and Mrs. Harrison decided to have a Picnic to celebrate Labor day.

75. Select the sentence that is written most correctly.
a. Each member of the Jameson family holds an advanced degree in either science or mathematics.
b. Each member of the Jameson family hold an advanced degree in either science or mathematics.
c. Each and every member of the Jameson family hold an advanced degree in either science or mathematics.

76. Select the sentence that is written most correctly.
a. Dr. Richard K Brown, CEO of the company, will speak to the scientists at Brookhaven National Laboratory on Wed at 9:00 A.M.
b. Dr Richard K Brown, C.E.O. of the company, will speak to the scientists at the Brookhaven National Laboratory on Wed. at 9:00 A.M.
c. Dr. Richard K. Brown, C.E.O. of the company, will speak to the scientists at the Brookhaven National Laboratory on Wed. at 9:00 A.M.

77. Select the sentence that is written most correctly.
a. A decision was made by the manager and will be followed by her subordinates.
b. A decision was made by the manager her subordinates will follow it.
c. The manager made a decision and her subordinates will follow it.

78. Select the sentence that is written most correctly.
a. The committee did their work very effectively.
b. The committee did their work very effective.
c. The committee did its work very effectively.

79. Select the sentence that is written most correctly.
   a. The bands performance has greatly bettered since they increased the length of their practice sessions.
   b. The band's performance has greatly improved since they increased the length of their practice sessions.
   c. The bands performance has greatly improved since they increased the length of their practice session's.

80. Select the sentence that is written most correctly.
   a. The consensus of opinion among the advertisers was that customers would be enticed by a free gift.
   b. The consensus of opinion among the advertisers was that customers would be enticed by a gift.
   c. The consensus among the advertisers was that customers would be enticed by a gift.

Section 3: Civil Service Skills

Customer Service— Questions 81 through 85

Select the best choice for each question.

81. Government offices strive to address customers' queries during a single visit or exchange whenever possible, a principle known as
   a. self-service communication.
   b. first contact resolution.
   c. interactive voice response.
   d. the abandonment rate.

82. Responses to citizen complaints should be
   a. processed twice annually to ensure uniformity of response.
   b. approved by a supervisor before they are delivered.
   c. delivered as quickly and accurately as possible.
   d. withheld until the citizen completes a customer satisfaction evaluation.

83. When scheduling an agency's office hours, a supervisor's primary consideration should be
   a. employees' personal commitments outside work.
   b. the schedules of other agencies with which the agency sometimes interacts.
   c. the time of year and its effect on electricity usage.
   d. the schedules of citizens who most often contact the agency.

84. Customers who request to speak to a supervisor should be
   a. allowed to do so in a timely manner whenever possible.
   b. informed that the help of a supervisor is not necessary to resolve their situation.
   c. prevented from distracting the supervisor from his or her duties.
   d. given an appointment at a later date to meet the supervisor.

85. Customers who contact an office by telephone and are put on hold more than one minute should
   a. not be informed of the projected wait time because inaccurate estimates anger customers.
   b. be informed of the projected wait time so they can make an informed decision about whether to wait.
   c. hear a recorded message encouraging them to resolve their matter via mail or in person.
   d. be offered a face-to-face appointment on the following day if their call is not handled within five minutes.

Memory—Questions 86 through 90

Take five minutes to study the following picture. Then, answer question 86 without looking back at the picture.

© Corbis

86. Who is holding a cellular telephone in the photograph?
   a. only the woman on the left
   b. only the woman in the middle
   c. only the woman on the right
   d. all three women

Take five minutes to study the following picture. Then answer questions 87 and 88 without looking back at the picture.

© Corbis

87. There are two women in the photograph. Which woman has hair long enough to cover her shoulder?
 a. only the woman on the left
 b. only the woman on the right
 c. both women
 d. neither woman

88. Which type of vehicle is visible in the photograph?
 a. a city bus
 b. a cable car
 c. a locomotive
 d. an airplane

Take five minutes to study the text that follows. Then, answer questions 89 and 90 without looking back at the text.

The following is the text of a notice posted in a government office. It instructs employees on the proper procedure for evacuating the office during a fire.
- Know the location of all stairwells, emergency exits, and fire extinguishers. Learn how to operate a fire extinguisher.
- If you see a fire, activate the nearest fire alarm. If you have a cell phone or are near a public telephone, call 911 to alert the fire department.
- If you do not have access to an alarm or a phone, inform other building occupants that they should vacate the building.
- If possible, assist others in evacuating the building.
- If the fire is small, use a fire extinguisher to extinguish the fire. Remember that you should never attempt to extinguish a fire when:

—you do not know what is fueling the fire (e.g., chemicals)
—you cannot keep a clear path between yourself and a fire exit
—the fire might block your path of escape
—the fire has spread to many locations
—the fire is spreading rapidly
—the fire is producing copious amounts of smoke
- Evacuate the building. If possible, close windows and doors if you are the last one to leave.
- Exit the building by stairwells. Do not use elevators.
- If you have not yet done so, notify the fire department. Report the location and nature of the fire.
- Do not reenter the building without the permission of the fire department.

89. According to the notice, people should not try to extinguish a fire on their own if they
 a. can detect the color blue in the burning flames.
 b. do not have the assistance of at least one other person.
 c. cannot maintain ready access to a fire exit.
 d. can contain the fire to a contained location.

90. According to the notice, why should people not use elevators during a fire?
 a. The fire might interrupt electrical service, rendering elevators inoperative.
 b. It is impossible to determine the fire conditions in an elevator shaft.
 c. An elevator is not always the quickest way to leave a building.
 d. The notice does not provide a reason people should not use elevators.

Coding—Questions 91 through 100

To answer questions 91 through 95, refer to the following scenario.

Each employee at a government office is assigned a unique identification code. The code is created according to the following rules:

4 digits = the first two digits represent an employee's last name; the second two digits represent the employee's first name. Digits are assigned accordingly:

0 = ABC
1 = DEF
2 = GHI
3 = JKL
4 = MNO
5 = PQR
6 = STU
7 = VWX
8 = YZ

1 letter = job grade. Jobs are graded 1 through 19; letters are assigned based on the numerical equivalent of the letter (i.e., A = 1, B = 2, C = 3, D = 4, etc.)

4 digits = month and date of birth (e.g., April 7 = 0407)

91. Marlene Romanoff is a grade 12 employee. Her birthday is December 24. What is her identification code?
   a. 4053AB2412
   b. 4053M2412
   c. 5440M1224
   d. 5440AB1224

92. Abdul Qoph is a grade 5 employee. His birthday is July 8. What is his identification code?
   a. 5400E0708
   b. 5400E78
   c. 0054E0708
   d. 0054E78

93. To whom might the identification code 6521R1115 belong?
   a. Barry Felton
   b. Spencer Henderson
   c. William Trieste
   d. Gerald Springer

94. Which of the following statements about the employee with identification code 0524D1102 must be true?
   a. The employee's birthday is May 24.
   b. The employee's birthday is November 2.
   c. The employee's last name begins with the letter D.
   d. The employee is a grade 8 employee.

95. Create an identification code for the following employee:
   Name: Rodriguez, Alexis
   Date of Birth: September 22
   Job Grade: 8
   a. 03540922H
   b. 03542209H
   c. 5403H0922
   d. 54032209H

To answer questions 96 through 100, refer to the following scenario.

A county animal control unit uses a code to log all complaints it receives. Each call receives a single code even if it includes multiple complaints. The code follows the rules below:

Subject of complaint

    C = cat
    D = dog
    H = horse
    R = reptile
    Z = none of the above

Nature of complaint (record all that apply)

    0 = noise
    1 = animal not properly restrained (e.g., no leash, not contained in enclosed area)
    2 = animal improperly fed, watered, or sheltered
    3 = animal not properly licensed
    4 = animal behaves menacingly toward human or other animal
    5 = abandoned animal
    6 = illegal animal breeding

The nature of complaint or complaints directly follows the code for the animal that is the subject of the complaint.

96. A citizen called animal control to complain that a neighbor's dog was barking and that the same neighbor owns a horse that is not properly fenced in. How should this complaint be coded?
   a. D0H1
   b. DH01
   c. 0DH1
   d. H10D

97. An animal control officer is flagged down by a citizen who directs the officer to a neighbor's house. There, the citizen points out that the neighbor owns a dog and a cat; he further notes that the dog is not receiving food or water and that neither the dog nor cat is properly licensed. How should this complaint be coded?
   a. DC23
   b. D3C23
   c. D23C3
   d. D2C3

98. Animal control receives a complaint of an abandoned horse that is not properly fed or watered. How should this complaint be coded?
   a. 25
   b. H5
   c. H2
   d. H25

99. The code Z5 could refer to
   a. a barking dog.
   b. an underfed horse.
   c. an abandoned pig.
   d. a menacing reptile.

100. An inspector discovers an illegal breeding facility at which the owner is breeding dogs, cats, horses, and ferrets. How should the inspector code this discovery?
   a. CDHZ6
   b. C6D6H6Z6
   c. CDHZ6666
   d. C6DHZ

Answers

Section 1: Mathematics

1. a. To add mixed numbers with uncommon denominators, first convert all mixed numbers to improper fractions. First, convert $3\frac{1}{2}$ to $\frac{7}{2}$, $4\frac{3}{4}$ to $\frac{19}{4}$, $3\frac{2}{3}$ to $\frac{11}{3}$, and $3\frac{1}{2}$ to $\frac{7}{2}$. Next, rewrite $\frac{7}{2}$, $\frac{19}{4}$, $\frac{11}{3}$, and $\frac{7}{2}$ over a common denominator. Use 12 because it is evenly divisibly by 2, 3, and 4; $\frac{7}{2} \times \frac{6}{6} = \frac{42}{12}$, $\frac{19}{4} \times \frac{3}{3} = \frac{57}{12}$, $\frac{11}{3} \times \frac{4}{4} = \frac{44}{12}$, and $\frac{7}{2} \times \frac{6}{6} = \frac{42}{12}$. Now, add the fractions: $\frac{42 + 57 + 44 + 42}{12} = \frac{185}{12}$. Finally, divide 185 by 12 to produce the result, $15\frac{5}{12}$.

2. d. Martine kept 2 of 8 equal slices, which can be represented by the fraction $\frac{2}{8}$. This reduces to $\frac{1}{4}$, which would mean he gave April the remaining $\frac{3}{4}$ of the pie. Mae took $\frac{1}{3}$ of April's portion. To determine the fraction of pie Mae took you must multiply the $\frac{1}{3}$ she took from April by the $\frac{3}{4}$ of the total that April got. To multiply fractions, multiply numerators, then denominators, and then reduce if necessary. $\frac{1}{3} \times \frac{3}{4} = \frac{3}{12}$, which reduces to $\frac{1}{4}$. Mae and Martine both had $\frac{1}{4}$ of the pie or 2 slices each for a total of 4 slices. With 8 original slices less the 4 that Mae and Martine ate, April must have eaten 4 slices.

3. b. To subtract, first rewrite each fraction over a common denominator 10 to get $\frac{6}{10} - \frac{2}{10}$, which equals $\frac{4}{10}$. This reduces to $\frac{2}{5}$.

4. c. To solve rate problems, apply the equation $rt = d$, where r equals rate, t equals time, and d equals distance. This problem provides the rate (55 miles per hour) and the time (3 hours 24 minutes). Before plugging numbers into the formula, rewrite 3 hours 24 minutes as a decimal. $\frac{24}{60}$ equals $\frac{2}{5}$, so 3 hours 24 minutes equals $3\frac{2}{5}$ hours, which equals 3.4 hours. Now plug values into the formula: $55(3.4) = d$. Multiply 55 and 3.4 to get 187.

5. b. To find the decimal equivalent, divide 5.5 by 100 to get 0.055. You also could simply move the decimal point 2 places to the left.

6. b. The x-axis is the horizontal axis of a graph, which in this graph shows the names of the counties.

7. a. The y-axis is the vertical axis of a graph, which in this graph shows the amount of recycling collected.

8. c. According to the graph, Dunn County produces less than half as much recycling as does Earvin County. Therefore, the data in the graph supports the conclusion that Dunn County does not need to collect its recycling as frequently as does Earvin County. Choice **a** relies on faulty reasoning; just because Berkeley County produces more recycling than does Floyd County does not mean that the former has a larger population. It is possible that Berkeley residents simply produce more recycling per capita. Because the graph includes no information about citizens' attitudes toward recycling, choice **b** cannot be correct. Because the graph does not break out the different types of items that are recycled, it is impossible to draw any conclusions about the amount of newspaper recycled, and therefore, choice **d** cannot be correct.

9. d. Joanne takes 45 minutes to complete *each* of two tasks; therefore, the two tasks take a total of 90 minutes, or 1 hour 30 minutes to complete. The third task takes 2 hours 10 minutes, meaning all 30 tasks take a total of 3 hours 40 minutes to complete.

10. a. The portion of seats on sale to the general public can be found by subtracting from the total the number of seats taken by friends and family of the cast and those given away on the radio. To arrive at how many seat are left after those taken by friends and family, multiply the total number of seats (296) by the portion of that amount that they did not take ($\frac{3}{8}$); $296 \times \frac{3}{8} = 111$. Next, subtract the number of VIP tickets given away on the radio from this amount to arrive at the number of seats taken by the general public; $111 - 37 = 74$. Lastly, divide this number by the total number of seats to determine the portion taken by the general public; $74 \div 296 = \frac{1}{4}$.

11. d. To add the fractions, first rewrite each fraction over a common denominator of 15 to get $\frac{10}{15} + \frac{3}{15}$, which equals $\frac{13}{15}$.

12. d. Both 55 and 120 are divisible by 5. Divide each by 5 to reduce $\frac{55}{120}$ to $\frac{11}{24}$.

13. d. There are a number of ways to arrive at the answer to this question. One way is to say Ken's bonus pay is $1\frac{1}{2}$ times his regular pay of $12.50 for the first four hours and 2 times that amount for hours worked over four hours. $\frac{1}{2}$ of Ken's regular pay would be $6.25, which when added to his regular pay equals a rate of $18.75. Ken's regular pay multiplied by 2 is $12.50 × 2 = $25.00 an hour. For the six hour shift described, Ken would get paid four hours at $18.75 an hour and two hours at $25.00 an hour; $18.75 × 4 = $75.00 and $25.00 × 2 = $50.00; $75.00 + $50.00 = $125.

14. d. Divide 72 by 10 to get 7 remainder 2, or $7\frac{2}{10}$. Reduce $\frac{2}{10}$ to $\frac{1}{5}$ to reach the final choice of $7\frac{1}{5}$.

15. a. Study the relationship between cost and gas mileage shown in the table. The data show neither an increase nor a decrease in gas mileage of an automobile as its cost increases. Therefore, the data show no relationship between cost and gas mileage. Choice **b** is contradicted by the data, as explained previously. Choice **c** cannot be correct because the table provides no data on the size and weight of the different automobiles listed. Because no data on actual sale price is provided, choice **d** also cannot be correct.

16. d. The range of a data set is the difference between the greatest and least values in the set. The greatest value in this set is 38 and the least value is 20, so the range of the data is $38 - 20$, which equals 18. Note that the question asks about highway mileage, so you must use the Gas Mileage for Highway column to answer this question.

17. c. To answer this question, take the retail price of each car and divide it by the number of miles per gallon it is able to drive in the city. In order from top to bottom: $16,600 \div 31 = $535.48; $22,100 \div 22 = $1,004.54; $27,800 \div 16 = $1,737.50; and $31,500 \div 27 = $1,166.66. The greatest of these results is $1,737.50, belonging to the Montannic.

18. c. $1.2 million can be written out as $1,200,000. A 4.5% raise as a decimal is $\frac{4.5}{100} = 0.045$. To calculate the raise, multiply: $1,200,000 × 0.045 = $54,000. His new salary is $1,200,000 + $54,000 = $1,254,000.

19. a. To subtract mixed numbers, convert them to improper fractions. Rewrite $7\frac{1}{5}$ as $\frac{36}{5}$ and $4\frac{4}{5}$ as $\frac{24}{5}$. Now subtract: $\frac{36-24}{5} = \frac{12}{5}$, which equals $2\frac{2}{5}$.

20. b. The decimal 0.7 is equal to the fraction $\frac{7}{10}$, which can be rewritten as $\frac{70}{100}$. Because a percent is the numerator of a fraction with a denominator of 100, 0.7 equals 70%.

21. b. Mr. Wallace wants to spend $80 on SDRAM, $700 on software (two programs costing $350 each), $65 on flash memory, and $165 on a scanner; $80 + $700 + $65 + $165 equals $1,010. If you selected choice **a**, you probably forgot to double $350 to account for the fact that Mr. Wallace plans to buy two software programs that cost $350 each.

22. b. To solve rate problems, apply the equation $rt = d$, where r equals rate, t equals time, and d equals distance. The problem provides time (12 hours) and rate (20 miles per hour). Plug these values into the formula and solve; $12 \times 20 = d$, so $d = 240$.

23. d. To divide fractions, multiply the dividend (the first fraction in the equation) by the reciprocal of the divisor (the second fraction in the equation). Thus, $\frac{2}{5} \div \frac{4}{7}$ should be rewritten as $\frac{2}{5} \times \frac{7}{4}$, which equals $\frac{14}{20}$. Divide numerator and denominator by 2 to reduce $\frac{14}{20}$ to $\frac{7}{10}$.

24. d. If Frank paid with his coupon he would pay 80% or $\frac{4}{5}$ of the total price of the jeans, which is $86. To arrive at the new price, multiply the original price by the fraction of that price he will be paying ($\frac{4}{5}$); $86.00 \times \frac{4}{5} = 68.80$.

25. d. To change a mixed number to a fraction, multiply the denominator by the whole number and then add to the numerator. Finally, write this amount over the denominator. So, $5\frac{1}{7}$ equals $\frac{35+1}{7} = \frac{36}{7}$.

26. c. To rewrite a decimal as a fraction, count the number of places in the decimal. The denominator of the fraction will be the digit 1 with as many zeros as the number of places you counted following it. In this case, the decimal 0.0034 has four places, so the denominator of the fraction will be a 1 and 4 zeros, i.e., 10,000. The numerator of the fraction is the decimal itself, less the decimal point and all consecutive zeros to the immediate right of the decimal point. Thus, the numerator of this fraction is 34, and the fraction is $\frac{34}{10,000}$.

27. a. The graph shows that 32% of household fires are caused by matches, more than any other single cause.

28. c. The question asks you to find 3% of 500; 3% of 100 is 3, so 3% of 500 is 5×3 (because 500 is 5×100). Thus, the answer to the question is 15.

29. d. The question asks you to determine what percentage of 40 is represented by 6. Use the translation technique to write an equation that asks "6 is what % of 40" as follows: $6 = \frac{x}{100} \times 40$. Next, divide both sides of the equation by 40 to get $\frac{6}{40} = \frac{x}{100}$. Now you can cross multiply to get $40x = 6,000$ and divide both sides by 40 to get $x = 15$.

30. a. To answer this question, you must first determine how much of the jackpot was given to each of Will, David, and June, and then take the sum of those subscriptions and subtract it from the total of $30,000 to determine how many Karen sold. Will and David each received 20% of the total of $30,000 which equals $6,000 each, or $12,000 when added together. Subtract $12,000 from the total of $30,000 to arrive at $18,000, the portion split by June and Karen. You can look at the fact that Karen receives 3 times the portion June gets as creating four equal parts with Karen receiving 3 of the 4 parts or $\frac{3}{4}$. To arrive at how much Karen was given, multiply the $18,000 she and June split by her portion of that amount ($\frac{3}{4}$); $18,000 × $\frac{3}{4}$ = $13,500.

31. b. To solve rate problems, apply the equation $rt = d$, where r equals rate, t equals time, and d equals distance. This problem is a little tricky because it provides two rates, Bill's (110 yards per minute) and Melissa's (95 yards per minute). However, because Bill and Melissa are walking directly toward each other, they approach each other at a rate equal to the sum of their two rates. That is, for every minute they walk, Bill and Melissa get 100 + 95, or 205, yards closer to each other. They approach each other at a rate of 205 yards per minute. Now, plug the rate and the distance (2,870 yards) into the formula and solve. $205t$ = 2,870; to solve, divide both sides by 205. The result is 14.

32. a. Thirty percent is equivalent to the fraction $\frac{3}{10}$. To determine the number of employees over the age of 50 you must multiply $\frac{3}{10}$ by 150, the total number of employees. $\frac{3}{10}$ × $\frac{150}{1}$ = $\frac{450}{10}$, which reduces to 45.

33. c. Add $4.99 and $2.69 to get $7.68. The two yogurts cost 2 × $0.60 = $1.20. Therefore, the total amount purchased is $7.68 + $1.20 = $8.88. To calculate the change, subtract $20.00 − $8.88 = $11.12.

34. a. To divide mixed numbers, first rewrite the mixed numbers as fractions. Rewrite $5\frac{1}{3}$ as $\frac{16}{3}$ and $1\frac{5}{9}$ as $\frac{14}{9}$. Next, multiply the dividend (the first fraction in the equation) by the reciprocal of the divisor (the second fraction in the equation). Thus, $\frac{16}{3} \div \frac{14}{9}$ should be rewritten as $\frac{16}{3} \times \frac{9}{14}$, which equals $\frac{144}{42}$. Rewrite $\frac{144}{42}$ as $3\frac{18}{42}$, and then reduce $\frac{18}{42}$ to $\frac{3}{7}$ by dividing numerator and denominator by 6. The correct answer is $3\frac{3}{7}$.

35. c. When both pipes are used to fill the pool, they fill the pool at a rate of $\frac{1}{10} + \frac{1}{8}$ per hour; $\frac{1}{10} + \frac{1}{8}$ equals $\frac{4}{40} + \frac{5}{40}$, or $\frac{9}{40}$, per hour. That means that the pipes fill slightly less than one-quarter of the pool each hour; therefore, the job takes a little more than four hours to complete. Use process of elimination to determine that choice **c** is the only possible answer.

36. c. The number of marbles is irrelevant, red marbles account for 5% or $\frac{1}{20}$ of the total weight. The total weight is 5 pounds, so to solve multiply 5 by the numerator and divide the product by the denominator; 5 × 1 = $\frac{5}{20}$, which reduces to $\frac{1}{4}$ pound.

37. c. First, rewrite $6\frac{1}{5}$ as an improper fraction by multiplying the whole number 6 by the denominator 5 and adding the product to the numerator 1 to get $\frac{31}{5}$. Next, multiply $\frac{31}{5}$ and $\frac{75}{1}$ to get $\frac{2,325}{5}$. Finally, divide 2,325 by 5 to get 465.

38. b. The range of a data set is the difference between the greatest and least values in the set. The greatest value in this set is 11 and the least value is 3, so the range of the data is 11 − 3, which equals 8.

39. d. To find the mean number of accidents per time period, add the different data points, and then divide by the number of time periods shown. The data is 11, 3, 5, 7, 9, 6, 5, and 3. The sum of the data is 49. Divide 49 by 8, the number of time periods shown, to get $6\frac{1}{8}$. Thus, the mean number of accidents per time period is between 6 and 7.

40. c. The y-axis is the vertical scale of the graph.

Section 2: Written Communication

41. c. The purpose of this passage is to explain the clerk of the court's job. The passage is informational, not persuasive, so choice **a** cannot be correct. Choices **b** and **d** refer to details of one paragraph of the passage; the correct answer to a main idea question must describe the entire passage, not just one small part of it.

42. b. The final paragraph states, "Although demanding, work in a clerk's office brings with it the satisfaction of knowing that one has performed an essential role in allowing our court system to function properly." This sentence suggests that the clerk of the court's office is a satisfying place to work. Choice **a** draws too strong a conclusion; although working in the clerk of the court's office requires special skills, that does not mean that "very few people are qualified" to work there. Choice **c** is contradicted by the statement "Organizational skill is obviously required of anyone working for the clerk." The court's seal is not even mentioned in the final paragraph, so choice **d** cannot be correct.

43. a. *Domain* means "area under control of a particular government, court, etc." It is the best choice. The clerk of the court works for federal, state, or local courts whose jurisdiction is local or regional, not national; therefore, choice **b** cannot be correct. The clerk of the court functions in a system governed by the rule of law, not by an individual or a political party, so choices **c** and **d** cannot be correct.

44. d. In the second paragraph, the passages states, "First and foremost, the clerk maintains the court's clerical records."

45. d. Use process of elimination to find the answer to this question. Choices **a** and **b** refer to specific details of the passage. They do not summarize the entire passage and, therefore, cannot sum up the author's main idea. Choice **c** is contradicted by the example of Texas's outsourcing of welfare benefits, which the author tells us has *not* improved services.

46. a. This is a tricky question, because choices **b** and **c** make sense in context; the state's computer system may indeed have been *broken* or *slow*. However, the word *antiquated* means *old* or *obsolete*. The word shares a root with the word *antique*, which should have helped you figure out that the word *antiquated* has something to do with age.

47. c. The passage states, "Unfortunately, the quality of service was initially poor, with many clients complaining that the call centers were difficult to reach *and that the information they provided was often inaccurate.*" This statement supports choice **c**. None of the other choices are supported by information in the passage.

48. b. The passage states, "Since contracting out operations, the city has reversed that $2 million loss, instead realizing an annual profit of $2 million; best of all, they've done it without significantly increasing course income." This statement supports the conclusion that the contractors who took control of New York City's golf courses used course income more efficiently than did the city, because they have increased profits and improved services without increasing income.

49. a. The discussion of the traits of a person with antisocial personality disorder in the middle of the passage specifies that such a person does not have distortions of thought, such as delusions of persecution. The passage speaks of the antisocial person as being inordinately self-confident (choice **b**) and of the person's emotional shallowness (choices **c** and **d**).

50. d. The third sentence of the passage speaks of con games. None of the other professions would suit an impulsive, shallow person who has been in trouble with the law.

51. b. The passage mentions emotional shallowness. The other choices hint at the ability to feel meaningful emotion.

52. b. The passage says that a person with antisocial personality disorder can mimic real emotion, thereby conning prison officials, judges, and psychiatrists. The other choices are mentioned in the passage, but not in connection with getting out of trouble with the law.

53. c. *Commemorative* means *preserving or honoring the memory of*. Thus, *celebratory* is closest in meaning to *commemorative*. *Funereal* (choice **a**) means *sad* or *somber*; *mnemonic* means *promoting memory*; and *exclusive* means *available to a select group only*.

54. a. The passage explains the process by which subjects for U.S. stamps are selected.

55. b. In paragraph 3, the passage states that the committee meets four times each year. The passage does not say how the rules for selecting a stamp were established, so choice **a** cannot be correct. The committee is appointed by the Postmaster General, but the passage does not say whether it is made up of former Postmasters General, so choice **c** cannot be correct. Choice **d** is contradicted in the first sentence of the final paragraph.

56. d. The final sentence of paragraph 2 states, "Prohibited subjects include individual towns, cities, elementary and secondary schools, hospitals, and libraries; fraternal, political, sectarian, and service organizations; and religious groups." Chicago (choice **a**) is an individual city, so it cannot be honored in a stamp. Likewise, the Republican Party (choice **c**) is a political organization, and so it cannot be honored on a stamp. The passage also points out that stamps may not depict living human beings; therefore, choice **b** cannot be correct.

57. b. The idea that employees will become more valuable if they take courses is stated in the fourth paragraph, which argues that the employer will have had a more sophisticated, more intelligent, and therefore more valuable and productive employee.

58. d. The writer of this passage states the opinion that a company that reimburses employees for all college courses, whether job related or not, offers a service to its employees, the entire company, and the greater community. The writer then proceeds to give reasons to persuade the reader of the validity of this statement.

59. a. By using a word associated with education, the writer is able to reinforce the importance of education and tuition reimbursement.

60. c. As used in the passage, *expendable* means *replaceable*. The writer uses the word immediately after saying that job security is a thing of the past. This clue tells you that workers do not feel they are important or valuable to a company that can fire them on a moment's notice.

61. c. The correct spelling is *debatable*.

62. a. The correct spelling is *sieve*.

63. b. The correct spelling is *feasible*.

64. a. The correct spelling is *rectify*.

65. c. The correct spelling is *deteriorating*.

66. a. *Opulent* means *luxurious*.

67. c. Take a look at the word *laborious*. You may notice that it includes the word *labor*, which means *hard work*.

68. b. *Pompous* means *stuck up* and *snobbish*, so *humble* is its opposite.

69. b. *Reciprocate* means *to repay*. The speaker in the sentence offers to repay a favor with a similar favor, so *reciprocate* is the best word for the blank. *Renege* (choice **a**) means *to go back on your work*. *Rejuvenate* (choice **c**) means *to modernize*.

70. a. *Incriminating* means *suggesting guilt*. Fingerprints on a murder weapon are definitely *incriminating* evidence. *Exonerating* (choice **b**) means *suggesting innocence*, which is the opposite of *incriminating*. *Dubious* (choice **c**) means *doubtful*.

71. b. Choices **a** and **c** consist of dependent clauses only, so they are not complete sentences.

72. a. Because the statement *Would you prefer sugar or artificial sweetener in your coffee* is a direct quote, it must be in quotation marks. Thus, choice **b** is incorrect. Because this statement is a question, it must end in a question mark. The entire sentence, however, is not a question; it is a statement of fact reporting what Humphrey asked. Thus, the sentence should not end in a question mark. Choice **c** ends in a question mark and is, therefore, incorrect.

73. c. The phrase *located along the railroad tracks* is a modifier describing *the community theater*. Choice **a** incorrectly states that it is *the noise of passing trains* rather than *the community theater* that is located along the tracks. Choice **b** is awkwardly and confusingly constructed; choice **c**, the correct answer, demonstrates how to express the same ideas much more clearly.

74. a. Choices **b** and **c** contain capitalization errors. In both, the word *Day* should be capitalized. In choice **b**, the word *Mrs.* should be capitalized. In choice **c**, the word *picnic* should not be capitalized.

75. a. The subject of the sentence is *each member*, which takes a singular verb. Therefore, choices **b** and **c**, in which the subject takes the plural verb *hold*, are incorrect.

76. c. Periods are correctly placed after all abbreviations in this sentence.

77. c. Each of the incorrect answers is written in the passive voice; the correct answer is written in the active voice, which is preferred.

78. c. *Committee* is a collective noun that takes a singular pronoun. Both incorrect choices use the plural pronoun *their* to refer to the committee.

79. b. Choice **a** is incorrect because *bands* should have an apostrophe and *bettered* is not an appropriate word choice. Choice **c** is incorrect because the word *sessions* contains an unnecessary apostrophe.

80. c. The phrase *consensus of opinion* is redundant; the word *consensus* means *unity of opinion*. Therefore, choices **a** and **b** are redundant. The term *free gift* in choice **a** is also redundant, because all gifts are free.

Section 3: Civil Service Skills

81. b. The correct term for this principle is *first contact resolution*.

82. c. The primary governing principle of customer service is to make things as easy and pleasant for the customer as possible. Choice **c** best articulates this principle. Each of the incorrect answers would result in an unnecessary delay in delivering service to the customer.

83. d. Once again, the correct answer reflects the need to place primary importance on the needs of citizens, the users of government services.

84. a. Choices **b** and **c** will almost certainly antagonize the customer, never a good idea when satisfying customer service is the goal. Choice **d** adds an unnecessary inconvenience and, therefore, will also probably annoy the customer. Only choice **a** reflects a "customer service first" attitude.

85. b. In general, the more accurate information you provide a customer, the better the customer's assessment of service will be. By informing customers of the approximate wait to speak with a representative, you allay their fears that they have been forgotten, that the call has been routed to a dead end, etc. Of course, some customers will be annoyed if the estimate turns out to be inaccurate, but not as annoyed as customers become when left on hold indefinitely with no idea of when they will ultimately be served.

86. a. Only one woman—the woman on the left—is holding a cell phone.

87. c. Both women have shoulder-length hair.

88. b. The vehicle is a cable car.

89. c. The notice states that "you should never attempt to extinguish a fire when . . . you cannot keep a clear path between yourself and the fire exit."

90. d. The notice simply states that people should not use the elevators; it does not explain the reasoning for this advice.

91. c. The first pair of digits in the code represent the employee's last name; the second pair represent the employee's first name. Marlene Romanoff's identification number should begin 54 (for the RO in Romanoff) 40 (for the MA in Marlene). Only choices **c** and **d** begin 5440; eliminate choices **a** and **b**. Job codes are a single letter; therefore, the two-letter job code AB that appears in choice **d** is incorrect. Choice **c** must be the correct answer by process of elimination.

92. a. Abdul Qoph's identification number should begin 54 (QO in Qoph) 00 (AB in Abdul). Eliminate choices **c** and **d**, which begin 0054. The code uses four digits to represent birthdays; therefore, choice **b** is incorrect. Choice **a** must be the correct answer by process of elimination.

93. d. This identification belongs to someone whose last name begins with the letter S, T, or U; the second letter in his last name is P, Q, or R. Only choices **c** and **d** meet this requirement; eliminate choices **a** and **b**. The employee's first name begins with the letter G, H, or I; this information allows you to eliminate choice **c**. The correct answer must be choice **d**.

94. b. The final four digits of the identification code represent the holder's birthday. The figures 1102 tell you that this employee's birthday is November 2.

95. c. The RO in Rodriguez is coded 54; the AL in Alexis is coded 03; the job grade 8 is coded H, because H is the eighth letter in the alphabet; the birthday September 22 is coded 0922. The correct identification number for Alexis Rodriguez is 5403H0922.

96. a. The rules of the code state, "The nature of complaint or complaints directly follows the code for the animal that is the subject of the complaint." Therefore, the code for a barking dog is D0 and the code for an improperly restrained horse is H1. The correct code for the incident described in the question is D0H1.

97. c. The code for a dog that is improperly fed and is not licensed is D23; the code for a cat that is not licensed is C3. The correct code for this incident is D23C3.

98. d. The code for a horse is H. The code for an abandoned animal is 5, and the code for improper food and water is 2. The code for this incident is H25.

99. c. The code Z refers to any animal other than a cat, dog, horse, or reptile. The code 5 refers to an abandoned animal. Thus, Z5 could refer to an abandoned pig.

100. b. The rules of the code state, "The nature of complaint or complaints directly follows the code for the animal that is the subject of the complaint." Therefore, the code for improper breeding of cats is C6; the code for improper breeding of dogs is D6, etc. The correct code for this incident is C6D6H6Z6.

5 ▶ CIVIL SERVICE PRACTICE EXAM 4

This fourth practice exam will continue to prepare you for the types of questions you will see on your civil service exam. The 100 multiple-choice questions that follow will test your knowledge of math, reading, spelling, grammar, civil service, memory, and coding.

Remember to read the complete answer explanation thoroughly, regardless of whether you answered the question correctly. Compare your score on this test to tests 1 through 3. Are there areas in which you need more improvement?

Civil Service Practice Exam 4

1.	ⓐ	ⓑ	ⓒ	ⓓ	36.	ⓐ	ⓑ	ⓒ	ⓓ	71.	ⓐ	ⓑ	ⓒ	
2.	ⓐ	ⓑ	ⓒ	ⓓ	37.	ⓐ	ⓑ	ⓒ	ⓓ	72.	ⓐ	ⓑ	ⓒ	
3.	ⓐ	ⓑ	ⓒ	ⓓ	38.	ⓐ	ⓑ	ⓒ	ⓓ	73.	ⓐ	ⓑ	ⓒ	
4.	ⓐ	ⓑ	ⓒ	ⓓ	39.	ⓐ	ⓑ	ⓒ	ⓓ	74.	ⓐ	ⓑ	ⓒ	
5.	ⓐ	ⓑ	ⓒ	ⓓ	40.	ⓐ	ⓑ	ⓒ	ⓓ	75.	ⓐ	ⓑ	ⓒ	
6.	ⓐ	ⓑ	ⓒ	ⓓ	41.	ⓐ	ⓑ	ⓒ	ⓓ	76.	ⓐ	ⓑ	ⓒ	
7.	ⓐ	ⓑ	ⓒ	ⓓ	42.	ⓐ	ⓑ	ⓒ	ⓓ	77.	ⓐ	ⓑ	ⓒ	
8.	ⓐ	ⓑ	ⓒ	ⓓ	43.	ⓐ	ⓑ	ⓒ	ⓓ	78.	ⓐ	ⓑ	ⓒ	
9.	ⓐ	ⓑ	ⓒ	ⓓ	44.	ⓐ	ⓑ	ⓒ	ⓓ	79.	ⓐ	ⓑ	ⓒ	
10.	ⓐ	ⓑ	ⓒ	ⓓ	45.	ⓐ	ⓑ	ⓒ	ⓓ	80.	ⓐ	ⓑ	ⓒ	
11.	ⓐ	ⓑ	ⓒ	ⓓ	46.	ⓐ	ⓑ	ⓒ	ⓓ	81.	ⓐ	ⓑ	ⓒ	ⓓ
12.	ⓐ	ⓑ	ⓒ	ⓓ	47.	ⓐ	ⓑ	ⓒ	ⓓ	82.	ⓐ	ⓑ	ⓒ	ⓓ
13.	ⓐ	ⓑ	ⓒ	ⓓ	48.	ⓐ	ⓑ	ⓒ	ⓓ	83.	ⓐ	ⓑ	ⓒ	ⓓ
14.	ⓐ	ⓑ	ⓒ	ⓓ	49.	ⓐ	ⓑ	ⓒ	ⓓ	84.	ⓐ	ⓑ	ⓒ	ⓓ
15.	ⓐ	ⓑ	ⓒ	ⓓ	50.	ⓐ	ⓑ	ⓒ	ⓓ	85.	ⓐ	ⓑ	ⓒ	ⓓ
16.	ⓐ	ⓑ	ⓒ	ⓓ	51.	ⓐ	ⓑ	ⓒ	ⓓ	86.	ⓐ	ⓑ	ⓒ	ⓓ
17.	ⓐ	ⓑ	ⓒ	ⓓ	52.	ⓐ	ⓑ	ⓒ	ⓓ	87.	ⓐ	ⓑ	ⓒ	ⓓ
18.	ⓐ	ⓑ	ⓒ	ⓓ	53.	ⓐ	ⓑ	ⓒ	ⓓ	88.	ⓐ	ⓑ	ⓒ	ⓓ
19.	ⓐ	ⓑ	ⓒ	ⓓ	54.	ⓐ	ⓑ	ⓒ	ⓓ	89.	ⓐ	ⓑ	ⓒ	ⓓ
20.	ⓐ	ⓑ	ⓒ	ⓓ	55.	ⓐ	ⓑ	ⓒ	ⓓ	90.	ⓐ	ⓑ	ⓒ	ⓓ
21.	ⓐ	ⓑ	ⓒ	ⓓ	56.	ⓐ	ⓑ	ⓒ	ⓓ	91.	ⓐ	ⓑ	ⓒ	ⓓ
22.	ⓐ	ⓑ	ⓒ	ⓓ	57.	ⓐ	ⓑ	ⓒ	ⓓ	92.	ⓐ	ⓑ	ⓒ	ⓓ
23.	ⓐ	ⓑ	ⓒ	ⓓ	58.	ⓐ	ⓑ	ⓒ	ⓓ	93.	ⓐ	ⓑ	ⓒ	ⓓ
24.	ⓐ	ⓑ	ⓒ	ⓓ	59.	ⓐ	ⓑ	ⓒ	ⓓ	94.	ⓐ	ⓑ	ⓒ	ⓓ
25.	ⓐ	ⓑ	ⓒ	ⓓ	60.	ⓐ	ⓑ	ⓒ	ⓓ	95.	ⓐ	ⓑ	ⓒ	ⓓ
26.	ⓐ	ⓑ	ⓒ	ⓓ	61.	ⓐ	ⓑ	ⓒ		96.	ⓐ	ⓑ	ⓒ	ⓓ
27.	ⓐ	ⓑ	ⓒ	ⓓ	62.	ⓐ	ⓑ	ⓒ		97.	ⓐ	ⓑ	ⓒ	ⓓ
28.	ⓐ	ⓑ	ⓒ	ⓓ	63.	ⓐ	ⓑ	ⓒ		98.	ⓐ	ⓑ	ⓒ	ⓓ
29.	ⓐ	ⓑ	ⓒ	ⓓ	64.	ⓐ	ⓑ	ⓒ		99.	ⓐ	ⓑ	ⓒ	ⓓ
30.	ⓐ	ⓑ	ⓒ	ⓓ	65.	ⓐ	ⓑ	ⓒ		100.	ⓐ	ⓑ	ⓒ	ⓓ
31.	ⓐ	ⓑ	ⓒ	ⓓ	66.	ⓐ	ⓑ	ⓒ						
32.	ⓐ	ⓑ	ⓒ	ⓓ	67.	ⓐ	ⓑ	ⓒ						
33.	ⓐ	ⓑ	ⓒ	ⓓ	68.	ⓐ	ⓑ	ⓒ						
34.	ⓐ	ⓑ	ⓒ	ⓓ	69.	ⓐ	ⓑ	ⓒ						
35.	ⓐ	ⓑ	ⓒ	ⓓ	70.	ⓐ	ⓑ	ⓒ						

Section 1: Mathematics

1. $\frac{58}{10} =$
   a. $5\frac{4}{5}$
   b. $\frac{10}{58}$
   c. $\frac{5}{29}$
   d. $5\frac{4}{10}$

2. Reduce $\frac{32}{55}$ to lowest terms.
   a. $\frac{1}{23}$
   b. $\frac{2}{11}$
   c. $\frac{55}{32}$
   d. The fraction cannot be reduced further.

3. $9\frac{3}{8} + 2\frac{7}{16} =$
   a. $11\frac{10}{24}$
   b. $11\frac{13}{16}$
   c. $6\frac{5}{16}$
   d. $12\frac{5}{8}$

4. $\frac{8}{9} - \frac{2}{3} =$
   a. 1
   b. $\frac{16}{27}$
   c. $1\frac{1}{3}$
   d. $\frac{4}{9}$

5. $3\frac{2}{3} \div 1\frac{1}{3} =$
   a. $4\frac{8}{9}$
   b. $2\frac{3}{4}$
   c. 5
   d. $\frac{4}{11}$

6. $\frac{8}{13} \times 2\frac{1}{6} =$
   a. $\frac{3}{4}$
   b. $\frac{8}{39}$
   c. $\frac{48}{169}$
   d. $1\frac{1}{3}$

7. $\frac{10}{11} \div \frac{12}{121} =$
   a. $9\frac{1}{6}$
   b. $\frac{6}{55}$
   c. $\frac{122}{121}$
   d. $\frac{98}{121}$

8. 5% of $\frac{1}{5}$ is _____.
   a. 1
   b. $\frac{1}{50}$
   c. $\frac{1}{100}$
   d. $\frac{1}{1,000}$

9. $1.01 \times 1.1 =$ _____.
   a. 1,111
   b. 2.11
   c. 11.11
   d. 1.111

10. What is the fraction equivalent of 95%?
    a. $\frac{9}{10}$
    b. $\frac{19}{20}$
    c. $\frac{9}{5}$
    d. $\frac{95}{10}$

11. What is the percent equivalent of $\frac{2}{5}$?
    a. 240%
    b. 2.4%
    c. 0.024%
    d. 24%

12. The first-place winner of a 200-yard dash had a time of 29.31 seconds. The time of the person finishing in second place was 32.06 seconds. By how many seconds did the first-place winner beat the second-place one?
    a. 2.75 seconds
    b. 3.77 seconds
    c. 3.75 seconds
    d. 2.77 seconds

CIVIL SERVICE PRACTICE EXAM 4

13. An office is processing printing jobs. One job will require $2\frac{2}{5}$ reams of paper, one will need $1\frac{2}{3}$ reams of paper, and one will require $\frac{2}{3}$ ream. How many reams of paper, total, are needed?
   a. $3\frac{6}{11}$ reams
   b. $4\frac{11}{15}$ reams
   c. $4\frac{1}{15}$ reams
   d. $3\frac{11}{15}$ reams

14. The base charge for a one-night stay at a hotel costs $122.50. The hotel, in addition, charges a 12% tax. What is the amount of the final bill?
   a. $137.20
   b. $136.20
   c. $14.70
   d. $134.50

15. The cost for lunch for a group of three friends at a local deli, including 18% tip, is $62.55. What was the bill before the tip?
   a. $53.01
   c. $9.54
   c. $72.09
   d. $61.44

16. A muffin recipe calls for $2\frac{1}{2}$ tablespoons of cocoa. This makes 18 muffins. If you want to make 81 muffins, how many tablespoons of cocoa would you need to use?
   a. $10\frac{3}{4}$
   b. 9
   c. $4\frac{1}{2}$
   d. $11\frac{1}{4}$

17. A small moving company was hired to transport the books from a business office to a new location. The movers required the use of 66 boxes, and each box contained, on average, 16 books. How many books, total, were moved?
   a. 82
   b. 462
   c. 1,400
   d. 1,056

18. A delivery truck has 420 packages onboard. Thirty percent of them exceed 5 pounds in weight. How many boxes have a weight of 5 pounds or less?
   a. 126
   b. 415
   c. 294
   d. 390

19. Two walkers take $\frac{3}{4}$ hour to jog one lap around a 2.5-mile track. If they walk for a total of 3 hours, how many total miles do they cover?
   a. 3
   b. 7.5
   c. 10
   d. 17.5

20. A couple has completed $\frac{3}{4}$ of an $8\frac{1}{4}$-mile hike. How many miles must they yet walk in order to complete the hike?
   a. $6\frac{3}{16}$
   b. $2\frac{1}{16}$
   c. $4\frac{1}{8}$
   d. 2

21. Thirty-six different office duties must be performed each day. They are distributed equally among nine employees. How many tasks must each employee complete?
a. 8
b. 5
c. 27
d. 4

22. One-hundred-twenty 7th graders attend a summer science camp. Ten percent are chosen as team leaders, while the remaining campers are divided equally into six teams. Excluding the team leaders, how many campers are on each team?
a. 15
b. 9
c. 18
d. 20

23. The planned length of a countertop is $9\frac{1}{6}$ feet. The customer wants to increase this by 20%. What would be the new length of the countertop after making such an increase?
a. 11 feet
b. 10 feet
c. $10\frac{1}{6}$ feet
d. $1\frac{5}{6}$ feet

24. An artist uses on average 5 canvases per month. If each canvas costs $3.82, how much would the artist spend in six months?
a. $19.10
b. $22.92
c. $42.02
d. $114.60

25. In preparation for a barbecue party, you buy 12.42 pounds of ground beef. You make burgers, the full-sized version of which require 0.30 pounds of ground beef each. How many such full-sized burgers can be made?
a. 42
b. 41
c. 40
d. 50

26. Three siblings co-own a bakery. The oldest of them owns $\frac{2}{5}$ of the bakery and the youngest owns $\frac{1}{4}$ of it. What fraction of the business does the third sibling own?
a. $\frac{3}{4}$
b. $\frac{7}{20}$
c. $\frac{2}{3}$
d. $\frac{3}{5}$

27. During a 12-day vacation, it rained 5 days. For approximately what percentage of the vacation did it not rain?
a. 12%
b. 58%
c. 42%
d. $\frac{7}{12}$%

28. A downhill extreme skier can reach speeds of 80 miles per hour. How many feet per minute is the skier moving?
a. 7,040 feet per minute
b. 117 feet per minute
c. 84,480 feet per minute
d. 1,408 feet per minute

29. Five trainees at a local supermarket were timed on how long it took them to completely ring up an order of groceries. Their times were $2\frac{1}{4}$ minutes, $2\frac{2}{3}$ minutes, $1\frac{5}{6}$ minutes, 2 minutes, and $3\frac{1}{3}$ minutes. What was the average time for these five trainees?

   a. $2\frac{1}{4}$ minutes

   b. $3\frac{1}{3}$ minutes

   c. $2\frac{5}{12}$ minutes

   d. $1\frac{5}{6}$ minutes

Refer to the following graph for questions 30 through 32:

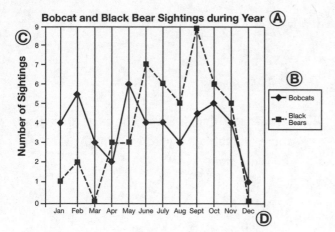

30. What letter corresponds to the *y*-axis?

   a. A
   b. B
   c. C
   d. D

31. Which month has the most bear sightings?

   a. September
   b. May
   c. December
   d. March

32. Which month has the fewest sightings of bobcats?

   a. January
   b. April
   c. July
   d. December

Refer to the following graph for questions 33 and 34:

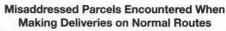
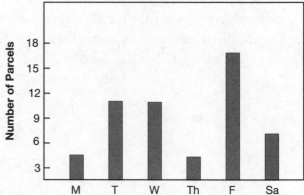

33. What is the range of the data?

   a. 15
   b. 3
   c. 12
   d. 9

34. What does the *y*-axis of the graph tell you?

   a. number of parcels delivered
   b. number of misaddressed parcels
   c. day of the week
   d. scale

For questions 35 through 37, there are 5,500 students enrolled in private high schools in Fall 2012 in City X. The percentages of these students who are freshmen, sophomores, juniors, and seniors are given in the pie chart.

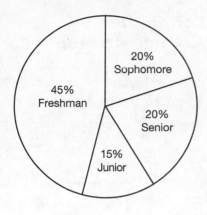

35. According to the pie chart, which category of student contributes the least amount to the total?
  a. freshmen
  b. sophomores
  c. juniors
  d. seniors

36. How many freshmen attend private high schools in City X in Fall 2012?
  a. 825
  b. 1,100
  c. 3,025
  d. 2,475

37. What is the ratio of freshmen to juniors?
  a. 1:1
  b. 4:3
  c. 3:1
  d. 1:3

Refer to the following chart for questions 38 through 40:

Miniature Golf Scores—Number of Strokes beyond Par		Course A	Course B
Team 1	Jodi	10	8
	Cassandra	18	13
	Mandi	11	9
Team 2	Joe	5	3
	Bryan	8	6
	Rick	8	6

38. What is the average score for all six players on Course A?
   a. 9
   b. 10
   c. 5
   d. 18

39. What is the range of scores for Course B?
   a. 13
   b. 7.5
   c. 10
   d. 3

40. Which of the following is a valid conclusion that can be deduced from the data provided?
   a. The range of scores on Course A is less than the range of scores on Course B.
   b. Mandi's average score on the two courses is 11.
   c. Rick played better than Bryan.
   d. The average score of all six players on Course B is lower than the average score of all six players on Course A.

Section 2:
Written Communication

Reading Comprehension—
Questions 41 through 60

Read the following passage. Then answer questions 41 through 45.

Greyhound racing is the sixth most popular spectator sport in the United States. Over the last decade, a growing number of racers have been adopted to spend their retirement as household pets, once their racing careers are over.

Many people <u>hesitate</u> to adopt a retired racing greyhound because they think only very old dogs are available. Actually, even champion racers only work until they are about three-and-a-half years old. Because greyhounds usually live to be 12 to 15 years old, their retirement is much longer than their racing careers.

People worry that a greyhound will be more nervous and active than other breeds and will need a large space to run. These are false impressions. Greyhounds have naturally sweet, mild dispositions, and while they love to run, they are sprinters rather than distance runners and are sufficiently exercised with a few daily laps around a fenced-in backyard.

Greyhounds do not make good watch-dogs, but they are very good with children, get along well with other dogs (and usually cats, as well), and are affectionate and loyal. They are intelligent, well-behaved dogs, usually house-broken in only a few days. A retired racing grey-hound is a wonderful pet for almost anyone.

41. Which of the following would be the best title for this passage?
   a. *The Popularity of Greyhound Racing*
   b. *Exercising Your Greyhound*
   c. *Nervousness and Hyperactivity in Greyhounds*
   d. *The Racing Greyhound: An Underrated Pet*

42. According to the passage, what is a failing of greyhounds?
   a. They are very anxious.
   b. They fight with cats.
   c. They are not good watchdogs.
   d. They dislike children.

43. As used in the passage, the word *hesitate* is closest in meaning to
   a. rush.
   b. dream.
   c. devise.
   d. resist.

44. According to the passage, racing greyhounds are
   a. sprinters.
   b. distance runners.
   c. expensive.
   d. excellent swimmers.

45. According to the passage, when are greyhounds often adopted?
   a. when they are puppies
   b. after their racing careers are over
   c. after they have been trained as guard dogs
   d. after they have been housebroken

Read the following passage. Then answer questions 46 through 50.

Millions of people in the United States are affected by eating disorders. More than 90% of those afflicted are adolescents or young adult women. Although all eating disorders share some common manifestations, anorexia nervosa, bulimia nervosa, and binge eating each have <u>distinctive</u> symptoms and risks.

People who intentionally starve themselves (even while experiencing severe hunger pains) suffer from anorexia nervosa. The disorder, which usually begins around the time of puberty, involves extreme weight loss to at least 15% below the individual's normal body weight. Many people with the disorder look emaciated but are convinced they are overweight. In patients with anorexia nervosa, starvation can damage vital organs such as the heart and brain. To protect itself, the body shifts into slow gear: Menstrual periods stop, blood pressure rates drop, and thyroid function slows. Excessive thirst and frequent urination may occur. Dehydration contributes to constipation, and reduced body fat leads to lowered body temperature and the inability to withstand cold. Mild anemia, swollen joints, reduced muscle mass, and light-headedness also commonly occur in anorexia nervosa.

People with bulimia nervosa consume large amounts of food and then rid their bodies of the excess calories by vomiting, abusing laxatives or diuretics, taking enemas, or exercising obsessively. Some use a combination of all these forms of purging. Individuals with bulimia who use drugs to stimulate vomiting, bowel movements, or urination may be in considerable danger, as this practice increases the risk of heart failure. Dieting heavily between episodes of binging and purging is common.

Binge-eating disorder is found in about 2% of the general population. As many as one-third of this group are men. It also affects older women, though with less frequency. Recent research shows that binge-eating disorder occurs in about 30% of people participating in medically supervised weight-control programs.

This disorder differs from bulimia because its sufferers do not purge. Individuals with binge-eating disorder feel that they lose control of themselves when eating. They eat large quantities of food and do not stop until they are uncomfortably full. Most sufferers are overweight or obese and have a history of weight fluctuations. As a result, they are prone to the serious medical problems associated with obesity, such as high cholesterol, high blood pressure, and diabetes. Obese individuals also have a higher risk for gallbladder disease, heart disease, and some types of cancer. Usually they have more difficulty losing weight and keeping it off than do people with other serious weight problems. Like anorexic and bulimic sufferers who exhibit psychological problems, individuals with binge-eating disorder have high rates of simultaneously occurring psychiatric illnesses, especially depression.

46. What is the primary purpose of this passage?
  a. to provide a definition of anorexia nervosa
  b. to prove bulimia nervosa is the most dangerous eating disorder
  c. to show how eating disorders affect more women than men
  d. to explain three kinds of eating disorders

47. According to the passage, people with binge-eating disorder are often
  a. emaciated.
  b. weak.
  c. overweight.
  d. elderly.

48. The passage supports which of the following conclusions?
  a. Binge-eating disorder affects more young women than men or older women.
  b. The first signs of anorexia nervosa usually appear after the sufferer turns 30.
  c. People with bulimia nervosa always diet between episodes of binging and purging.
  d. People with bulimia nervosa tend to avoid overeating.

49. According to the passage, the health risks of bulimia nervosa are made worse by
  a. excess calories.
  b. drug use.
  c. dieting.
  d. constipation.

50. As used in the passage, the word *distinctive* is closest in meaning to
  a. unique.
  b. strange.
  c. short.
  d. heavy.

Read the following passage. Then answer questions 51 through 55.

No longer is asthma considered a condition with isolated, acute episodes of bronchospasm. Rather, asthma is now understood to be a chronic inflammatory disorder of the airways—that is, inflammation makes the airways chronically sensitive. When these hyperresponsive airways are irritated, airflow is limited, and attacks of coughing, wheezing, chest tightness, and breathing difficulty occur.

Asthma involves complex interactions among inflammatory cells, mediators, and the cells and tissues in the airways. The interactions result in airflow limitation from acute bronchoconstriction, swelling of the airway wall, increased mucus secretion, and airway remodeling. The inflammation also causes an increase in airway responsiveness. During an asthma attack, the patient attempts to compensate by breathing at a higher lung volume in order to keep the air flowing through the constricted airways, and the greater the airway limitation, the higher the lung volume must be to keep airways open. The morphologic changes that occur in asthma include bronchial infiltration by inflammatory cells. Key effector cells in the inflammatory response are the mast cells, T lymphocytes, and eosinophils. Mast cells and eosinophils are also significant participants in allergic responses, hence the similarities between allergic reactions and asthma attacks. Other changes include mucus plugging of the airways, interstitial edema, and microvascular leakage. Destruction of bronchial epithelium and thickening of the subbasement membrane is also characteristic. In addition, there may be hypertrophy and hyperplasia of airway smooth muscle, increase in goblet cell number, and enlargement of submucous glands.

51. Which sentence best summarizes the main idea of the passage?
    a. Asthma is similar to allergic reactions because mast cells and eosinophils are also significant participants in allergic responses.
    b. Asthma attacks are dangerous because the patient attempts to compensate by breathing at a higher lung volume in order to keep the air flowing through the constricted airways.
    c. Asthma is a chronic inflammatory disorder of the airways that involves complex interactions among inflammatory cells, mediators, and the cells and tissues in the airways.
    d. Asthma mainly manifests itself with isolated, acute episodes of bronchospasm, as well as hypertrophy and hyperplasia of airway smooth muscle and an increase in goblet cell number.

52. In this passage, the word *chronic* is closest in meaning to
    a. rare.
    b. continual.
    c. various.
    d. difficult.

53. The passage supports which of the following conclusions?
    a. Mediators affect the cells and tissues in the airways.
    b. Bronchoconstriction results in free flow of air.
    c. Gland enlargement is not a side effect of asthma.
    d. Stress is not a significant trigger of asthma.

54. According to the passage, a morphologic change that occurs in asthma is
    a. swelling of the airway wall.
    b. increased mucus secretion.
    c. airway remodeling.
    d. bronchial infiltration by inflammatory cells.

55. According to the passage, asthma can cause all the following EXCEPT
    a. wheezing.
    b. throat irritation.
    c. chest tightness.
    d. breathing difficulty.

Read the following passage. Then answer questions 56 through 60.

The human body can tolerate only a small range of temperature, especially when the person is engaged in vigorous activity. Heat reactions usually occur when large amounts of water and/or salt are lost through excessive sweating following strenuous exercise. When the body becomes overheated and cannot eliminate this excess heat, heat exhaustion and heatstroke are possible.

Heat exhaustion is generally characterized by clammy skin, fatigue, nausea, dizziness, profuse perspiration, and sometimes fainting, resulting from an inadequate intake of water and the loss of fluids. First aid treatment for this condition includes having the victim lie down, raising the feet 8 to 12 inches, applying cool, wet cloths to the skin, and giving the victim sips of salt water (1 teaspoon per glass, half a glass every 15 minutes) over a 1-hour period.

Heatstroke is much more serious; it is an immediate life-threatening situation. The characteristics of heatstroke are a high body temperature (which may reach 106°F or more); a rapid pulse; hot, dry skin; and a blocked sweating mechanism. Victims of this condition may be unconscious, and first aid measures should be directed at quickly cooling the body. The victim should be placed in a tub of cold water or repeatedly sponged with cool water until his or her temperature is sufficiently lowered. Fans or air conditioners will also help with the cooling process. Care should be taken, however, not to overchill the victim once the temperature is below 102°F.

56. The author's main purpose in writing this passage is to
   a. argue that heatstroke is not as dangerous as heat exhaustion.
   b. explain the dangers of and treatments for heat exhaustion and heatstroke.
   c. report about the most serious instances of heatstroke to ever occur in the United States.
   d. propose that there needs to be more research about heatstroke and heat exhaustion.

57. According to the passage, what is NOT a symptom of heatstroke?
   a. rapid pulse
   b. a blocked sweating mechanism
   c. dizziness
   d. dry skin

58. In paragraph 3, the author suggests that
   a. heat exhaustion sufferers can be treated with wet cloths to the skin.
   b. only those with professional training can aid heatstroke sufferers.
   c. heatstroke is not a life-threatening condition.
   d. it is important to monitor the temperature of heatstroke sufferers.

59. According to the passage, heat exhaustion is often caused by
   a. intake of water.
   b. drinking salt water.
   c. loss of fluids.
   d. exposure to cold water.

60. As used in the passage, the word *tolerate* most nearly means
   a. watch.
   b. enjoy.
   c. show.
   d. stand.

Spelling—Questions 61 through 65
Select the choice that is spelled correctly.

61. The winning team was particularly _____ in Sunday's football game.
   a. agressive
   b. aggressive
   c. aggresive

62. She _____ flyers to announce her upcoming yard sale.
   a. circulatcd
   b. sirculated
   c. circelated

63. Which of the following words is spelled correctly?
   a. quarentine
   b. metropalis
   c. heirloom

64. Which of the following words is spelled correctly?
   a. jargun
   b. lacquer
   c. chaffeur

65. Which of the following words is spelled correctly?
   a. intersept
   b. phenomanon
   c. monologue

Vocabulary—Questions 66 through 70
Select the best answer for each question.

66. Find the word that is closest in meaning to the underlined word.
   precipitate a result
   a. accelerate
   b. halt
   c. interrupt

67. Find the word that is closest in meaning to the underlined word.
   a tumultuous storm
   a. violent
   b. orderly
   c. constant

68. Find the word that is most nearly the opposite of the underlined word.
   a laborious project
   a. tiresome
   b. fascinating
   c. effortless

69. Find the word that best completes the sentence.
   We _____ the attic of a lot of old junk during spring cleaning.
   a. amended
   b. purged
   c. enthralled

70. Find the word that best completes the sentence.
   The _____ old man never indulged in long speeches.
   a. verbose
   b. poignant
   c. laconic

Grammar—Questions 71 through 80
Select the best choice for each question.

71. Which of the following is a complete sentence?
   a. The other night.
   b. We came home from the animal shelter with a serene, affectionate cat.
   c. The project I spent the last two months developing was a success because.

72. Select the sentence that is written most correctly.
   a. The best-selling book was written by a new author.
   b. A new author wrote best-selling book.
   c. A new author wrote the best-selling book.

73. Select the sentence that is written most correctly.
   a. Much to his delight, Grant got to the station just in time for the train's arrival.
   b. Much to his delight, Grant got to the station just in time for the train's arrived.
   c. Much to his delight, Grant got to the station just in time for the train's coming arrival.

74. Select the sentence that is written most correctly.
   a. The president made his inaugural address on January 20th.
   b. The President made his inaugural address on January 20th.
   c. The president made his inaugural address on january 20th.

75. Select the sentence that is written most correctly.
   a. Dr Andress began preparing for surgery at 5:30 in the morning.
   b. Dr. Andress began preparing for surgery at 5:30 in the morning.
   c. Dr. Andress began preparing for Surgery at 5:30 in the morning.

76. Select the sentence that is written most correctly.
   a. In contrast, cell phones can be taken anywhere, to most earlier communication technologies.
   b. In contrast to most earlier communication technologies, anywhere is the place cell phones can be taken.
   c. In contrast to most earlier communication technologies, cell phones can be taken anywhere.

77. Select the sentence that is written most correctly.
   a. Ms. Blau the chair of the committee on public works projects, has scheduled a meeting for this Tuesday.
   b. Ms. Blau, the chair of the committee on public works projects, has scheduled a meeting for this Tuesday.
   c. Ms. Blau the chair of the committee on public works projects has scheduled a meeting for this Tuesday.

78. Select the sentence that is written most correctly.
   a. Samantha is accompanying Luis and me to the theater tomorrow.
   b. Samantha is accompanying Luis and I to the theater tomorrow.
   c. Samantha, she is accompanying Luis and me to the theater tomorrow.

79. Select the sentence that is written most correctly.
   a. We will need tents, dried food, warm clothing sleeping bags, and a box of matches for the camping trip.
   b. We will need tents, dried food, warm clothing, sleeping bags, and a box of matches for the camping trip.
   c. We will need tents, dried food, warm clothing, sleeping, bags, and a box of matches for the camping trip.

80. Select the sentence that is written most correctly.

    a. All movie genres, such as comedy and science fiction, include some wonderful example of filmmaking.

    b. All movie genre, such as comedy and science fiction, include some wonderful examples of filmmaking.

    c. All movie genres, such as comedy and science fiction, include some wonderful examples of filmmaking.

Section 3: Civil Service Skills

Customer Service—Questions 81 through 85

Select the best answer for each question.

81. Customers may register complaints using each of the following options EXCEPT

    a. the Internet.

    b. in person.

    c. text message.

    d. the telephone.

82. A customer who lodges a complaint over the Internet should immediately receive

    a. a thorough solution to his or her problem.

    b. directions to the head office.

    c. a telephone call.

    d. an auto-reply message.

83. Appointments should be offered by agencies whose walk-in customers typically have to wait for a meeting for more than

    a. 15 minutes.

    b. 20 minutes.

    c. 25 minutes.

    d. 30 minutes.

84. What is the 2005 report focused on making government services "market-based, customer-centric, and customer-focused"?

    a. *The U.S. General Services Administration*

    b. *The Citizen Service Levels Interagency Committee*

    c. *FirstGov*

    d. *Really Simple Syndication*

85. When possible, customer queries should be resolved

    a. during first contact.

    b. after two detailed meetings.

    c. over the telephone only.

    d. by a manager only.

Memory—Questions 86 through 90

Take five minutes to study the following picture. Then, answer questions 86 through 88 without looking back at the picture.

86. The amount of sales tax in this urban enterprise zone is
   a. 3%.
   b. 3.5%.
   c. 4%.
   d. 4.5%.

87. The cross street occurs at
   a. Monmouth St. and Newark Av.
   b. Newark Av. And Monmouth St.
   c. Monmouth St. and Metro Av.
   d. Newark St. and Metro Av.

88. Which of the following signs does NOT appear in the photo?
   a. One Way
   b. No Vehicles Over 4 Tons
   c. Speed Limit 30
   d. No Trucks Over 4 Tons

Take five minutes to study the text that follows. Then, answer questions 89 and 90 without looking back at the text.

The following is the text of a notice posted in a government office. It instructs employees on the proper procedure for basic filing.

- Organize files according to category, which may precede two or more subcategories.
- Files must be organized in alphabetical order. The previous method of organization according to date has been discontinued.
- Names of individuals are alphabetized according to the first letter of the last name.
- Last names with prefixes are alphabetized according to the first letter of the prefix. For example, the name *van Gogh* would be filed under *V* rather than *G*.

- Paired individuals are filed according to the last name that comes first in the alphabet. For example, John Zeibler and Marjorie Allan should be filed as *Allan and Ziebler*.
- Business and company names are alphabetized according to the first letter in the company's name.
- All active and closed files must be kept for 25 years.
- Closed files must be discarded after 25 years to allow room for new files.
- Discarding of outdated files must be performed every Thursday.

89. According to the notice, files were previously organized according to
   a. first name.
   b. last name.
   c. company.
   d. date.

90. According to the notice, which files should be discarded?
   a. all files older than 25 years
   b. closed files older than 25 years
   c. open files older than 25 years
   d. files with names beginning in prefixes

Coding—Questions 91 through 100

To answer questions 91 through 95, refer to the following scenario.

Each employee at a government office is given a key code for access to the building. The code is created according to the following rules:
   2 letters = employee's initials
   4 digits = employee's date of birth
      (e.g., March 27 = 0327)

2 letters = employee's department. Letters are assigned accordingly:

CC = City Clerk
CM = City Manager
CS = Customer Service
ED = Economic Department
FD = Finance Department
HR = Human Resources
IT = Information Technology
PA = Public Affairs
TA = Tax Assessor's Office

91. Sheila Jackson works in the Human Resources Department. Her birthday is February 12. What is her key code?
a. SJ0212HR
b. SJHR2012
c. HRSJ2012
d. 2012HRSJ

92. Herman Munson works in the Customer Service Department. His birthday is July 7. What is his key code?
a. HR0707CS
b. HM0707HR
c. HM0707CS
d. CS0707HM

93. To whom might the key code KE0915ED belong?
a. Edward Dwyer
b. Janelle Scarano
c. Danica Kersh
d. Kevin Elbert

94. Which of the following statements about the employee with the key code PE1031CM must be true?
a. The employee's last name begins with D.
b. The employee's birthday is October 31.
c. The employee works in the Customer Service Department.
d. The employee's first name begins with O.

95. Create a key code for the following employee:
Date of Birth: April 10
Department: Information Technology
Name: Catherine Hall
a. 0410ITCH
b. CH0404IT
c. CH0410IT
d. IT0410CH

To answer questions 96 through 100, refer to the following scenario.

A safety compliance organization uses a code to log all safety violations. The code follows the rules below:

Nature of violation (record all that apply)
A = accident
B = behavior safety
Ca = chemical related
Cb = construction
D = dangerous gas related
Ea = electrical related
Eb = faulty evacuation procedures
F = fire related
M = machine related
P = pathogens
Sa = sanitation related
Sb = scaffolding

Subject of violation
1 = corporation
2 = government agency
3 = hospital
4 = nonprofit
5 = private business
6 = residential building
The subject of the violation directly follows the code(s) for the nature(s) of the violation.

96. A citizen reports a local grocery store that has not disposed of its trash for over two weeks. How should the violation be coded?
a. Sa5
b. 5Sa
c. S5a
d. aS5

97. A safety inspector investigates a pharmaceutical corporation that has been illegally disposing of toxic chemicals in a public lake. During the investigation, the inspector also discovers that technicians at the corporation have failed to contain noxious gases that have escaped into the workplace. How should the violation be coded?
a. Ca1D
b. CaD1
c. 1DCa
d. CbD1

98. The safety compliance organization receives a complaint that an apartment building has faulty wiring. How should this complaint be coded?
a. Eb6
b. Ea5
c. D6
d. Ea6

99. The code Cb4 could refer to
a. a hospital that has been dumping solid waste illegally.
b. a clothing store that does not provide fire exits.
c. an animal shelter with unstable stairways.
d. a movie theater without safely situated aisles.

100. A safety inspector investigates a corporation that has received several complaints about the manufacturing plant of an international steel corporation. Several employees have been injured by poorly maintained machines and electrical fires. Others have slipped on floors slick with oil. How should this violation be coded?
a. AEa1M
b. PEaM3
c. AEaM1
d. SaSb5

Answers

Section 1: Mathematics

1. **a.** Convert an improper fraction to a mixed number by dividing the denominator into the numerator; this will result in a whole number and a remainder, the latter of which is expressed as the numerator of a fraction with the same denominator as the original improper fraction. Doing so yields $\frac{58}{10} = 5\frac{8}{10}$ $= 5\frac{4}{5}$. Choices **b** and **c** are incorrect because they are the reciprocals of the given improper fraction. Choice **d** is incorrect because the fractional part (remainder) is expressed incorrectly.

2. **d.** To reduce a fraction to lowest terms, write the numerator and denominator as products of their factors, and cancel all those that are common to both the numerator and denominator: $\frac{32}{55} = \frac{2 \cdot 2 \cdot 2 \cdot 2 \cdot 2}{5 \cdot 11}$. Since there are no factors common to both the numerator and denominator, the fraction cannot be reduced further. Choice **a** is incorrect because you cannot subtract the numerator from the denominator. Choice **b** mistakenly cancels the power 5 with the factor of 5 in the denominator. Choice **c** is the reciprocal of the given fraction.

3. **b.** $9\frac{3}{8} + 2\frac{7}{16} = 9\frac{6}{16} + 2\frac{7}{16} = (9 + 2) + (\frac{6}{16} + \frac{7}{16})$ $= 11\frac{13}{16}$. Choice **a** adds the fractional parts incorrectly. Choice **c** subtracts the fractions instead of adding them. Choice **d** does not find a least common denominator before adding the fractional parts.

4. **d.** $\frac{8}{9} - \frac{2}{3} = \frac{8}{9} - \frac{4}{9} = \frac{8-4}{9} = \frac{4}{9}$. Choice **a** subtracts the numerators and denominators without first finding a common denominator. Choice **b** multiplies the fractions; it doesn't subtract them. Choice **c** adds instead of subtracts the fractions, and then converts the result to a mixed number.

5. **b.** $3\frac{2}{3} \div 1\frac{1}{3} = \frac{11}{3} \div \frac{4}{3} = \frac{11}{3} \times \frac{3}{4} = \frac{11}{4} = 2\frac{3}{4}$. Choice **a** multiplies the fractions instead of dividing them; choice **c** adds them. Choice **d** is incorrect because it is the reciprocal of the correct answer.

6. **d.** $\frac{8}{13} \times 2\frac{1}{6} = \frac{8}{13} \times \frac{13}{6} = \frac{8}{6} = \frac{4}{3} = 1\frac{1}{3}$. Choice **a** is the reciprocal of the correct answer. Choice **b** treats the mixed number as $2 \times \frac{1}{6}$, which is incorrect. Choice **c** divides the fractions instead of multiplying them.

7. **a.** $\frac{10}{11} \div \frac{12}{121} = \frac{10}{11} \times \frac{121}{12} = \frac{5 \cdot \cancel{2}}{\cancel{11}} \times \frac{11 \cdot \cancel{11}}{6 \cdot \cancel{2}} = \frac{55}{6} = 9\frac{1}{6}$. Choice **b** is the reciprocal of the correct answer. Choice **c** adds the fractions instead of dividing them, and choice **d** subtracts them.

8. **c.** $5\% = \frac{5}{100} = \frac{1}{20}$. So, 5% of $\frac{1}{5}$ is $\frac{1}{20}(\frac{1}{5}) = \frac{1}{100}$. Choice **a** is incorrect because 5% does not equal 5—you must divide 5 by 100. Choice **b** is incorrect because 5% does not equal 5 divided by 10—you must divide 5 by 100 instead of 10. Choice **d** is incorrect because 5% does not equal 5 divided by 1,000—you must divide 5 by 100 instead of 1,000.

9. **d.** Multiply the numbers as if they were whole numbers to get 1,111. Then, move the decimal point three places to the left to get 1.111. Choice **a** does not insert the decimal point. Choice **b** adds the decimals rather than multiplying them. In choice **c**, the decimal point is in the wrong location.

10. **b.** $95\% = \frac{95}{100}$, which simplifies to $\frac{19}{20}$ upon canceling a 5 in the numerator and denominator. Choice **a** = 90%, not 95%. Choice **c** misinterprets the meaning of a percent, which is not found by simply dividing the digits. Choice **d** is incorrect because you should divide 95 by 100, not 10.

11. a. $2\frac{2}{5} = 2.40$, and then moving the decimal point two places to the right gives the equivalent percent of 240%. Choice **b** is incorrect because 2.4 is the decimal equivalent of $2\frac{2}{5}$. To get the percent equivalent, move the decimal point two places to the right. Choice **c** is incorrect because when converting the decimal equivalent of $2\frac{2}{5}$ to a percent, you moved the decimal point two places to the left instead of to the right. Choice **d** is incorrect because you did not move the decimal point two places to the right when converting the decimal equivalent of $2\frac{2}{5}$ to a percent—you only moved it one place.

12. a. Subtract the first place time from the second place time: $32.06 - 29.31 = 2.75$ seconds. Choices **b** and **c** don't borrow correctly. Choice **d** adds the hundredths digits instead of subtracting them.

13. b. Add the three fractions together:
$2\frac{2}{5} + 1\frac{2}{3} + \frac{2}{3} = (2 + 1) + (\frac{2}{5} + \frac{2}{3} + \frac{2}{3})$

$\qquad = 3 + \frac{2}{5} + \frac{4}{3}$

$\qquad = 3 + \frac{6}{15} + \frac{20}{15}$

$\qquad = 3\frac{26}{15}$

$\qquad = 4\frac{11}{15}$

The fractional part is incorrect in choice **a**. Choice **c** is incorrect because it does not include the fraction of a ream from the third project. Choice **d** does not carry the whole part when simplifying the improper fraction that arose from adding the fractional parts.

14. a. First, determine the amount of the tax: $0.12(\$122.50) = \$14.70$. Now, add this to the amount before tax to get the final bill amount: $\$122.50 + \$14.70 = \$137.20$. Choice **b** does not carry 1 to the ones place. Choice **c** is just the tax amount, not the total bill. Choice **d** interprets 12% as \$12—you must compute 12% of \$122.50.

15. a. Let x be the amount of the bill before tip. Then, the 18% tip is $0.18x$. When the two dollar amounts are added, the sum is \$62.55: $x + 0.18x = 62.55$. Simplify the left-side of the equation to get $1.18x = 62.55$. Finally, divide both sides by 1.18: $x = \frac{\$62.55}{1.18} = \$53.01$. Choice **b** is the amount of the tip only. Choice **c** adds 18% of \$62.55 (the amount that already contained the tip) to \$62.55. Choice **d** treats 18% as 0.018 instead of 1.8.

16. d. Let x be the number of tablespoons needed to bake 81 muffins. First, rewrite $2\frac{1}{2}$ as a mixed number $\frac{5}{2}$. Then, set up the following proportion: $\frac{2\frac{1}{2}}{18} = \frac{x}{81}$. To solve for x, cross-multiply: $18x = 81(2\frac{1}{2})$. This simplifies to get $18x = 81(\frac{5}{2})$, so that dividing both sides by 18 yields
$x = \frac{81}{18}(\frac{5}{2}) = \frac{\cancel{9} \times 9 \times 5}{\cancel{9} \times 2 \times 2} = \frac{45}{4} = 11\frac{1}{4}$.
Choice **a** divides incorrectly when simplifying the proportion. Choice **b** forgets to include the fractional part of $2\frac{1}{2}$ when setting up the proportion. Choice **d** forgets to include the whole part of $2\frac{1}{2}$ when setting up the proportion.

17. d. Multiply the number of boxes used by the number of books per box: $66(16) = 1,056$. Choice **a** adds the number of boxes to the average number of books per box instead of multiplying them. Choice **b** multiplies the tens place incorrectly. Choice **d** rounds each of the numbers to the nearest ten before multiplying, which produces an inaccurate count.

18. c. If 30% of the boxes exceed 5 pounds in weight, the remainder of the boxes (70%) have a weight of 5 pounds or less. To determine this amount, multiply 0.70 times 420: 0.70(420) = 294. Choice **a** is the number of boxes whose weight exceeds 5 pounds. Choice **b** subtracts the weight from the number of boxes. Choice **d** is incorrect because 30% does not equal 30. You must multiply 0.30 times the original amount (420) in order to determine the number of boxes whose weight exceeds 5 pounds.

19. c. Let x represent the number of laps completed in 3 hours. Convert $\frac{3}{4}$ to the decimal 0.75 and set up the following proportion:

$$\frac{1 \text{ lap}}{0.75 \text{ hours}} = \frac{x \text{ laps}}{3 \text{ hours}}$$

To solve the proportion, cross-multiply to get the equation, $0.75x = 3$. Solve the equation by dividing both sides by 0.75 to get $x = 4$. This is the total number of laps completed. Each lap is 2.5 miles, so the total miles the walkers completed is $2.5 \times 4 = 10$ miles.

20. b. Multiply the two fractions to determine the number of miles they have completed: $\frac{3}{4}(8\frac{1}{4}) = \frac{3}{4} \times \frac{33}{4} = \frac{99}{16} = 6\frac{3}{16}$ miles. Now, subtract this from the total number of miles for the entire hike: $8\frac{1}{4} - 6\frac{3}{16} = 8\frac{4}{16} - 6\frac{3}{16} = 2\frac{1}{16}$ miles. Choice **a** is the number of miles the couple have already walked, not the amount that needs to still be completed. Choice **c** is exactly half of the total distance covered by the hike, not $\frac{1}{4}$ of the hike (which is the portion that still needs to be completed). Choice **d** does not include the remainder when dividing.

21. d. Divide the total number of duties that must be completed by the number of employees: $\frac{36}{9} = 4$ tasks per employee. Choice **a** is twice the number of tasks each employee is assigned. Choice **b** divides incorrectly—this would be the number of tasks each employee would be assigned if there were 45 duties, not 36. Choice **c** subtracts the number of employees from the total number of tasks instead of dividing.

22. c. The number of team leaders is 10% of 120: 0.10(120) = 12. So, the number of remaining campers is $120 - 12 = 108$. Dividing this by 6 yields 18. Choice **a** assumes there are 100 campers all told, not 120. Choice **b** is incorrect because it is half of the correct answer. Choice **d** is incorrect because this number includes team leaders.

23. a. First, note that 20% is equivalent to $\frac{20}{100} = \frac{1}{5}$. So, 20% of $9\frac{1}{6}$ feet is $\frac{1}{5} \times (9\frac{1}{6}) = \frac{1}{5} \times \frac{55}{6} = \frac{11}{6} = 1\frac{5}{6}$ feet. Thus, the length of the countertop upon implementing such an increase would be $9\frac{1}{6} + 1\frac{5}{6} = (9 + 1) + (\frac{1}{6} + \frac{5}{6}) = 10 + 1 = 11$ feet. Choice **b** only adds the whole parts of the lengths—it should be 1 foot larger. Choice **c** forgets to include the fractional part of the length corresponding to a 20% increase. Choice **d** is only the amount of additional footage added to the countertop, which needs to be added to the length of the existing countertop.

24. d. Each canvas costs $3.82. Five canvases per month cost $3.82 \times 5 = \$19.10$. For six months, the total cost is $\$19.10 \times 6 = \$114.60$. Choice **a** is incorrect because it is only the cost per month.

25. b. Divide the total amount of ground beef by the amount of ground beef used for a single burger: $\frac{12.42}{0.30} = 41.4$. This number must be rounded *down* to 41 because beyond this, a 42nd full-sized burger cannot be made. Choice **a** rounds up instead of down. Choice **c** divides 12 by 0.3 rather than dividing 12.42 by 0.3. Choice **d** is the number of quarter-pounders (0.25 pounds of beef used for each burger).

26. b. Subtract the sum of the fractions of the bakery owned by the oldest and youngest sibling from 1 to obtain the fraction of the bakery owned by the third sibling: $1 - (\frac{2}{5} + \frac{1}{4}) =$ $1 - (\frac{8}{20} + \frac{5}{20}) = 1 - \frac{13}{20} = \frac{7}{20}$. Choices **a** and **d** do not account for the fraction of the bakery owned by the oldest and youngest siblings, respectively. Choice **c** adds the fractions by adding the numerators and denominators instead of getting a least common denominator.

27. b. It did not rain for 7 of 12 days. Since $\frac{7}{12} =$ 0.583, conclude that it did not rain for about 58% of the vacation. Choice **a** is incorrect because 12 is the number of days of vacation, not the percentage of days it did not rain. Choice **c** is the percentage of the vacation for which it *did* rain. Choice **d** is does not convert $\frac{7}{12}$ (which is the *fraction* of days it did not rain) to a percentage correctly.

28. a. Use the fact that 1 mile = 5,280 feet and that 1 hour = 60 minutes to change the units, as follows:

80 ~~miles~~	5,280 feet	1 ~~hour~~
1 ~~hour~~	1 ~~mile~~	60 minutes

Pay particular attention to the canceling of units. Multiplying through gives 7,040 feet per minute. Choice **b** is the approximate number of feet per second, not minute. Choice **c** is the number of inches per minute, not feet per minute. Choice **d** is the number of inches per second, not feet per minute.

29. c. Add the numbers together and divide by 5:
$$\frac{2\frac{1}{4} + 2\frac{2}{3} + 1\frac{5}{6} + 2 + 3\frac{1}{3}}{5} = \frac{\frac{9}{4} + \frac{8}{3} + \frac{11}{6} + 2 + \frac{10}{3}}{5}$$
$$= \frac{\frac{27 + 32 + 22 + 24 + 40}{12}}{5}$$
$$= \frac{145}{12(5)} = \frac{29}{12}$$
$$= 2\frac{5}{12} \text{ minutes}$$
Choice **a** is the median time, not the average time. Choice **b** is the maximum time; choice **d** is the minimum time.

30. c. The vertical axis is the y-axis, which is labeled as C. Choice **a** is the title of the graph. Choice **b** is the legend of the graph. Choice **d** is the x-axis.

31. a. There are nine sightings in this month, and this is the highest point (for bears) shown on the line graph. Choice **b** is incorrect because there is one month with a greater number of bear sightings. Choice **c** is the month with the fewest bear sightings. Choice **d** is incorrect because there are several months with more bear sightings.

32. d. There is only one sighting in this month, and this is the lowest point on the bobcat portion of the line graph. Choices **a** and **b** are incorrect because there is one month with fewer bobcat sightings. Choice **c** is incorrect because there are several months with fewer bobcat sightings.

33. c. Subtract the smallest value (3) from the largest value (15): $15 - 3 = 12$. Choice **a** is the maximum value, not the range. Choice **b** is the minimum value, not the range. Choice **d** is the *mode* (that is, the value that occurs the most often), not the range.

34. b. Compute 25% of 500: $0.25(500) = 125$. Choice **a** is incorrect because this information is not provided in the data. Choice **c** is incorrect because this is described by the *x*-axis, not the *y*-axis. Choice **d** is the distance between hash marks on the *y*-axis, not the nature of what these numbers represent.

35. c. Fifteen percent is the smallest percentage of the four listed in the graph. Choice **a** is incorrect because this category accounts for most of these students, not the smallest amount. Choices **b** and **c** are incorrect because these categories contribute more than the juniors category.

36. d. 45% of 5,500 is $0.45(5,500) = 2,475$. Choice **a** is the number of juniors, not freshmen. Choice **b** is the number of sophomores (and the number of seniors), not the number of freshmen. Choice **c** is the number of non-freshmen.

37. c. Divide the percentage of freshmen by the percentage of juniors, and simplify: $\frac{45}{15} = \frac{3}{1}$. So, the ratio is 3:1. Choice **a** assumes an equal number of freshmen and juniors, which is not the case. Choice **b** is incorrect because this ratio compares sophomore to juniors, or seniors to juniors. Choice **d** is written backwards—it is the ratio of juniors to freshmen.

38. b. Add the six scores and divide by 6: $\frac{10+18+11+5+8+8}{6} = \frac{60}{6} = 10$. Choice **a** is the median score (that is, the average of the two middle scores, assuming the scores are arranged in increasing order), not the average score. Choice **c** is the minimum score on Course A, not the average. Choice **d** is the maximum score on Course A, not the average.

39. c. Subtract the minimum score on Course B (3) from the maximum score on Course B (13): $13 - 3 = 10$. Choice **a** is the maximum score on Course B, not the range. Choice **b** is the average score on Course B, not the range. Choice **d** is the minimum score on Course B, not the range.

40. d. The average score of all six players on Course B is 7.5, while the average score of all six players on Course A is 10. Choice **a** is incorrect because the range of scores for Course A is $18 - 5 = 13$, while the range of scores for Course B is $13 - 3 = 10$. Choice **b** is incorrect because Mandi's average is $\frac{11+9}{2} = \frac{20}{2} = 10$, not 11. Choice **c** is incorrect because their scores on both courses are identical.

Section 2: Written Communication

41. d. A good title gives a strong impression of a passage's main idea. The main focus of this passage is to dispel assumptions about pet racing greyhounds and highlight how they actually make excellent pets. Choices **a** and **b** illustrate minor details in the passage, but fail to capture the main idea. Choice **c** is contradicted by information in paragraph 3.

42. c. Paragraph 4 begins by stating, "Greyhounds do not make good watchdogs, but they are very good with children, get along well with other dogs (and usually cats, as well)." This statement confirms choice **c** and contradicts choices **b** and d. Information in paragraph 3 contradicts choice **a**.

43. d. Reread the sentence, substituting each choice for the word *hesitate*. Of the four choices, only choice **d** makes sense in context. Choice **a**, *rush*, has the opposite meaning of *hesitate*.

44. a. The final sentence of paragraph 3 supports choice **a** and contradicts choice **b**. There is no information in the passage that supports either choice **c** or choice **d**.

45. b. The second sentence of the passage supports choice **b** and contradicts choice **a**. Choices **c** and **d** are also contradicted by information in the passage.

46. d. The primary purpose of the passage is to explain three kinds of eating disorders: anorexia nervosa, bulimia nervosa, and binge-eating disorder. Choice **a** only describes the purpose of paragraph 2; it does not sum up the purpose of the entire passage. Choice **c** is a minor detail in the passage and hardly illustrates its primary purpose. There is no evidence in the passage to support choice **b**.

47. c. Paragraph 4 states that most binge eaters "are overweight or obese." Choice **a** describes anorexia nervosa sufferers. Information in paragraph 3 contradicts choice **d**.

48. a. Paragraph 4 indicates that only one-third of binge eaters are men, and it affects older women less frequently. Based on this information, one can conclude that younger women suffer from the disorder more often than men or older women. Paragraph 2 states that anorexia nervosa "usually begins around the time of puberty," which contradicts choice **b**. Paragraph 3 states that dieting between episodes of binging and purging is common, but not something that always occurs, so choice **c** is incorrect. Information in paragraph 3 also contradicts choice **d**.

49. b. People with bulimia nervosa risk heart failure by using drugs to help them rid their bodies of excess calories. It is this ridding that is a health risk, not the calories themselves, so choice **a** is incorrect. Although paragraph 3 mentions that people with bulimia nervosa often diet heavily, it does not indicate that dieting poses a risk, so choice **c** is incorrect. Choice **d**, constipation, is only mentioned in the paragraph about anorexia nervosa.

50. a. Reread the sentence, substituting each choice for the word *distinctive*. Of the four choices, only choice **a** makes sense in context.

51. c. Choice **c** sums up the most important ideas in the passage. Choices **a** and **b** are important details, but they do not illustrate the most important ideas that run throughout the entire passage. The passage begins by stating, "No longer is asthma considered a condition with isolated, acute episodes of bronchospasm," which contradicts choice **d**.

52. b. Reread the sentence, substituting each choice for the word *continual*. Of the four choices, only choice **b** makes sense in context.

53. a. The second paragraph begins with the statement, "Asthma involves complex interactions among inflammatory cells, mediators, and the cells and tissues in the airways." This indicates that mediators affect cells and tissues in the airways. Choices **b** and **c** are directly contradicted by the passage. Choice **d** is incorrect because stress is not mentioned in the passage at all.

54. d. The second paragraph directly states, "The morphologic changes that occur in asthma include bronchial infiltration by inflammatory cells." Choices **a**, **b**, and **c** are effects of the interactions among inflammatory cells, mediators, and the cells and tissues in the airways, not examples of morphologic changes.

55. b. The second sentence of the passage lists a number of symptoms of asthma, but throat irritation is not included in the list. Asthma is a respiratory condition, not an illness that causes an irritated throat.

56. b. The main purpose of this passage is to explain the dangers and treatments of heat exhaustion and heatstroke. Choice **a** is contradicted by the first sentence of paragraph 3. No information in the passage supports either choice **c** or choice **d**.

57. c. Paragraph 2 indicates that dizziness is a symptom of heat exhaustion, but it is not included among the symptoms of heatstroke in paragraph 3.

58. d. Paragraph 3 ends by stating, "Care should be taken, however, not to overchill the victim once the temperature is below 102°F." This detail indicates that it is important to monitor the temperature of heatstroke sufferers. Choice **a** refers to information in paragraph 2, not paragraph 3. Choice **c** is contradicted by the first sentence of paragraph 3.

59. c. Choice **c** is directly supported by information in paragraph 2. The paragraph also states that heat exhaustion is caused by "inadequate intake of water," which contradicts choice **a**. Drinking salt water is a treatment, not a cause, of heat exhaustion, so choice **b** is incorrect, too. Choice **d** is a treatment of heatstroke, not a cause of heat exhaustion.

60. d. Reread the sentence, substituting each choice for the word *tolerate*. Of the four choices, only choice **d** makes sense in context.

61. b. The correct spelling is *aggressive*.

62. a. The correct spelling is *circulated*.

63. c. The correct spellings of **a** and **b** are *quarantine* and *metropolis*.

64. b. The correct spellings of **a** and **c** are *jargon* and *chauffeur*.

65. c. The correct spellings of **a** and **b** are *intercept* and *phenomenon*.

66. a. *Accelerate* is the word that is closest in meaning to *precipitate*.

67. a. *Violent* is the word that is closest in meaning to *tumultuous*.

68. c. The word *laborious* means *requiring hard work*, so the word most nearly its opposite is *effortless*.

69. b. Choices **a** and **c** can be eliminated because neither makes sense in the context of this sentence. The word *amended* means *altered* and *fascinating* means *very interesting*. When something has been *purged*, it has been *cleaned out*.

70. c. A *laconic* person is *someone who does not speak much*, so such a person is not likely to indulge in long speeches. Choice **a**, *verbose*, means *talkative*. Choice **b**, *poignant*, means *emotional*.

71. b. Choices **a** is a sentence fragment lacking both a subject and a verb. Choice **c** is a sentence fragment because it needs a complete phrase after the conjunction *because*.

72. c. Choice **a** uses the passive voice when a better alternative written in the active voice— choice **c**—is available. Choice **b** is missing the article *the*.

73. a. In choice **b**, the past-tense verb *arrived* is used incorrectly in place of the noun *arrival*. Choice **c** contains a redundancy because *coming* and *arrival* share the same meaning.

74. a. Choice **b** is incorrect because a title such as president should only be capitalized when placed at the beginning of a sentence or used to identify a proper name, such as *President Washington*. Choice **c** is incorrect because days of the month, such as *January*, should be capitalized.

75. b. Choice **a** is incorrect because an abbreviation, such as *Dr.*, should end with a period. Choice **c** is incorrect because *surgery* is capitalized incorrectly.

76. c. Choice **a** is incorrect because the clause *cell phones can be taken anywhere* is placed in the middle of the phrase *In contrast to most earlier communication technologies* mistakenly. Choice **b** is awkwardly and confusingly worded; choice **c** is a much better formulation of the same idea, so it is the better answer.

77. b. Choice **a** is missing a comma to offset *the phrase the chair of the committee on public works projects* from *Ms. Blau*. Choice **c** is missing both commas needed to offset the phrase.

78. a. Choice **b** incorrectly uses *I* where it should use *me*. Omit Luis from the sentence; would you say *Samantha is accompanying me to the theater tomorrow* or *Samantha is accompanying Luis and me to the theater tomorrow*? Because the sentence calls for an indirect object, the word *me* should be used, not *I*. Choice **c** is incorrect because its use of both *Samantha* and the pronoun *she* is redundant.

79. b. When you write a list of items, separate each item on the list with a comma. Choice **a** omits the comma between *warm clothing* and *sleeping bag*. Choice **c** contains a comma between *sleeping* and *bag*. One cannot bring an intangible state, such as *sleeping*, so this comma is incorrect.

80. c. Choice **a** is incorrect because the plural verb *includes* does not agree with the plural subject *movie genres*. The subject *movie genre* should be in the plural form in choice **b**. Only choice **c** contains proper subject-verb agreement.

Section 3: Civil Service Skills

81. c. While the Internet, the telephone, and an in-person visit allow a customer to lodge a detailed official complaint, brief text messages are not as conducive to doing so.

82. d. An auto-reply message should be sent to a customer upon receipt of his or her complaint. Such messages confirm that the complaint has been received and offer alternative suggestions for resolving the issue.

83. a. The understanding that good customer service does not waste the customer's time is the key to answering this question. No walk-in customer should be expected to wait more than 15 minutes. Appointments are set to minimize customer wait time.

84. b. In October 2005, the federal government commissioned *The Citizen Service Levels Interagency Committee* (*CSLIC*) to improve customer service procedures among government agencies.

85. a. Prompt action is one of the keys to excellent customer service. Queries should be resolved during first contact with customers whenever possible.

86. b. A sign labeled Urban Enterprise Zone informs the reader that sales tax is 3.5% in the zone.

87. a. According to the sign at the top of the photo, the cross streets are Monmouth St. and Newark Av.

88. c. No speed limit sign is visible in this photo.

89. d. The second bullet point of the notice indicates that "The previous method of organization according to date has been discontinued."

90. b. The final bullet point of the notice indicates that "Closed files must be discarded after 25 years to allow room for new files."

91. a. The first pair of letters in the code represent the employee's name; the following four digits represent the employee's birthday; the final two letters represent the employee's department. Sheila Jackson's key code should begin with her initials (SJ). Only choices **a** and **b** begin with SJ, so choices **c** and **d** can be eliminated. Choice **b** can then be eliminated because it follows the first two letters with two more letters instead of four digits. Therefore, the correct answer can only be choice **a**.

92. c. Choice **a** is incorrect because HR is the code for the Human Resources department, not Herman Munson's initials (HM). Since Herman Munson does not work for the Human Resources Department, choice **b** can be eliminated as well. Choice **d** is incorrect because it reverses the employee's name and his department, which should be placed at the end of the key code.

93. d. The first two letters of the key code indicate the employee's initials. The first two letters of this particular key code are KE. Choice **d** is the only one that has a name with these initials.

94. b. The four digits in the key code indicate the employee's birthday; the first two digits indicate the month and the last two indicate the day. An employee with the digits 1031 in the middle of his or her key code was born on October 31.

95. c. The employee's name is coded according to his or her initials. They are followed by digits indicating his or her birthday. The code is completed with two letters indicating the employee's department. Only choice **c** presents the correct letters and digits in the correct order.

96. a. The rules of the code state "The subject of the violation directly follows the code for the nature of the violation." The subject of this particular violation is a grocery store, which is a private business. So the code for a private business, 5, should follow the code for a sanitation-related violation, *Sa*, because that is what failing to dispose of trash is.

97. b. The rules state that all violations must be included in the code. This particular scenario includes two violations involving chemicals (*Ca*) and gas (*D*), so both need to be included in the code and both need to precede the number indicating the subject of the violation.

98. d. Faulty wiring is an electrical-related violation, so it should be coded *Ea*. An apartment building is a residential building, so it should be coded *6*.

99. c. Unstable stairways are a construction-related safety violation and an animal shelter is a nonprofit.

100. c. The corporation described in this question is guilty of three violations: slick floors are accident violations (*A*), electrical fires are filed as electrical-related violations (*Ea*), and dangerous machines are machine violations (*M*). All three of these violations need to be included in the code before the digit *1*, indicating that a corporation is the subject of these violations.

6 ▶ CIVIL SERVICE PRACTICE EXAM 5

This fifth practice exam in the book will continue to prepare you for the types of questions you will see on your civil service exam. The 100 multiple-choice questions that follow will test your knowledge of math, reading, spelling, grammar, civil service, memory, and coding.

Remember to read the entire answer explanation thoroughly, regardless of whether you answered the question correctly. Compare your score on this test to tests 1 through 4. Are there areas in which you need more improvement?

Civil Service Practice Exam 5

1.	ⓐ	ⓑ	ⓒ	ⓓ
2.	ⓐ	ⓑ	ⓒ	ⓓ
3.	ⓐ	ⓑ	ⓒ	ⓓ
4.	ⓐ	ⓑ	ⓒ	ⓓ
5.	ⓐ	ⓑ	ⓒ	ⓓ
6.	ⓐ	ⓑ	ⓒ	ⓓ
7.	ⓐ	ⓑ	ⓒ	ⓓ
8.	ⓐ	ⓑ	ⓒ	ⓓ
9.	ⓐ	ⓑ	ⓒ	ⓓ
10.	ⓐ	ⓑ	ⓒ	ⓓ
11.	ⓐ	ⓑ	ⓒ	ⓓ
12.	ⓐ	ⓑ	ⓒ	ⓓ
13.	ⓐ	ⓑ	ⓒ	ⓓ
14.	ⓐ	ⓑ	ⓒ	ⓓ
15.	ⓐ	ⓑ	ⓒ	ⓓ
16.	ⓐ	ⓑ	ⓒ	ⓓ
17.	ⓐ	ⓑ	ⓒ	ⓓ
18.	ⓐ	ⓑ	ⓒ	ⓓ
19.	ⓐ	ⓑ	ⓒ	ⓓ
20.	ⓐ	ⓑ	ⓒ	ⓓ
21.	ⓐ	ⓑ	ⓒ	ⓓ
22.	ⓐ	ⓑ	ⓒ	ⓓ
23.	ⓐ	ⓑ	ⓒ	ⓓ
24.	ⓐ	ⓑ	ⓒ	ⓓ
25.	ⓐ	ⓑ	ⓒ	ⓓ
26.	ⓐ	ⓑ	ⓒ	ⓓ
27.	ⓐ	ⓑ	ⓒ	ⓓ
28.	ⓐ	ⓑ	ⓒ	ⓓ
29.	ⓐ	ⓑ	ⓒ	ⓓ
30.	ⓐ	ⓑ	ⓒ	ⓓ
31.	ⓐ	ⓑ	ⓒ	ⓓ
32.	ⓐ	ⓑ	ⓒ	ⓓ
33.	ⓐ	ⓑ	ⓒ	ⓓ
34.	ⓐ	ⓑ	ⓒ	ⓓ
35.	ⓐ	ⓑ	ⓒ	ⓓ

36.	ⓐ	ⓑ	ⓒ	ⓓ
37.	ⓐ	ⓑ	ⓒ	ⓓ
38.	ⓐ	ⓑ	ⓒ	ⓓ
39.	ⓐ	ⓑ	ⓒ	ⓓ
40.	ⓐ	ⓑ	ⓒ	ⓓ
41.	ⓐ	ⓑ	ⓒ	ⓓ
42.	ⓐ	ⓑ	ⓒ	ⓓ
43.	ⓐ	ⓑ	ⓒ	ⓓ
44.	ⓐ	ⓑ	ⓒ	ⓓ
45.	ⓐ	ⓑ	ⓒ	ⓓ
46.	ⓐ	ⓑ	ⓒ	ⓓ
47.	ⓐ	ⓑ	ⓒ	ⓓ
48.	ⓐ	ⓑ	ⓒ	ⓓ
49.	ⓐ	ⓑ	ⓒ	ⓓ
50.	ⓐ	ⓑ	ⓒ	ⓓ
51.	ⓐ	ⓑ	ⓒ	ⓓ
52.	ⓐ	ⓑ	ⓒ	ⓓ
53.	ⓐ	ⓑ	ⓒ	ⓓ
54.	ⓐ	ⓑ	ⓒ	ⓓ
55.	ⓐ	ⓑ	ⓒ	ⓓ
56.	ⓐ	ⓑ	ⓒ	ⓓ
57.	ⓐ	ⓑ	ⓒ	ⓓ
58.	ⓐ	ⓑ	ⓒ	ⓓ
59.	ⓐ	ⓑ	ⓒ	ⓓ
60.	ⓐ	ⓑ	ⓒ	ⓓ
61.	ⓐ	ⓑ	ⓒ	
62.	ⓐ	ⓑ	ⓒ	
63.	ⓐ	ⓑ	ⓒ	
64.	ⓐ	ⓑ	ⓒ	
65.	ⓐ	ⓑ	ⓒ	
66.	ⓐ	ⓑ	ⓒ	
67.	ⓐ	ⓑ	ⓒ	
68.	ⓐ	ⓑ	ⓒ	
69.	ⓐ	ⓑ	ⓒ	
70.	ⓐ	ⓑ	ⓒ	

71.	ⓐ	ⓑ	ⓒ	
72.	ⓐ	ⓑ	ⓒ	
73.	ⓐ	ⓑ	ⓒ	
74.	ⓐ	ⓑ	ⓒ	
75.	ⓐ	ⓑ	ⓒ	
76.	ⓐ	ⓑ	ⓒ	
77.	ⓐ	ⓑ	ⓒ	
78.	ⓐ	ⓑ	ⓒ	
79.	ⓐ	ⓑ	ⓒ	
80.	ⓐ	ⓑ	ⓒ	
81.	ⓐ	ⓑ	ⓒ	ⓓ
82.	ⓐ	ⓑ	ⓒ	ⓓ
83.	ⓐ	ⓑ	ⓒ	ⓓ
84.	ⓐ	ⓑ	ⓒ	ⓓ
85.	ⓐ	ⓑ	ⓒ	ⓓ
86.	ⓐ	ⓑ	ⓒ	ⓓ
87.	ⓐ	ⓑ	ⓒ	ⓓ
88.	ⓐ	ⓑ	ⓒ	ⓓ
89.	ⓐ	ⓑ	ⓒ	ⓓ
90.	ⓐ	ⓑ	ⓒ	ⓓ
91.	ⓐ	ⓑ	ⓒ	ⓓ
92.	ⓐ	ⓑ	ⓒ	ⓓ
93.	ⓐ	ⓑ	ⓒ	ⓓ
94.	ⓐ	ⓑ	ⓒ	ⓓ
95.	ⓐ	ⓑ	ⓒ	ⓓ
96.	ⓐ	ⓑ	ⓒ	ⓓ
97.	ⓐ	ⓑ	ⓒ	ⓓ
98.	ⓐ	ⓑ	ⓒ	ⓓ
99.	ⓐ	ⓑ	ⓒ	ⓓ
100.	ⓐ	ⓑ	ⓒ	ⓓ

Section 1: Mathematics

1. $3\frac{2}{7} =$

   a. $\frac{6}{7}$

   b. $\frac{23}{7}$

   c. $\frac{32}{7}$

   d. $\frac{7}{23}$

2. Reduce $\frac{24}{64}$ to lowest terms.

   a. $\frac{2}{6}$

   b. $\frac{3}{8}$

   c. $\frac{1}{40}$

   d. $\frac{3}{64}$

3. $5\frac{1}{4} - (2\frac{3}{8} + 1\frac{7}{8}) =$

   a. 1

   b. $1\frac{1}{4}$

   c. $4\frac{1}{2}$

   d. $2\frac{11}{12}$

4. $5.7 - 2.3 =$

   a. 3.4

   b. 5.3

   c. 8.0

   d. 10.3

5. $3 \times 2\frac{5}{6} =$

   a. $6\frac{5}{6}$

   b. $8\frac{1}{2}$

   c. $1\frac{1}{17}$

   d. $5\frac{5}{6}$

6. $\frac{2}{5} \div 5\frac{1}{2} =$

   a. $2\frac{1}{5}$

   b. $\frac{5}{11}$

   c. $\frac{4}{55}$

   d. $5\frac{9}{10}$

7. $\frac{8}{11} \times 1\frac{5}{6} =$

   a. $1\frac{1}{3}$

   b. $\frac{3}{4}$

   c. $\frac{48}{121}$

   d. $1\frac{20}{33}$

8. 90% of 30 is _____.

   a. 27

   b. 30

   c. 60

   d. 120

9. $2.012 - 0.334 =$ _____.

   a. 1.9786

   b. 2.346

   c. 1.788

   d. 1.678

10. What is the decimal equivalent of $\frac{22}{25}$?

   a. 0.22

   b. 0.40

   c. 0.88

   d. 0.80

11. What is the fraction equivalent of 58%?

   a. $\frac{21}{50}$

   b. $\frac{17}{50}$

   c. $\frac{29}{50}$

   d. $\frac{36}{100}$

12. Matilda bought 5.48 ounces of fudge and her friend, Sue, bought 4.79 ounces. How many more ounces of fudge would they have to buy in order to have a combined total of 15 ounces of fudge?

   a. 10.27 ounces

   b. 9.52 ounces

   c. 5.73 ounces

   d. 4.73 ounces

13. If a carpenter trims $1\frac{1}{2}$ inches from a wall molding that is $18\frac{3}{4}$ inches long, how much of the wall molding is left?

a. $17\frac{1}{2}$

b. $17\frac{1}{4}$

c. $18\frac{5}{4}$

d. $19\frac{1}{4}$

14. A restaurant bill comes to $86.90 before tax. If 6% sales tax is added to this amount, what is the amount of the final bill?

a. $5.21

b. $91.11

c. $92.11

d. $91.25

15. The cost of an office copier, with 5% discount, is $1,275. What is the original cost of the copier?

a. $1,275

b. $1,500

c. $5,500

d. 25,500

16. A store has a sale on holiday candy—3 candy bars for $0.84. How much would 14 candy bars cost?

a. $2.94

b. $5.88

c. $3.92

d. $11.76

17. While stacking cans of soup on a shelf at a grocery store, the stock person formed 3 rows of cans, one behind the other. Each row consisted of 24 cans lengthwise and the cans were all stacked 4 high. How many cans of soup were stacked on this shelf?

a. 192

b. 72

c. 288

d. 96

18. An intramural tennis team has an annual budget of $850. Forty-five percent of this budget is used to purchase equipment. How much money remains for other expenses?

a. $382.50

b. $467.50

c. $425.00

d. $805.00

19. It took Sue $1\frac{3}{4}$ hours to walk $5\frac{1}{4}$ miles. How fast, on average, was she walking?

a. 9 miles per hour

b. $3\frac{1}{2}$ miles per hour

c. 3 miles per hour

d. $\frac{1}{3}$ mile per hour

20. Nick has $2\frac{5}{8}$ hours in which to complete a qualifying exam. At the moment when he looked at his watch, $\frac{8}{9}$ of his time had elapsed. How much more time does Nick have to complete the exam?

a. $\frac{7}{24}$ hour

b. $2\frac{61}{64}$ hours

c. $1\frac{2}{3}$ hours

d. $2\frac{1}{3}$ hours

21. A box holds 12 reams of paper and weighs 15.6 pounds. Assuming the weight of the box is negligible, how much does each ream of paper weigh?

a. 3.6 pounds

b. 1.56 pounds

c. 1.3 pounds

d. 2 pounds

22. Sixty college students are hired to work at the county fair. Twenty-five percent of them are assigned to work at the food booths, one-fifth of them are assigned cleanup duty, and the rest of them are assigned to rides and games. How many of them are in charge of rides and games?
   a. 15
   b. 12
   c. 33
   d. 27

23. Mason got 20 miles per gallon with his old car. His mileage per gallon increased by 60% when he started driving his new SUV. How many miles per gallon does he get with his new SUV?
   a. 28
   b. 32
   c. 26
   d. 12

24. Your hybrid SUV averages 32 miles for every $1\frac{1}{4}$ gallons of fuel used. How many miles could be driven on 15 gallons of fuel?
   a. 480 miles
   b. 600 miles
   c. 256 miles
   d. 384 miles

25. The value of a new computer reduces to 0.7 of its value after one year. If you bought the computer on January 2, 2011, for $950, what is its worth on January 2, 2012?
   a. $760
   b. $190
   c. $66.50
   d. $883.50

26. If a three-vegetable soup contains $\frac{3}{4}$ tomatoes and $\frac{1}{8}$ squash, what fraction of onions are in the soup?
   a. $\frac{1}{8}$
   b. $\frac{3}{8}$
   c. $\frac{6}{8}$
   d. $\frac{7}{8}$

27. A local movie theater shows 14 separate films. Three of these movies are rated G and are appropriate for all ages. Approximately what percentage of movies are appropriate for all ages?
   a. $\frac{3}{14}$%
   b. 14%
   c. 21%
   d. 79%

28. A roller coaster, at its top speed, moves at 75 miles per hour. How many feet per second is it moving at this speed?
   a. 51 feet per second
   b. 15 feet per second
   c. 6,600 feet per second
   d. 110 feet per second

29. A small deli is open 2 hours during lunch. The number of customers they served on the five weekdays, Monday through Friday, this week are 158, 170, 164, 121, and 192. What is the average number of customers served during lunchtime?
   a. 161
   b. 121
   c. 192
   d. 164

Refer to the following graph for questions 30 through 32:

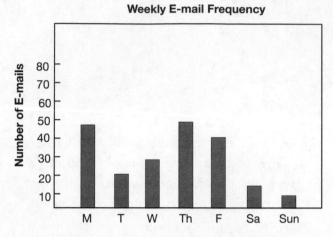

Weekly E-mail Frequency

30. What is the range of the data shown in the graph?
   a. 10
   b. 40
   c. 50
   d. 30

31. What information is displayed on the *x*-axis of the graph?
   a. the title of the graph
   b. number of e-mails
   c. days of the week
   d. the real numbers

32. The average number of e-mails recovered in one week is _____.
   a. 30
   b. 40
   c. 10
   d. 50

Refer to the following pie chart for questions 33 and 34.

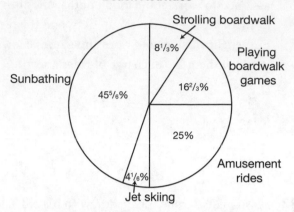

Beach Activities

33. According to the pie chart, the least common beach activity is _____.
   a. strolling the boardwalk
   b. amusement rides
   c. sunbathing
   d. Jet skiing

34. Suppose 500 tourists were asked to provide their favorite beach activity, and the data was used to form the pie chart. How many tourists answered "amusement rides"?
   a. 125
   b. about 83
   c. 250
   d. 100

Refer to the following chart for questions 35 through 37.

Age Group	Number of Hours Daily Spent Outside, on Average
Less than 4 years old	8
Between 4 and 7 years old	7
Between 7 and 10 years old	7
Between 10 and 13 years old	5.5
Between 13 and 15 years old	4.5
Between 15 and 18 years old	4

35. The average number of hours spent outside, across age groups, is _____.

a. 6

b. 6.25

c. 8

d. 4

36. What conclusion is best supported by the data given in this table?

a. No person has ever spent fewer than 4 hours outside.

b. Younger people spend more time outside, on average, than older people.

c. No teenager spends more than 7 hours outside.

d. People over 27 years of age spend 0 hours outside.

37. The range of the data is _____.

a. 4 hours

b. 7 hours

c. 8 hours

d. 6 hours

Refer to the following chart for questions 38 through 40.

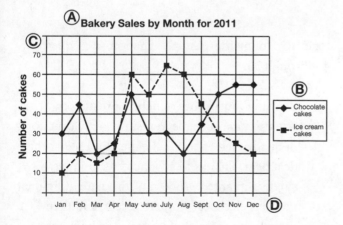

38. What letter corresponds to the *x*-axis of the graph?

a. A

b. B

c. C

d. D

39. What letter corresponds to the legend of the graph?

a. A

b. B

c. C

d. D

40. Which of the following is a valid conclusion that can be deduced from the graph?

a. The maximum number of chocolate cakes sold in any month is 70.

b. The minimum number of ice cream cakes sold in any month is 5.

c. There is a month in which the number of chocolate cakes sold is equal to the number of ice cream cakes sold.

d. Ice cream cakes sell better than chocolate cakes during the summer months.

Section 2: Written Communication

Reading Comprehension— Questions 41 through 60

Read the following passage. Then answer questions 41 through 45.

The worst and longest economic crisis in the modern industrial world, the Great Depression in the United States had devastating consequences for American society. At its lowest depth (1932 and 1933), more than 16 million people were unemployed, more than 5,000 banks had closed, and over 85,000 businesses had failed. Millions of Americans lost their jobs, their savings, and even their homes. The homeless built shacks for temporary shelter— these emerging shantytowns were nicknamed Hoovervilles: a bitter <u>homage</u> to President Herbert Hoover, who refused to give government assistance to the jobless. The effects of the Depression—severe unemployment rates and a sharp drop in the production and sales of goods—could also be felt abroad, where many European nations still struggled to recover from World War I.

Although the stock market crash of 1929 marked the onset of the Great Depression, it was not the cause of it. Deep, underlying fissures already existed in the economy of the Roaring Twenties. For example, the tariff and war-debt policies after World War I contributed to the instability of the banking system. American banks made loans to European countries following World War I. However, the United States kept high tariffs on goods imported from other nations. These policies worked against one another. If other countries could not sell goods in the United States, they could not make enough money to pay back their loans or to buy American goods.

41. This passage was mostly likely written to
  a. show how the Great Depression affected Europeans.
  b. explain the causes and effects of the Great Depression.
  c. prove that the Great Depression was not as bad as people think.
  d. warn readers that a great depression could happen again.

42. There is enough information in this passage to show that
  a. American banks had no role in causing the Great Depression.
  b. President Herbert Hoover is mainly responsible for the Great Depression.
  c. the Great Depression was a direct result of the stock market crash of 1929.
  d. the Great Depression was not caused by a single event.

43. How many people did the Great Depression leave unemployed?
  a. 1,932
  b. 5,000
  c. 85,000
  d. 16 million

44. As it is used in the passage, the word <u>homage</u> most nearly means
  a. tribute.
  b. picture.
  c. speech.
  d. building.

45. According to the passage, the U.S. government helped cause the Great Depression by
  a. lending money to European countries, while keeping high tariffs on goods imported from other nations.
  b. forcing other countries to sell goods in the United States, where they could not make enough money to pay back their loans.
  c. allowing the homeless to build temporary shacks called Hoovervilles.
  d. deciding to enter the unpopular war, World War I.

Read the following passage. Then answer questions 46 through 50.

By using tiny probes as neural prostheses, scientists may be able to restore nerve function in quadriplegics and make the blind see or the deaf hear. Thanks to advanced techniques, a single implanted probe can stimulate individual neurons electrically or chemically and then record responses. Preliminary results suggest that the microprobe telemetry systems can be permanently implanted and replace damaged or missing nerves.

The tissue-compatible microprobes represent an advance over the typical aluminum wire electrodes used in studies of the cortex and other brain structures. Researchers accumulate much data using traditional electrodes, but there is a question of how much damage they cause to the nervous system. Microprobes, which are about as thin as a human hair, cause minimal damage and disruption of neurons when inserted into the brain.

In addition to recording nervous system impulses, the microprobes have minuscule channels that open the way for delivery of drugs, cellular growth factors, neurotransmitters, and other neuroactive compounds to a single neuron or to groups of neurons. Also, patients who lack certain biochemicals could receive doses via prostheses. The probes can have up to four channels, each with its own recording/stimulating electrode.

46. The author's main purpose is to
   a. prove that microprobes do more damage than good.
   b. show how microprobes have already cured people.
   c. explain the possible uses of microprobes.
   d. refute claims that microprobes do not damage the nervous system.

47. It can be inferred from this passage that
   a. microprobes function better than natural nerves.
   b. microprobes are extremely small.
   c. microprobes can be used to help speechless people talk.
   d. microprobes can be dangerous if inserted in the brain.

48. As it is used in the passage, the word <u>accumulate</u> most nearly means
   a. dispose.
   b. create.
   c. gather.
   d. imitate.

49. With which of the following statements would the author most likely agree?
   a. Microprobes are promising tools for healing nerve damage.
   b. Microprobes are too risky to be used on actual patients.
   c. Microprobes need to be tested more extensively before being used.
   d. Microprobes will be replaced by even better probes in the near future.

50. According to the passage, microprobes have channels that open the way for all the following EXCEPT
   a. neurotransmitters.
   b. cellular growth factors.
   c. drugs.
   d. electrodes.

Read the following passage. Then answer questions 51 through 55.

Milton Hershey was born near the small village of Derry Church, Pennsylvania, in 1857. It was a modest beginning that did not <u>foretell</u> his later popularity. Milton only attended school through the fourth grade; at that point, he was apprenticed to a printer in a nearby town. Fortunately for all chocolate lovers, Milton did not excel as a printer. After a while, he left the printing business and was apprenticed to a Lancaster, Pennsylvania candy maker. It was apparent he had found his calling in life, and at the age of 18, he opened his own candy store in

Philadelphia. In spite of his talents as a candy maker, the shop failed after six years.

It may come as a surprise to current Milton Hershey fans, but his first candy success came with the manufacture of caramel. After the failure of his Philadelphia store, Milton headed for Denver, where he learned the art of making caramels. There he took a job with a local manufacturer who insisted on using fresh milk in making his caramels; Milton saw that this made the caramels especially tasty. After a time in Denver, Milton once again attempted to open his own candy-making businesses, in Chicago, New Orleans, and New York City. Finally, in 1886, he went to Lancaster, Pennsylvania, where he raised the money necessary to try again. This company— the Lancaster Caramel Company—established Milton's reputation as a master candy maker.

In 1893, Milton attended the Chicago International Exposition, where he saw a display of German chocolate-making implements. Captivated by the equipment, he purchased it for his Lancaster candy factory and began producing chocolate, which he used for coating his caramels. By the next year, production had grown to include cocoa, sweet chocolate, and baking chocolate. The Hershey Chocolate company was born in 1894 as a subsidiary of the Lancaster Caramel Company. Six years later, Milton sold the caramel company, but retained the rights, and the equipment, to make chocolate. He believed that a large market of chocolate consumers was waiting for someone to produce reasonably priced candy. He was right.

51. What is this passage about?
   a. a man who formed his own candy business and later became a chocolate manufacturer
   b. a young man who was an apprentice printer, but quit printing because he did not excel at it
   c. an international exposition that featured revolutionary new equipment for chocolate manufacturing
   d. an extremely successful chocolate company that continues to be profitable to this day

52. As used in the passage, the word *foretell* most nearly means
   a. encourage.
   b. predict.
   c. believe.
   d. labor.

53. Milton Hershey did all the following EXCEPT
   a. work as an apprentice printer.
   b. make chocolate-covered caramels.
   c. form a subsidiary of the Lancaster Caramel Company.
   d. manufacture chocolate-making equipment.

54. It can be inferred from the passage that
   a. Milton Hershey never really experienced failure.
   b. Milton Hershey ran his caramel company until his death.
   c. Milton Hershey was not successful at everything he did.
   d. Milton Hershey regretted having to move from Philadelphia.

55. Milton Hershey attempted to start candy-making businesses in all the following cities EXCEPT
   a. Philadelphia.
   b. Denver.
   c. Chicago.
   d. New Orleans.

Read the following passage. Then answer questions 56 through 60.

For centuries, time was measured by the position of the sun with the use of sundials. Noon was recognized when the sun was the highest in the sky, and cities would set their clocks by this apparent solar time, even though some cities would often be on a slightly different time. Daylight saving time (DST), sometimes called summer time, was <u>instituted</u> to make better use of daylight. Thus, clocks are set forward one hour in the spring to move an hour of daylight from the morning to the evening and then set back one hour in the fall to return to normal daylight.

Benjamin Franklin first conceived the idea of daylight saving during his tenure as an American delegate in Paris in 1784 and wrote about it extensively in his essay, "An Economical Project." It is said that Franklin awoke early one morning and was surprised to see the sunlight at such an hour. Always the economist, Franklin believed the practice of moving the time could save on the use of candlelight, as candles were expensive at the time.

The U.S. Congress passed the Standard Time Act of 1918 to establish standard time and preserve and set daylight saving time across the continent. This act also devised five time zones throughout the United States: Eastern, Central, Mountain, Pacific, and Alaska. The first time zone was set on "the mean astronomical time of the seventy-fifth degree of longitude west from Greenwich" (England). In 1919, this act was repealed.

President Roosevelt established year-round daylight saving time (also called war time) from 1942 to 1945. However, after this period, each state adopted its own DST, which proved to be disconcerting to television and radio broadcasting and transportation. In 1966, President Lyndon Johnson created the Department of Transportation and signed the Uniform Time Act. As a result, the Department of Transportation was given the responsibility for the time laws. During the oil embargo and energy crisis of the 1970s, President Richard Nixon extended DST through the Daylight Saving Time Energy Act of 1973 to conserve energy further. This law was modified in 1986, and daylight saving time was reset to begin on the first Sunday in April (to spring ahead) and end on the last Sunday in October (to fall back).

56. Which of the following best expresses the main idea of the passage?
   a. Benjamin Franklin first conceived daylight saving time while working as an American delegate in Paris.
   b. President Roosevelt established year-round daylight saving time in 1942.
   c. Clocks are set forward one hour in the spring and then set back one hour in the fall.
   d. Daylight saving time, a way to make better use of daylight, has gone through many changes throughout the years.

57. According to the passage, daylight saving time was reset in 1986 to end on
   a. the last Sunday in October.
   b. the first Sunday in April.
   c. the second Sunday in October.
   d. the last Sunday in April.

58. It can be inferred from the passage that
   a. President Nixon wanted to eliminate daylight saving time.
   b. daylight saving time helps to lower energy bills.
   c. daylight saving time never changed again after 1986.
   d. President Roosevelt ensured that each state had its own daylight saving time.

59. As used in the passage, the word <u>instituted</u> most nearly means
  a. held.
  b. arrested.
  c. introduced.
  d. educated.

60. According to the passage, the Daylight Saving Time Energy Act was enacted in
  a. 1784.
  b. 1918.
  c. 1966.
  d. 1973.

Spelling—Questions 61 through 65

Select the choice that is spelled correctly.

61. The fresh peach was particularly _____.
  a. succulant
  b. suculent
  c. succulent

62. Although the _____ was untamed, the settlers managed to make a home there.
  a. fronteir
  b. fronteer
  c. frontier

63. Which of the following words is spelled correctly?
  a. fidelity
  b. concievable
  c. perpetuel

64. Which of the following words is spelled correctly?
  a. wimper
  b. superstision
  c. vibration

65. Which of the following words is spelled correctly?
  a. disolve
  b. hideous
  c. glamor

Vocabulary—Questions 66 through 70

Select the best answer for each question.

66. Find the word that is closest in meaning to the underlined word.
  a <u>judicious</u> decision
  a. timely
  b. sensible
  c. curious

67. Find the word that is closest in meaning to the underlined word.
  an <u>atrocious</u> disaster
  a. unusual
  b. skeptical
  c. terrible

68. Find the word that is most nearly the opposite of the underlined word.
  an <u>audacious</u> risk
  a. measured
  b. cautious
  c. silent

69. Find the word that best completes the sentence.
  Our swim in the cool water was incredibly _____.
  a. invigorating
  b. plaintive
  c. whimsical

70. Find the word that best completes the sentence. The chicks were _____ to predators when their mother went hunting for food.
  a. wondrous
  b. spurious
  c. vulnerable

Grammar—Questions 71 through 80
Select the best choice for each question.

71. Which of the following is a complete sentence?
  a. Alex returned the ship to shore because the water was growing very turbulent.
  b. Because the water was growing very turbulent, Alex the ship to shore.
  c. Alex returned the ship to shore the water was growing very turbulent.

72. Select the sentence that is written most correctly.
  a. Patrice mentally imagined she would cross the finish line before the other runners.
  b. Patrice imagined she would cross the finish line completely before the other runners.
  c. Patrice imagined she would cross the finish line before the other runners.

73. Select the sentence that is written most correctly.
  a. The painter's studio was alighted by the sunlight streaming through the windows.
  b. The sunlight streaming through the windows illuminated the painter's studio.
  c. The painters studio was illuminated by the sunlight streaming through the windows.

74. Select the sentence that is written most correctly.
  a. The group set up their tent at the campsite swift.
  b. The group set up its tent at the campsite swiftly.
  c. The group set up their tent at the campsite swiftly.

75. Select the sentence that is written most correctly.
  a. Samantha Juste, D.D.S., is scheduled for surgery on Mon. at 10:00 A.M.
  b. Samantha Juste, DD, is scheduled for surgery on Mon at 10:00 A.M.
  c. Samantha Juste, D.D.S., is scheduled for surgery on Mon at 10.00 A.M.

76. Select the sentence that is written most correctly.
  a. Each person in the lounge is responsible for cleaning up after him- or herself.
  b. Each person in the lounge is responsible for cleaning up after him or themselves.
  c. Each person in the lounge is responsible for cleaning up after theirselves.

77. Select the sentence that is written most correctly.
  a. John F. Kennedy elementary school will be closed on Presidents Day.
  b. John F. Kennedy Elementary School will be closed on Presidents day.
  c. John F. Kennedy Elementary School will be closed on Presidents Day.

78. Select the sentence that is written most correctly.
  a. Sunning on the rock, today the green and yellow lizard could not have been happier.
  b. Sunning on the rock, the green and yellow lizard could not have been happier today.
  c. The green and yellow lizard today, sunning on the rock, could not have been happier.

79. Select the sentence that is written most correctly.
  a. "Are you going to study with me on Thursday?" Nathan inquired.
  b. "Are you going to study with me on Thursday," Nathan inquired?
  c. "Are you going to study with me on Thursday, Nathan inquired."

80. Select the sentence that is written most correctly.
  a. Frankie was intrigued by the television special about owls.
  b. Frankie was intrigued by the television special of owls.
  c. The television special about owls intrigued Frankie.

Section 3: Civil Service Skills

Customer Service— Questions 81 through 85

Select the best choice for each question.

81. At least 80% of incoming customer queries made by telephone should be handled within
  a. 30 seconds.
  b. 60 seconds.
  c. 30 minutes.
  d. 60 minutes.

82. A customer with limited English skills should be provided with
  a. a translator who speaks multiple languages.
  b. the number of a customer service agent in the customer's native country.
  c. the url of a text-translating website.
  d. a translator who speaks his or her language expertly.

83. A customer service agent who cannot resolve a problem should express
  a. frustration to the customer.
  b. curiosity to the customer.
  c. regret to the customer.
  d. indifference to the customer.

84. If a customer sends an e-mail query to the wrong agency, that e-mail should be
  a. sent to the U.S. General Services Administration.
  b. sent to a bulk folder.
  c. redirected by whoever receives the message.
  d. deleted.

85. The most common complaint of customers who send e-mail queries is that they
  a. miss the human contact of a telephone conversation.
  b. do not know where to send their e-mails.
  c. have trouble figuring out how to send an e-mail.
  d. do not always receive replies to their e-mails.

Memory—Questions 86 through 90

Take five minutes to study the following picture. Then, answer questions 86 through 88 without looking back at the picture.

86. The person on the far right-hand side of the photo is wearing
   a. a long-sleeved shirt.
   b. shorts.
   c. a baseball cap.
   d. a jacket.

87. The street sign indicates
   a. don't walk.
   b. walk.
   c. yield.
   d. one way.

88. How many traffic cones are visible on the left-hand side of the photo?
   a. 1
   b. 4
   c. 8
   d. 16

Take five minutes to study the following picture. Then, answer questions 89 and 90 without looking back at the picture.

89. The 2-hour parking rule is in effect until
   a. 8 A.M.
   b. 11 A.M.
   c. 1 P.M.
   d. 4 P.M.

90. What vehicles may park in this zone for over two hours?
   a. all towing vehicles
   b. vehicles with a zone 1 permit
   c. all vehicles parked before 10 A.M.
   d. no vehicles

Coding—Questions 91 through 100

To answer questions 91 through 95, refer to the following scenario.

The city sanitation department logs violations according to the following coding rules:

Address
Digits indicating building number
Four letters indicating first two letters of street name and type (example: Elm Street = ElSt)

Violation
   1 = refuse thrown in street
   2 = refuse left on front, side, or rear of property
   3 = ragweed, tall weeds, and/or grass must be cut
   4 = unapproved container used for refuse
   5 = unapproved container used for recyclables
   6 = improper use of litter receptacle
   7 = refuse set out too early
   8 = recycling set out too early
   9 = improper use of recyclable receptacle
   10 = recyclable cardboard and/or papers not tied properly
   11 = refuse left on sidewalk
   12 = other violations

Digits indicating violation must follow digits and letters indicating street name.

91. The person residing 7 Rubarb Lane has been putting out his recyclables at 3 P.M. However, sanitation law indicates recyclables must be put out after 5 P.M. How should this violation be coded?
   a. 8RuLa7
   b. RuLn87
   c. 7RuLn8
   d. 7RuLa8

92. A stationery store located at 362 Front Street has been putting its refuse in a blue recyclable bin instead of a metal or plastic trash can. How should this violation be coded?
   a. 36FrSe5
   b. 362FrSt04
   c. 362FrSt4
   d. 382FrS4

93. On July 15th, Aubrey Mitchell at 54 Pyle Drive violated local sanitation laws by allowing the refuse in her trash can to spill over into the street. How should her violation be coded?
   a. 54PyDr1
   b. 15AuMi5
   c. 15JuPy4
   d. 54AuMi1

94. A code reading 999MaAv9 could represent
   a. refuse left on the sidewalk at 999 Marshall Street.
   b. a citizen's personal firewood supply being stored in a recyclable bin.
   c. a citizen who has used a city Dumpster to dispose of personal trash.
   d. uncut ragweed at 99 Maple Avenue.

95. A report of loose trash left at the side of a house at 211 Oak Park Drive was coded 211OPDr2. It contains which of the following errors?
   a. The street name contains too many letters.
   b. The street name should be coded Pa.
   c. The street name should be coded Oa.
   d. The street name is in the wrong place.

To answer questions 96 through 100, refer to the following scenario.

A city's department of motor vehicles logs moving violations according to a specific code. The code begins with the first three digits or letters of the violator's license plate number. The code is completed with the following violation rules:

Infraction violations
A = disobeying traffic warnings at construction site
B = driving in bicycle lane
C = driving over double solid lines
D = display of light source impairing vision of drivers
E = driving against traffic on a one-way street
F = driving on sidewalk

Misdemeanor violations
g = driving the wrong way on a divided highway
h = failure to yield right of way to blind pedestrian
i = unauthorized moving of tow truck
j = reckless driving
k = failure to obey officer's command at tollbooth
l = riding unauthorized vehicle on hiking trail
m = driving vehicle under the influence of drugs or alcohol

Felony violations
nn = causing injury or death while driving under the influence of drugs or alcohol

Multiple violations are logged multiple times alphabetically (e.g., a driver who has crossed double solid lines after failing to obey an officer's command at a tollbooth would be logged as Ck).

96. A man has just exited a party at which he drank four cocktails. On his way home, he drove his car into a bicycle lane. If his license number is 902YAK, how should his violation be coded?
   a. YAKBM
   b. 902Bm
   c. YAKBB
   d. 902BM

97. A young woman is showing off to her friends by weaving her car on the road deliberately. She ends her stunt by driving up on the sidewalk. Her license number is KP09112. How should her violation be coded?
   a. KP0jF
   b. FKP0j
   c. 112C
   d. KP0Fj

98. A man is guilty of a felony violation. Which of the following codes is the only one that could be assigned to his violation?
   a. 745Enn
   b. B62NN
   c. nn90Y
   d. LMNn

99. A worker at the department of motor vehicles logs a violation as ACFghk. The driver committed which of the following violations?
- **a.** disobeying traffic warnings at construction site
- **b.** driving over double solid lines
- **c.** driving on sidewalk
- **d.** failure to yield right of way to blind pedestrian

100. A woman has been driving with her brights on. Doing so has caused an oncoming driver to swerve dangerously. A police officer pulls her over and writes her a ticket. Which of the following codes is the only one that could be assigned to her violation?
- **a.** V66Eji
- **b.** dI43
- **c.** 5G5D
- **d.** M99we

Answers

Section 1: Mathematics

1. b. Convert a mixed number to an improper fraction by multiplying the denominator of the fractional part by the whole number, then add the numerator to it, and finally, put that number over the denominator of the fractional part. Doing so yields $3\frac{2}{7} = \frac{7(3)+2}{7} = \frac{23}{7}$. Choice **a** multiplies the whole part of the mixed number by the fractional part, which is not a correct interpretation of a mixed number. Choice **c** simply moves the whole part of the mixed number as a digit into the numerator of the fractional part, which is not a correct interpretation of a mixed number. Choice **d** is the reciprocal of the correct answer.

2. b. Write the numerator and denominator as products of their factors, and cancel all those that are common to both the numerator and denominator: $\frac{24}{64} = \frac{4 \cdot 2 \cdot 3}{4 \cdot 2 \cdot 8} = \frac{3}{8}$. Choice **a** treats the 4s as though they were factors when they are simply digits. Choice **c** subtracts the numerator from the denominator, which is not how to simplify a fraction. Choice **d** does not cancel the common factor of 8 from the denominator.

3. a. $5\frac{1}{4} - (2\frac{3}{8} + 1\frac{7}{8}) = 5\frac{1}{4} - 3\frac{10}{8}$. To subtract the two mixed numbers, first convert them to improper fractions. $5\frac{1}{4} = \frac{21}{4}$; $3\frac{10}{8} = \frac{34}{8}$. Subtract $\frac{21}{4} - \frac{34}{8}$ by using a common denominator of 4 and 8 is 8. Rewrite $\frac{21}{4}$ by multiplying by $\frac{2}{2}$ to get $\frac{44}{8}$. So $\frac{42}{8} - \frac{34}{8} = \frac{8}{8}$, which is 1. Choice **a** is the correct answer. Choice **b** subtracts the fractional parts incorrectly. Choice **c** does not distribute the negative sign through the parentheses. Choice **d** does not find a least common denominator before adding and subtracting the fractional parts.

4. a. Line up the decimal points and subtract as you would with whole numbers to get $5.7 - 2.3 = 3.4$.

5. b. $3 \times 2\frac{5}{6} = 3 \times \frac{3 \times 17}{6} = \frac{51}{6} = 8\frac{3}{6} = 8\frac{1}{2}$. Choice **a** does not first convert the mixed number to an improper fraction and then multiply the numerators and the denominators. Choice **c** divides the fractions instead of multiplying them. Choice **d** adds the fractions instead of multiplying them.

6. c. $\frac{2}{5} \div 5\frac{1}{2} = \frac{2}{5} \div \frac{11}{2} = \frac{2}{5} \times \frac{2}{11} = \frac{2 \times 2}{5 \times 11} = \frac{4}{55}$. Choice **a** multiplies the fractions instead of dividing them; choice **b** multiplies them, and then takes the reciprocal. Choice **d** adds the fractions instead of dividing them.

7. a. $\frac{8}{11} \times 1\frac{5}{6} = \frac{8}{11} \times \frac{11}{6} = \frac{8 \times 11}{11 \times 6} = \frac{8}{6} = \frac{4}{3} = 1\frac{1}{3}$. Choice **b** is the reciprocal of the correct answer. Choice **c** divides the fractions instead of multiplying them. Choice **d** incorrectly treated the mixed number as $1 \times \frac{5}{6}$.

8. a. First, write 90% as the fraction $\frac{90}{100}$. Multiply 30 by $\frac{90}{100}$ to get $\frac{2,700}{100}$, which is 27.

9. d. Arrange the numbers vertically, lining up the decimal points. Then, subtract as you would whole numbers, keeping the location of the decimal point fixed.

$$\begin{array}{r} 2\overset{1}{.}\,\overset{9}{0}\,\overset{10}{1}\,\overset{1}{2} \\ -0\,.\,3\quad 3\quad 4 \\ \hline 1\,.\,6\quad 7\quad 8 \end{array}$$

Choice **a** is incorrect because it subtracts 0.0334, not 0.334, from 2.012. Choice **b** adds the decimals rather than subtracting them. Choice **c** does not borrow correctly.

10. c. $\frac{22}{25} = \frac{22 \times 4}{25 \times 4} = \frac{88}{100} = 0.88$. Choice **a** is incorrect because you must first obtain an equivalent fraction whose denominator is 100 before moving the decimal point two places to the left in the numerator to get the decimal equivalent of a fraction. Choice **b** is incorrect because you canceled a pair of 2s in the numerator and denominator, and then converted the resulting fraction to a decimal. The 2s are not factors, they are digits, and so, cannot be canceled in this manner. Choice **d** is incorrect because you did not divide correctly; the fraction to which this is equal is $\frac{20}{25}$.

11. c. To get the fraction equivalent of 58%, divide 58 by 100 to get $\frac{58}{100}$, which reduces to $\frac{29}{50}$.

12. d. Add the amounts they currently have, and then subtract that sum from 15: $15 - (5.48 + 4.79) = 4.73$ ounces. Choice **a** is the number of ounces of fudge they currently have, not how much they need to purchase. Subtract this from 15. Choice **b** does not account for the amount of fudge Sue currently has. Choice **c** does not borrow correctly when subtracting.

13. b. To subtract $18\frac{3}{4} - 1\frac{1}{2}$, first subtract the fractional part. Rewrite the second fraction over a common denominator of 4 to get $\frac{3}{4} - \frac{2}{4}$, which equals $\frac{1}{4}$. Next, subtract $18 - 1$, which equals 17. Therefore, the correct answer is $17\frac{1}{4}$. Choice **a** is incorrect because it subtracts the fractions incorrectly. Choice **c** is incorrect because it adds the fractional parts. Choice **d** is incorrect because it adds the whole numbers instead of subtracting them.

14. c. First, determine the amount of the tax: $0.06(\$86.90) = \$5.21$. Now, add this to the amount before tax to get the final bill amount: $\$86.90 + \$5.21 = \$92.11$. Choice **a** is just the amount of tax, which then must be added to the original bill amount. Choice **b** does not carry 1 to the ones place when adding the tax to the original bill amount. Choice **d** computes 5% sales tax, not 6%.

15. d. Since the original price of the copier is unknown, use variable x for this amount. Then, write an equation from the problem. If 5% of the original price of the copier x is \$1,275, the equation for this problem can be $.05x = 1,275$. Solve by dividing both sides by .05 to get $x = \$25,500$.

16. c. Let x be the cost for 14 candy bars. Set up the following proportion: $\frac{3}{\$0.84} = \frac{14}{x}$. To solve for x, cross-multiply: $3x = 14(\$0.84)$. This simplifies to $3x = \$11.76$, so that dividing both sides by 3 yields $x = \$3.92$. Choice **a** assumes that four candy bars cost \$0.84, not three. Choice **b** assumes that two candy bars cost \$0.84, not three. Choice **d** assumes that each candy bar costs \$0.84, not three.

17. c. Multiply the number of rows (3) times the number of cans per row (24) times the number of cans stacked high (4): $3 \times 24 \times 4 = 288$ cans. Choice a assumes that there are only two rows of cans, not three. Choice **b** does not account for the fact that the rows are stacked four high. Choice **d** only accounts for one of the three rows of cans.

18. b. If 45% of the budget is used to purchase equipment, the remainder of the budget (55%) can be used for other expenses. To determine this amount, multiply 0.55 times \$850: $0.55(\$850) = \$467.50$. Choice **a** is incorrect because this is the amount spent on equipment. Choice **c** is incorrect because this assumes that 50% of the budget is used for equipment, not 45%. Choice **d** is incorrect because 45% does not equal \$45. You must multiply 0.45 times the original amount (\$850) in order to determine the percentage.

19. c. Apply the formula $D = R \times T$ with $D = 5\frac{1}{4}$ miles and $T = 1\frac{3}{4}$ hours:

$$5\frac{1}{4} \text{ miles} = (1\frac{3}{4} \text{ hours}) \times T$$

$$T = \frac{5\frac{1}{4} \text{ miles}}{1\frac{3}{4} \text{ hours}} = \frac{\frac{21}{4}}{\frac{7}{4}} \text{ miles per hour}$$

$$= 3 \text{ miles per hour}$$

Choice **a** is incorrect because instead of using $D = R \times T$, you used $D \times R = T$.
Choice **b** is incorrect because instead of using $D = R \times T$, you used $D - T = R$.
Choice **d** is incorrect because you divided incorrectly.

20. a. Multiply the two fractions to determine the number of hours that have elapsed: $\frac{8}{9}(2\frac{5}{8}) = \frac{8}{9} \times \frac{21}{8} = \frac{7}{3} = 2\frac{1}{3}$ hours. Now, subtract this from the total amount of time allotted to take the exam: $2\frac{5}{8} - 2\frac{1}{3} = \frac{21}{8} - \frac{7}{3} = \frac{63}{8} - \frac{56}{24} = \frac{7}{24}$ hour. Choice **b** mistakenly divides the two fractions to get the amount of time that had elapsed instead of multiplying. Choice **c** subtracts $\frac{8}{9}$ from $2\frac{5}{8}$ instead of multiplying. Choice **d** is the amount of time that has elapsed, not the amount of time he still has to complete the exam.

21. c. Divide the total weight by the number of reams of paper: $\frac{15.6}{12} = 1.3$ pounds. Choice **a** subtracts the number of reams from the total weight instead of dividing. Choice **b** assumes there were only 10 reams in the box, not 12. Choice **d** is the result of rounding the two numbers to the nearest ten before dividing. This does not yield an accurate weight for each ream of paper.

22. c. Determine the number in charge of the food booths and the number assigned cleanup duty; then, subtract the sum of these two numbers from 60. Observe that 25% of 60 is $0.25(60) = 15$. Also, one-fifth of 60 is $\frac{1}{5}(60) = 12$. So, the number in charge of rides and games is $60 - (15 + 12) = 60 - 27 = 33$. Choice **a** is the number in charge of the food booths. Choice **b** is the number assigned cleanup duty. Choice **d** is the number not in charge of rides and games.

23. b. Compute 60% of 20: $0.60(20) = 12$. Now, add this to the original 20 miles per gallon to conclude that he gets $20 + 12 = 32$ miles per gallon with his new SUV. Choice a computes a 40% increase instead of a 60% increase. Choice c is incorrect because 60% does not equal 6. You need to compute 60% of 20 and add this to 20 to get his new mileage per gallon. Choice **d** is the number of additional miles per gallon gained; you need to add this to 20.

24. d. Let x be the number of miles that can be driven on 15 gallons of fuel. Set up the following proportion: $\frac{32}{\frac{5}{4}} = \frac{x}{15}$. To solve for x, cross-multiply: $32(15) = \frac{5}{4}x$. Now, multiply both sides by $\frac{4}{5}$ to isolate x on the right side; then, simplify: $x = \frac{4}{5} \times 32(15) = 384$ miles. Choice **a** assumes you get 32 miles per gallon, not per $1\frac{1}{4}$ gallons. Choice **b** solves the proportion incorrectly by multiplying both sides by $\frac{5}{4}$, not $\frac{4}{5}$. Choice **c** is the mileage for 10 gallons, not 15 gallons.

25. a. Multiply the amount for which you purchased the computer by 0.7: $\$950(0.7) = \$760$. Choice **b** is the amount by which the computer's value depreciates. Subtract this from \$950 to get its current value. Choice **c** is the amount by which the computer's value would have depreciated if 0.7 had been 0.07. Choice **d** is the amount the computer would have been worth if it had depreciated to 0.07 of its value instead of 0.7 of its value.

26. a. Since the number of onions is unknown, let variable x be the fraction of onions in the soup. The entire soup can be thought of as 1. Write an equation from the problem: $\frac{3}{4} + \frac{1}{8} + x = 1$. Add $\frac{3}{4}$ and $\frac{1}{8}$ by first rewriting each fraction over the common denominator 8 to get $\frac{6}{8} + \frac{1}{8}$, which equals $\frac{7}{8}$. So, the resulting equation is $\frac{7}{8} + x = 1$. To solve this equation, subtract $\frac{7}{8}$ from both sides to get $x = 1 - \frac{7}{8} = \frac{1}{8}$.

27. c. Three of fourteen films are suitable for all ages. To determine the equivalent percentage, divide 3 by 14, and then move the decimal point two places to the right: $\frac{3}{14} \approx 0.214$, which is equivalent to approximately 21%. Choice **a** is incorrect because you did not convert the fraction to a percentage correctly. Choice **b** is incorrect because you interpreted the number of films offered as the percentage suitable for all ages. Choice **d** is incorrect because this is the percentage of films that have some age restriction.

28. d. Use the fact that 1 mile = 5,280 feet and that 1 hour = 3,600 seconds to change the units, as follows:

75 ~~miles~~	5,280 feet	1 ~~hour~~
1 ~~hour~~	1 ~~mile~~	3,600 seconds

Pay particular attention to the canceling of units. Multiplying through gives 110 feet per second. Choice **a** is incorrect because when converting units, it multiplies instead of dividing. Choice **b** uses the wrong conversion factors. Use the fact that 1 mile = 5,280 feet and that 1 hour = 3,600 seconds to change the units. Choice **c** is incorrect because 1 hour = 3,600 seconds, not 60 seconds.

29. a. Add the numbers together and divide by 5: $\frac{158 + 170 + 164 + 121 + 192}{5} = 161$. Choice **b** is the minimum number of customers served on these five days, not the mean. Choice **c** is the maximum number of customers served and choice **d** is the median number.

30. b. Compute the difference between the maximum y-value and the minimum y-value: $50 - 10 = 40$. Choice **a** is the minimum value, not the range. Subtract this from 50. Choice **c** is the maximum value, not the range. Subtract 10 from this. Choice **d** is the average value.

31. c. The days of the week are displayed on the horizontal axis of the graph. Choice **a** is incorrect because the title of the graph is at the top: "Weekly E-mail Frequency." Choice **b** is the scale for the y-axis. Choice **d** is not a feature of this particular graph.

32. a. Add the heights of each of the seven bars, and divide the sum by 7: $\frac{45 + 20 + 30 + 50 + 40 + 15 + 10}{7} = \frac{210}{7} = 30$. Choice **b** is is the range, not the average. Choice **c** is the minimum, and choice **d** is the maximum.

33. d. This is the case because $4\frac{1}{6}\%$ is the smallest percentage of all of the pieces. Choice **a** is incorrect because there is a wedge with an even lower percentage. Choice **b** is incorrect because there are other wedges with lower percentages. Choice **c** is incorrect because this is the most common, not least common.

34. a. Compute 25% of 500: $0.25(500) = 125$. Choice **b** is the number who chose playing boardwalk games. Choice **c** is double the correct answer and constitutes 50% of the total number polled. Choice **d** is 20% of the total number polled, not 25%.

35. a. Add the six numbers in the second column and divide the sum by 6: $\frac{8 + 7 + 7 + 5.5 + 4.5 + 4}{6} = \frac{36}{6} = 6$. Choice **b** is the median, not the mean. Choice **c** is the maximum; choice **d** is the minimum.

36. b. Reading down the columns from top to bottom, we see that as the age increases, the number of hours spent outside (i.e., the value in the second column) decreases. Choices **a** and **c** are incorrect because the data provided is *average* data. Some people could spend fewer than 4 or 7 hours outside assuming others spent more than 4 or 7 hours outside to balance it out when computing the average. Choice **d** is incorrect because such data is not provided in the table, so this conclusion cannot be drawn.

37. a. Compute the difference between the largest amount of time spent outside and the shortest amount of time spent outside: 8 hours – 4 hours = 4 hours. Choice **b** is the mode (i.e., the value occurring most often in the second column). Choice **c** is the maximum value. Choice **d** is the mean.

38. d. The x-axis is the vertical axis of a graph. Choice **a** is the title of the graph. Choice **b** is the legend of the graph. Choice **c** is the y-axis of the graph.

39. b. The legend is the small portion that indicates what the different curves (in this case, line graphs) represent. Choice **a** is the title of the graph. Choice **c** is the y-axis of the graph. Choice **d** is the x-axis of the graph.

40. d. This can be observed by comparing the number of each type of cake sold during May through August. Choice **a** is incorrect because the maximum number sold is 55. Choice **b** is incorrect because the minimum number sold is 10. Choice **c** is incorrect because the line graphs never coincide directly on any of the twelve months.

Section 2: Written Communication

41. b. Paragraph 1 describes some of the effects of the Great Depression and paragraph 2 explains some causes of it.

42. d. Paragraph 2 shows that the Great Depression was caused by a number of factors and not the stock market crash of 1929. This supports choice **d** and contradicts choice **c**. Choice **a** is also contradicted by paragraph 2.

43. d. Choice **d** is directly stated in paragraph 1. Choice **a** indicates a year of the depression's lowest depth. Choice **b** indicates how many banks closed during the depression. Choice **c** indicates how many businesses failed.

44. a. Reread the sentence, substituting each choice for the word *homage*. Of the four choices, only choice **a** makes sense in context.

45. a. Paragraph 2 states that the two policies described in choice **a** worked against each other and helped cause the Great Depression.

46. c. The passage explains how microprobes may be able to restore nerve functions in people. Although there is some concern that they might damage the nervous system, the passage states that they cause minimal damage, which contradicts choices **a** and **d**. The first sentence states that microprobes "may be able to restore nerve function," which means they have not been used this way yet and that choice **b** is incorrect.

47. b. Paragraph 1 states that microprobes can be implanted under the skin and paragraph 2 states that they are "thin as a human hair." Choices **a** and **c** are not indicated in the passage. Choice **d** is contradicted by the final sentence of paragraph 2.

48. c. Reread the sentence, substituting each choice for the word *accumulate*. Of the four choices, only choice **c** makes sense in context.

49. a. The author champions the positive uses of microprobes and refutes claims that they cause damage. Choice **b** is contradicted by information in paragraph 2. There is no evidence that supports choices **c** and **d** in the passage.

50. d. Each channel of a microprobe has its own electrode, but electrodes are not among the things for which the channels open the way. Information in paragraph 3 supports this conclusion.

51. a. The main idea refers to the most important points of a passage while avoiding details not present in it. Choice **a** accomplishes this well. Choice **b** is a pretty good summary of the first paragraph, but it does not capture the most important points of the entire passage. Choice **c** only refers to a single detail in the final paragraph. Choice **d** refers to information not present in the passage at all.

52. b. Reread the sentence, substituting each choice for the word *foretell*. Of the four choices, only choice **b** makes sense in context.

53. d. According to the passage, Milton Hershey did each answer choice except for choice **d**. Paragraph 4 states that Hershey merely purchased chocolate-making equipment that had been made in Germany.

54. c. According to the first paragraph, Milton Hershey was not a very good printer and he opened a candy store that failed. This means he was not successful at everything he did, which supports choice **c** and contradicts choice **a**.

55. b. Although Milton Hershey did work for a candy manufacturer in Denver, the passage does not state that he tried to open his own candy-making business there.

56. d. The main idea refers to the most important points of a passage. Choice **d** accomplishes this well. Choices **a**, **b**, and **c** all refer to specific details that do not capture the most important idea of the entire passage.

57. a. The final paragraph of the passage states "This law was modified in 1986, and daylight saving time was reset to begin on the first Sunday in April (to spring ahead) and end on the last Sunday in October (to fall back)." Choice **b** indicates the day daylight saving time was set to begin in 1986. Choices **c** and **d** are not mentioned in the passage at all.

58. b. According to the passage, energy conservation is one of the benefits of daylight saving time. Using less energy results in lower energy bills. Choices **a** and **d** are contradicted by information in the final paragraph. There is no information in the passage that supports choice **c**, which is untrue.

59. c. Reread the sentence, substituting each choice for the word *instituted*. Of the four choices, only choice **c** makes sense in context.

60. d. The final paragraph of the passage states "President Richard Nixon extended DST through the Daylight Saving Time Energy Act of 1973 to conserve energy further." Choice **a**, 1784, indicates the year Benjamin Franklin conceived of daylight saving time. Choice **b**, 1918, indicates the year Congress passed the Standard Time Act. Choice **c**, 1966, indicates the year President Johnson created the Department of Transportation and signed the Uniform Time Act.

61. c. The correct spelling is *succulent*.

62. c. The correct spelling is *frontier*.

63. a. The correct spelling is *fidelity*.

64. c. The correct spelling is *vibration*.

65. b. The correct spelling is *hideous*.

66. b. *Sensible* is the word that is closest in meaning to *judicious*.

67. c. *Terrible* is the word that is closest in meaning to *atrocious*.

68. b. The word *audacious* means *daring*, so the word most nearly its opposite is *cautious*.

69. a. *Invigorating* means *brisk* or *refreshing*, which is the effect of a swim in cool water. Choice **b**, *plaintive*, means *sad*. Choice **c**, *whimsical*, means *fanciful*.

70. c. Choices **a** and **b** can be eliminated because neither makes sense in the context of this sentence. The word *wondrous* means *amazing* and *spurious* means *false*. When something is *vulnerable*, it is in danger.

71. a. Choice **b** is missing the verb *returned*. Choice **c** needs the conjunction *because* to join the two clauses: *Alex returned the ship to shore* and *the water was growing very turbulent*.

72. c. The phrase "mentally imagined" is redundant because one can only imagine something mentally, which means *in the mind*. Choice **b** is redundant because one can only cross a finish line *completely*. Therefore, choices **a** and **b** are redundant.

73. b. Choices **a** and **c** are incorrect because they are both written in the passive voice. Additionally, the word *alighted*, meaning *landed*, is used incorrectly in choice **a**, and the word *painter's* is missing its apostrophe in choice **c**.

74. b. *Group* is a collective noun that takes a singular pronoun. Both incorrect choices use the plural pronoun *their* to refer to the group. Choice **a** also makes the mistake of using the adjective *swift* to modify *set up* instead of the adverb *swiftly*.

75. a. Periods are placed after all abbreviations correctly in choice **a**.

76. a. The subject of the sentence is each person, which takes a singular pronoun. Choice **b** uses the plural pronoun *themselves* incorrectly. Choice **c** uses *theirselves*, which is not a real word.

77. c. Choices **a** and **b** contain capitalization errors. In choice **a**, *elementary school* is part of a school's proper name, so it should be capitalized. In choice **b**, the word *day* should be capitalized because it is part of the name of a holiday.

78. b. The phrase *sunning on the rock* is a modifier describing *the green and yellow lizard*. Choice **a** incorrectly states that *today*, rather than *the green and yellow lizard*, is *sunning on the rock*. Choice **c** is awkwardly and confusingly constructed; choice **b**, the correct answer, demonstrates how to express the same ideas much more clearly.

79. a. Because the statement *Are you going to study with me on Thursday* is a quote, it must end in a question mark. The entire sentence, however, is not a question; it is a statement of fact reporting what Nathan asked. Thus, the sentence should not end in a question mark, as choice **b** does. Since the entire sentence is not a quote, it should not end with quotation marks, as choice **c** does.

80. c. Each of the incorrect answers is written in the passive voice; the correct answer is written in the active voice, which is preferred.

Section 3: Civil Service Skills

81. b. Prompt customer service is good customer service. According to U.S. government customer service policies, 80% of incoming calls during business hours should be handled within 60 seconds.

82. d. Customers with limited English skills should be provided with a translator with expertise in the customer's language. Quality of translation is more important than the quantity of languages the translator speaks, so choice **a** is incorrect.

83. c. Customer service agents must be polite to customers under all circumstances. Even if the customer becomes abusive when his or her problem is not resolved, agents must express regret for failing to resolve it.

84. a. All misdirected e-mails should be sent to the U.S. General Services Administration, which is responsible for forwarding them to the proper agencies.

85. d. The most common complaint of customers who send e-mail queries is that they do not always receive replies to their e-mails. That's why it is so important to send an auto-reply message to all queries.

86. b. There is a man in the center of the photo wearing a baseball cap and a child wearing a jacket, but the man at the far right is wearing shorts.

87. a. Only one street sign is visible in this photo, and it is an electric sign displaying a hand indicating *don't walk*.

88. c. There are 8 traffic cones visible on the left-hand side of this photo.

89. d. According to the top sign, the 2-hour parking rule is in effect from 8 A.M. until 4 P.M.

90. b. The top sign specifies *Any vehicles without Zone 1 Permit parked over 2 Hrs* beneath *Tow-Away Zone.*

91. d. Although the word *Lane* is usually abbreviated as *Ln*, the directions indicate that this is not how it should be coded here. So choices **b** and **c** can be eliminated. Choice **a** confuses the building's street number with the digit indicating the violation.

92. c. The code should indicate the address 362 Front Street (coded *362FrSt*) where the violation *unapproved container used for refuse* (coded *4*) has taken place.

93. a. Do not be thrown off by irrelevant details that should not be included in the code, such as the violator's name or the date of the violation. The code should only include the address at which the violation occurred (coded here as *54PyDr*) and the nature of the violation (coded here as *1*).

94. b. The code ends with the digit *9*, which indicates *improper use of recyclable receptacle.* Storing one's private firewood supply in a bin designated for recyclable papers, plastics, and metals would be considered improper use. Choice **a** is incorrect because the code *999MaAv9* indicates an avenue, not a street. *Improper use of a city receptacle* is not mentioned among the violations, so choice **c** is incorrect. The violation *ragweed, tall weeds, and/or grass must be cut* is coded with a *3*, not a *9*, so choice **d** is incorrect.

95. c. The initials of *Oak Park* are *OP*, but street names should not be coded according to initials. They are supposed to be coded according to the first two letters of the street name. Therefore, *Oak Park* should be coded *Oa*, as it is in choice **c**.

96. b. This code should begin with the first three numbers or letters of the driver's license plate number, which are *902*. It should end with the code for *driving in bicycle lane*, which is *B*, and *driving vehicle under the influence of drugs or alcohol*, which is *m*. Choice **d** is incorrect because the misdemeanor violations are coded in lower case.

97. d. Choice **a** can be eliminated because the codes for *driving on sidewalk* (*F*) and *reckless driving* (*j*) are not ordered alphabetically. Choice **b** is also incorrect because the license plate code is placed between the letters indicating the two violations.

98. a. Choice **a** is the only answer that ends with the sole felony violation code, *nn*. This code is mistakenly placed in capital letters in choice **b** and at the beginning of the code in choice **c**. Choice **d** only logs one *n* when there should be two.

99. d. The first three numbers or letters in the code indicate the driver's license number, not the violations. Choices **a**, **b**, and **c** all mistake the driver's license number for violations. The final three letters of the code refer to violations, and *h*, which indicates *failure to yield right of way to blind pedestrian*, is among them.

100. c. The driver in this scenario has committed violation *D*, *display of light source impairing vision of drivers*. The only answer that places *D* in the correct spot is choice **c**.

7 ▶ CIVIL SERVICE PRACTICE EXAM 6

This sixth practice exam will continue to prepare you for the types of questions you will see on your civil service exam. The 100 multiple-choice questions that follow will test your knowledge of math, reading, spelling, grammar, civil service, memory, and coding.

Remember to read the entire answer explanation thoroughly, regardless of whether you answered the question correctly. Compare your score on this test to tests 1 through 5. Are there areas in which you need more improvement?

Civil Service Practice Exam 6

1. ⓐ ⓑ ⓒ ⓓ	36. ⓐ ⓑ ⓒ ⓓ	71. ⓐ ⓑ ⓒ
2. ⓐ ⓑ ⓒ ⓓ	37. ⓐ ⓑ ⓒ ⓓ	72. ⓐ ⓑ ⓒ
3. ⓐ ⓑ ⓒ ⓓ	38. ⓐ ⓑ ⓒ ⓓ	73. ⓐ ⓑ ⓒ
4. ⓐ ⓑ ⓒ ⓓ	39. ⓐ ⓑ ⓒ ⓓ	74. ⓐ ⓑ ⓒ
5. ⓐ ⓑ ⓒ ⓓ	40. ⓐ ⓑ ⓒ ⓓ	75. ⓐ ⓑ ⓒ
6. ⓐ ⓑ ⓒ ⓓ	41. ⓐ ⓑ ⓒ ⓓ	76. ⓐ ⓑ ⓒ
7. ⓐ ⓑ ⓒ ⓓ	42. ⓐ ⓑ ⓒ ⓓ	77. ⓐ ⓑ ⓒ
8. ⓐ ⓑ ⓒ ⓓ	43. ⓐ ⓑ ⓒ ⓓ	78. ⓐ ⓑ ⓒ
9. ⓐ ⓑ ⓒ ⓓ	44. ⓐ ⓑ ⓒ ⓓ	79. ⓐ ⓑ ⓒ
10. ⓐ ⓑ ⓒ ⓓ	45. ⓐ ⓑ ⓒ ⓓ	80. ⓐ ⓑ ⓒ
11. ⓐ ⓑ ⓒ ⓓ	46. ⓐ ⓑ ⓒ ⓓ	81. ⓐ ⓑ ⓒ ⓓ
12. ⓐ ⓑ ⓒ ⓓ	47. ⓐ ⓑ ⓒ ⓓ	82. ⓐ ⓑ ⓒ ⓓ
13. ⓐ ⓑ ⓒ ⓓ	48. ⓐ ⓑ ⓒ ⓓ	83. ⓐ ⓑ ⓒ ⓓ
14. ⓐ ⓑ ⓒ ⓓ	49. ⓐ ⓑ ⓒ ⓓ	84. ⓐ ⓑ ⓒ ⓓ
15. ⓐ ⓑ ⓒ ⓓ	50. ⓐ ⓑ ⓒ ⓓ	85. ⓐ ⓑ ⓒ ⓓ
16. ⓐ ⓑ ⓒ ⓓ	51. ⓐ ⓑ ⓒ ⓓ	86. ⓐ ⓑ ⓒ ⓓ
17. ⓐ ⓑ ⓒ ⓓ	52. ⓐ ⓑ ⓒ ⓓ	87. ⓐ ⓑ ⓒ ⓓ
18. ⓐ ⓑ ⓒ ⓓ	53. ⓐ ⓑ ⓒ ⓓ	88. ⓐ ⓑ ⓒ ⓓ
19. ⓐ ⓑ ⓒ ⓓ	54. ⓐ ⓑ ⓒ ⓓ	89. ⓐ ⓑ ⓒ ⓓ
20. ⓐ ⓑ ⓒ ⓓ	55. ⓐ ⓑ ⓒ ⓓ	90. ⓐ ⓑ ⓒ ⓓ
21. ⓐ ⓑ ⓒ ⓓ	56. ⓐ ⓑ ⓒ ⓓ	91. ⓐ ⓑ ⓒ ⓓ
22. ⓐ ⓑ ⓒ ⓓ	57. ⓐ ⓑ ⓒ ⓓ	92. ⓐ ⓑ ⓒ ⓓ
23. ⓐ ⓑ ⓒ ⓓ	58. ⓐ ⓑ ⓒ ⓓ	93. ⓐ ⓑ ⓒ ⓓ
24. ⓐ ⓑ ⓒ ⓓ	59. ⓐ ⓑ ⓒ ⓓ	94. ⓐ ⓑ ⓒ ⓓ
25. ⓐ ⓑ ⓒ ⓓ	60. ⓐ ⓑ ⓒ ⓓ	95. ⓐ ⓑ ⓒ ⓓ
26. ⓐ ⓑ ⓒ ⓓ	61. ⓐ ⓑ ⓒ	96. ⓐ ⓑ ⓒ ⓓ
27. ⓐ ⓑ ⓒ ⓓ	62. ⓐ ⓑ ⓒ	97. ⓐ ⓑ ⓒ ⓓ
28. ⓐ ⓑ ⓒ ⓓ	63. ⓐ ⓑ ⓒ	98. ⓐ ⓑ ⓒ ⓓ
29. ⓐ ⓑ ⓒ ⓓ	64. ⓐ ⓑ ⓒ	99. ⓐ ⓑ ⓒ ⓓ
30. ⓐ ⓑ ⓒ ⓓ	65. ⓐ ⓑ ⓒ	100. ⓐ ⓑ ⓒ ⓓ
31. ⓐ ⓑ ⓒ ⓓ	66. ⓐ ⓑ ⓒ	
32. ⓐ ⓑ ⓒ ⓓ	67. ⓐ ⓑ ⓒ	
33. ⓐ ⓑ ⓒ ⓓ	68. ⓐ ⓑ ⓒ	
34. ⓐ ⓑ ⓒ ⓓ	69. ⓐ ⓑ ⓒ	
35. ⓐ ⓑ ⓒ ⓓ	70. ⓐ ⓑ ⓒ	

Section 1: Mathematics

1. $\frac{41}{6} =$
 a. $4\frac{1}{6}$
 b. $6\frac{5}{6}$
 c. $41\frac{1}{6}$
 d. $5\frac{5}{6}$

2. Reduce $\frac{18}{108}$ to its lowest terms.
 a. $\frac{1}{90}$
 b. $\frac{1}{6}$
 c. $\frac{2}{12}$
 d. $\frac{1}{10}$

3. $32\frac{3}{4} - 15\frac{1}{2} =$
 a. $17\frac{1}{4}$
 b. $17\frac{1}{2}$
 c. $18\frac{1}{2}$
 d. $19\frac{3}{4}$

4. $\frac{13}{16} + \frac{2}{3} + \frac{5}{8} =$
 a. $\frac{20}{27}$
 b. $\frac{101}{144}$
 c. $2\frac{5}{48}$
 d. $\frac{48}{101}$

5. $4\frac{1}{4} \times 2\frac{2}{17} =$
 a. $\frac{1}{9}$
 b. 9
 c. $\frac{289}{144}$
 d. $8\frac{1}{34}$

6. $\frac{4}{7} \div 7 =$
 a. 4
 b. $\frac{4}{49}$
 c. $12\frac{1}{4}$
 d. $\frac{1}{4}$

7. $2\frac{4}{5} \times \frac{5}{14} =$
 a. $\frac{1}{2}$
 b. 2
 c. $7\frac{21}{25}$
 d. 1

8. 250% of 1.8 is _____.
 a. 450
 b. 4.5
 c. 45
 d. 0.045

9. $5.3 - 1.97 =$ _____.
 a. 4.43
 b. 3.43
 c. 3.33
 d. 7.27

10. What is the percent equivalent of $\frac{21}{40}$?
 a. 0.00525%
 b. 5.25%
 c. 52.5%
 d. 0.525%

11. What is the decimal equivalent of 0.5%?
 a. 0.005
 b. 0.05
 c. 0.5
 d. 50

12. The weight on a produce scale registers 17.03 ounces. If you remove a bag of peaches, the new weight registers 6.87 ounces. How many ounces does the bag of peaches weigh?
 a. 11.16 ounces
 b. 11.26 ounces
 c. 23.90 ounces
 d. 10.16 ounces

13. A muffin recipe calls for $2\frac{1}{4}$ cups of all-purpose white flour, $1\frac{1}{3}$ cups of whole wheat flour, and $\frac{3}{8}$ cup of buckwheat flour. How much total flour is being used?

    a. $1\frac{5}{8}$ cups

    b. $3\frac{1}{3}$ cups

    c. $3\frac{23}{24}$ cups

    d. $3\frac{7}{12}$ cups

14. A lunch bill comes to $27.25. If you want to leave a 15% tip, what is the total cost of the bill?

    a. $4.09

    b. $27.25

    c. $31.34

    d. $33.44

15. A dinner bill was $68.20. Don gave the waiter $80 and told him to keep the change as a tip. What percent tip did the waiter receive? Round to the nearest tenth of a percent.

    a. 11.8%

    b. 14.8%

    c. 17.3%

    d. 20%

16. Raymond pedals his bike 8 feet in 2 seconds. How far does he move in one minute?

    a. 240 feet

    b. 480 feet

    c. 960 feet

    d. 120 feet

17. A tree farmer wishes to plant 22 rows of trees, each containing 48 trees. How many trees will he plant?

    a. 70

    b. 1,000

    c. 1,056

    d. 192

18. A total of 450 employees work at a local department store. If 16% of employees work part-time and the others work full-time, how many workers in the company are full-time?

    a. 72

    b. 366

    c. 378

    d. 552

19. Anne rode her bicycle 17.08 miles on a spring day. The trip took 2.8 hours to complete. What was her average speed for the ride?

    a. 14.28 miles per hour

    b. 6 miles per hour

    c. 6.1 miles per hour

    d. 5.6 miles per hour

20. A chili recipe calls for $2\frac{1}{4}$ pounds of ground beef. Tom has enough ground beef for $\frac{5}{8}$ of the recipe. How much ground beef does he have?

    a. $1\frac{13}{32}$ pounds

    b. $\frac{5}{18}$ pounds

    c. $3\frac{3}{5}$ pounds

    d. $1\frac{5}{8}$ pounds

21. A bag weighs 3 pounds 4 ounces and contains 13 identical packages of chocolate. How much does each package weigh?

    a. 52 ounces

    b. 13 ounces

    c. 2 ounces

    d. 4 ounces

22. A 9-hour workday is divided into segments devoted to different tasks. Fifteen percent of the day is set aside for lunch. Three-tenths of the day is devoted to participation in off-site workshops. The rest of the day is devoted to completing routine work. How many minutes of the day are devoted to routine work?
  a. 297 minutes
  b. 459 minutes
  c. 162 minutes
  d. 243 minutes

23. A student typically spends $1\frac{1}{3}$ hours per day studying for the ACT exam during the summer. In the weeks leading up to the exam, the student increases her study time by 40%. How many minutes per day does she now spend studying?
  a. 32 minutes
  b. 100 minutes
  c. 112 minutes
  d. 120 minutes

24. On a trail map, $1\frac{1}{4}$ inches represents $2\frac{1}{2}$ miles. How many inches correspond to $10\frac{1}{4}$ miles?
  a. 5
  b. $5\frac{1}{8}$
  c. $5\frac{1}{2}$
  d. 9

25. A phone company charges $0.15 per minute of data sharing. If a customer uses 1.5 hours worth of data for a call, how much is the total charge?
  a. $9.00
  b. $13.00
  c. $13.50
  d. $15.00

26. A restaurant is divided into three main seating areas. One-fifth is reserved for private, banquet-style rooms and one-third is reserved for bar seating. The rest of the restaurant is devoted to traditional table seating arrangements. What fraction of the restaurant is devoted to traditional table seating arrangements?
  a. $\frac{2}{3}$
  b. $\frac{4}{5}$
  c. $\frac{7}{15}$
  d. $\frac{3}{4}$

27. If a college student sleeps 18 out of 24 hours one Saturday, what percentage of the day is she awake?
  a. 10%
  b. 25%
  c. 50%
  d. 75%

28. At the batting cages, a speed pitch machine will pitch a baseball at 65 miles per hour. How many inches per minute is such a pitch moving?
  a. 1.144 inches per minute
  b. 68,640 inches per minute
  c. 5,720 inches per minute
  d. 95 inches per minute

29. A botanist takes temperature readings four times a day in the greenhouse to monitor temperature controls. The readings she has from today are:
65.2°F, 66.1°F, 65.3°F, and 65.7°F.
What is the average temperature for the day, rounded to the nearest tenth of a degree?
  a. 65.6°F
  b. 65.5°F
  c. 65.2°F
  d. 66.1°F

Refer to the following graph for questions 30 through 32.

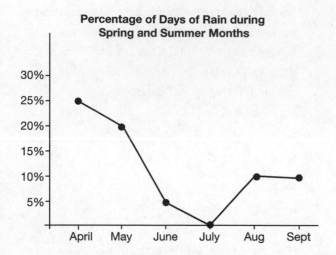

Percentage of Days of Rain during Spring and Summer Months

Refer to the following graph for questions 33 through 35.

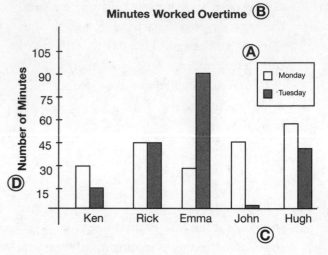

Minutes Worked Overtime

30. What information does the *x*-axis provide?
   a. month
   b. percentage of days it rained
   c. number of days its rained
   d. likelihood of rain during winter months

31. Which month had the highest percentage of days with rain?
   a. April
   b. May
   c. July
   d. August

32. What is the range of the data, measured as a percent?
   a. 0
   b. 25
   c. 10
   d. $11\frac{2}{3}$

33. What is A?
   a. title of the graph
   b. legend
   c. *x*-axis
   d. *y*-axis

34. How many minutes overtime, total, did Emma work on Monday and Tuesday?
   a. 105
   b. 90
   c. 30
   d. 120

35. How many more minutes, total, did the five employees work overtime on Monday than on Tuesday?
   a. 25
   b. 195
   c. 210
   d. 0

For questions 36 and 37, use the following data chart.

IMPROVEMENT IN MOBILITY		
NUMBER OF WEEKS IN PHYSICAL THERAPY	DEGREES THAT THE ELBOW CAN BEND	DEGREES THAT THE TORSO CAN BEND
1	40	45
2	50	50
3	55	60
4	63	62
5	66	70
6	71	70
7	73	78
8	76	85

36. What is the range of degrees of movement of the elbow?
a. 40 degrees
b. 63 degrees
c. 36 degrees
d. 76 degrees

37. What is the average number of degrees the torso can bend over the 8-week physical therapy treatment?
a. 61.75 degrees
b. 40 degrees
c. 65 degrees
d. 70 degrees

Refer to the following pie chart for questions 38 through 40:

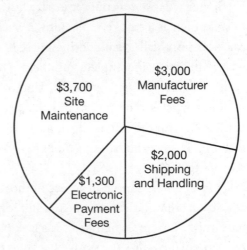

Monthly Expenditures Incurred When Running an Online Business

$3,000 Manufacturer Fees

$3,700 Site Maintenance

$2,000 Shipping and Handling

$1,300 Electronic Payment Fees

38. What are the monthly average expenses?
a. $1,300
b. $2,000
c. $2,500
d. $3,700

39. What percentage of the total monthly expenses does site maintenance account for?
   a. 37%
   b. 50%
   c. 30%
   d. 63%

40. What is the ratio of manufacturer fees to shipping and handling fees?
   a. 3:2
   b. 2:3
   c. 20:13
   d. 37:30

Section 2: Written Communication

Reading Comprehension— Questions 41 through 70

Read the following passage. Then answer questions 41 through 45.

One of the most hazardous conditions a firefighter will ever encounter is a backdraft (also known as a smoke explosion). A backdraft can occur in the hot-smoldering phase of a fire when burning is incomplete and there is not enough oxygen to <u>sustain</u> the fire. Unburned carbon particles and other flammable products, combined with the intense heat, may cause instantaneous combustion if more oxygen reaches the fire.

Firefighters should be aware of the conditions that indicate the possibility for a backdraft to occur. When there is a lack of oxygen during a fire, the smoke becomes filled with carbon dioxide or carbon monoxide and turns dense gray or black. Other warning signs of a potential backdraft are little or no visible flame, excessive heat, smoke leaving the building in puffs, muffled sounds, and smoke-stained windows.

Proper ventilation will make a backdraft less likely. Opening a room or building at the highest point allows heated gases and smoke to be released gradually. However, suddenly breaking a window or opening a door is a mistake, because it allows oxygen to rush in, causing an explosion.

41. The author's main purpose in this passage is to
   a. prove that a backdraft is the single most dangerous situation a firefighter can face.
   b. show the best way to prevent a backdraft with proper ventilation.
   c. explain the causes, dangers, warning signs, and preventions of backdrafts.
   d. tell a dramatic story about a firefighter caught in a backdraft.

42. According to the passage, all the following are potential warning signs of a backdraft EXCEPT
   a. little or no visible flame.
   b. muffled sounds.
   c. smoke-stained windows.
   d. unburned carbon particles.

43. The final paragraph of the passage suggests that
   a. instantaneous combustion is not a factor of backdrafts.
   b. a backdraft occurs before the end of a fire.
   c. backdrafts are known by several different names.
   d. there are ways to prevent a backdraft.

44. According to the passage, a poor method of preventing a backdraft is
   a. opening a room or building at the highest point.
   b. filling the smoke with carbon dioxide.
   c. suddenly breaking a window.
   d. smothering the flame with a blanket.

45. As used in the passage, the word *sustain* most nearly means
   a. maintain.
   b. regain.
   c. train.
   d. explain.

Read the following passage. Then answer questions 46 through 50.

Today, bicycles are elegantly simple machines that are common around the world. Many people ride bicycles for recreation, whereas others use them as a means of transportation. The first bicycle, called a <u>draisienne</u>, was invented in Germany in 1818 by Baron Karl de Drais de Sauerbrun. Because it was made of wood, the draisienne wasn't very <u>durable</u> nor did it have pedals. Riders moved it by pushing their feet against the ground.

In 1839, Kirkpatrick Macmillan, a Scottish blacksmith, invented a much better bicycle. Macmillan's machine had tires with iron rims to keep them from getting worn down. He also used foot-operated cranks, similar to pedals, so his bicycle could be ridden at a quick pace. It didn't look much like the modern bicycle, though, because its back wheel was substantially larger than its front wheel. Although Macmillan's bicycles could be ridden easily, they were never produced in large numbers.

In 1861, Frenchman Pierre Michaux and his brother Ernest invented a bicycle with an improved crank mechanism. They called their bicycle a <u>vélocipède</u>, but most people called it a "bone shaker" because of the jarring effect of the wood and iron frame. Despite the unflattering nickname, the vélocipède was a hit. After a few years, the Michaux family was making hundreds of the machines annually, mostly for fun-seeking young people.

Ten years later, James Starley, an English inventor, made several innovations that revolutionized bicycle design. He made the front wheel many times larger than the back wheel, put a gear on the pedals to make the bicycle more efficient, and lightened the wheels by using wire spokes. Although this bicycle was much lighter and less tiring to ride, it was still clumsy, extremely top-heavy, and ridden mostly for entertainment.

It wasn't until 1874 that the first truly modern bicycle appeared on the scene. Invented by another Englishman, H. J. Lawson, the safety bicycle would look familiar to today's cyclists. The safety bicycle had equal-sized wheels, which made it much less prone to toppling over. Lawson also attached a chain to the pedals to drive the rear wheel. By 1893, the safety bicycle had been further improved with air-filled rubber tires, a diamond-shaped frame, and easy braking. With the improvements provided by Lawson, bicycles became extremely popular and useful for transportation. Today, they are built, used, and enjoyed all over the world.

46. The author's primary purpose in writing this passage is to
   a. explain how the bicycle was first invented.
   b. prove the bicycle is the best form of transportation.
   c. describe improvements in the bicycle throughout the years.
   d. define the terms *vélocipède* and *bone shaker*.

47. Which of the following would be the most uncomfortable bicycle to ride?
   a. Starley's bicycle
   b. the vélocipède
   c. the modern bicycle
   d. the safety bicycle

48. The passage suggests that James Starley
   a. made a better bicycle than the Michaux brothers.
   b. made few adjustments to the bicycle.
   c. invented the bicycle used currently.
   d. invented the safety bicycle.

49. As used in the passage, the word *durable* most nearly means
   a. cheap.
   b. attractive.
   c. sturdy.
   d. common.

50. Based on the passage, which of the following words best sums up Baron Karl de Drais de Sauerbrun?
   a. gentleman
   b. perfectionist
   c. failure
   d. innovator

Read the following passage. Then answer questions 51 through 55.

The walnut tree produces wood that is used for countless purposes, and is considered the finest wood in the world. The wood is easy to work with, yet it is very hard and durable—and when it is polished, it produces a rich, dark <u>luster</u>. It also shrinks and swells less than any other wood, which makes it especially desirable for fine furniture, flooring, and even gunstocks.

In fact, just about every part of the walnut is unusually hard and strong. The nut of the tree is encased inside a very hard shell, which itself is enclosed in a leathery outer covering called a husk. It requires real effort to break through those layers to get at the tasty meat inside.

Every part of the walnut is useful to people. The outer husk produces a dark reddish stain that is hard to remove from the hands of the person who opens the nut, and this pigment is widely used in dyes and wood stains. The inner shell is used as an abrasive to clean jet engines. The meat of the nut is extensively used in cooking, ice cream, and flavorings. And, of course, it can just be eaten raw.

Walnut trees exude a chemical into the soil near their roots, which can be poisonous to some trees and shrubs. Fruit trees, for example, will not survive if planted too close to a walnut. Many other plants, such as maple trees or ivy, are not affected by the walnut's presence, and are well suited to grow in its vicinity.

51. The author's main idea is best summarized by which of the following?
   a. Because the walnut is so hard, accessing the meat inside can be very difficult.
   b. The walnut tree has many uses, including providing building materials and food, although it can be poisonous to other plants.
   c. Walnuts can be used in variety of recipes, including salads, breads, cakes, cookies, and poultry dishes.
   d. Walnut trees exude a chemical that can be poisonous to some trees and shrubs, but other plants are not affected by it.

52. Based on the passage, which of the following is likely NOT something the walnut tree provides?
   a. a fertilizer for fruit trees
   b. a material for a dresser
   c. a coloring for wooden chairs
   d. a bread ingredient

53. As it is used in the passage, the word *luster* most nearly means
   a. cover.
   b. wood.
   c. shine.
   d. fruit.

54. According to the passage, the walnut tree can be used to make all the following EXCEPT
  a. furniture.
  b. engines.
  c. flooring.
  d. guns.

55. According to the passage, which part of the walnut tree is like leather?
  a. the wood
  b. the husk
  c. the pigment
  d. the nut

Read the following passage. Then answer questions 56 through 60.

The late 1980s found the landscape of popular music in America dominated by a distinctive style of rock and roll known as glam rock, or hair metal—so called because of the overstyled hair, makeup, and wardrobe worn by the genre's *ostentatious* rockers. Bands like Poison, Whitesnake, and Mötley Crüe popularized glam rock with their power ballads and flashy style, but the product had worn thin by the early 1990s. Just as superficial as the 1980s, glam rockers were shallow, short on substance, and musically inferior.

In 1991, a Seattle-based band called Nirvana shocked the corporate music industry with the release of its debut single, "Smells Like Teen Spirit," which quickly became a huge hit all over the world. Nirvana's distorted, guitar-laden sound and thought-provoking lyrics were the antithesis of glam rock, and the youth of America were quick to pledge their allegiance to the brand new movement known as grunge.

Grunge actually got its start in the Pacific Northwest during the mid-1980s. Nirvana had simply mainstreamed a sound and culture that got its start years before with bands like Mudhoney, Soundgarden, and Green River. Grunge rockers derived their fashion sense from the youth culture of the Pacific Northwest: a melding of punk rock style and outdoor clothing like flannels, heavy boots, worn-out jeans, and corduroys. At the height of the movement's popularity, when other Seattle bands like Pearl Jam and Alice in Chains were all the rage, the trappings of grunge were working their way to the height of American fashion. Like the music, the teenagers were fast to embrace the grunge fashion, because it represented defiance against corporate America and shallow pop culture.

The popularity of grunge music was ephemeral; by the mid- to late 1990s, its influence on American culture had all but disappeared, and most of its recognizable bands were nowhere to be seen on the charts. The heavy sound and themes of grunge were replaced on the radio waves by boy bands like the Backstreet Boys, and the bubblegum pop of Britney Spears and Christina Aguilera.

There are many reasons why the Seattle sound faded out of the mainstream as quickly as it rocketed to prominence, but the most glaring reason lies at the defiant, antiestablishment heart of the grunge movement itself. It is very hard to buck the trend when you are the one setting it, and many of the grunge bands were never comfortable with the fame that was thrust on them. Ultimately, the simple fact that many grunge bands were so against mainstream rock stardom eventually took the movement back to where it started: underground. The fickle American mainstream public, as quick as they were to hop on to the grunge bandwagon, were just as quick to hop off and move on to something else.

56. As used in the passage, the word *ostentatious* most nearly means
  a. rich.
  b. angry.
  c. tasteful.
  d. showy.

57. The author's purpose in writing this passage is to
  a. describe how grunge sounded.
  b. explain the history of a kind of music.
  c. show how music changed in the 2000s.
  d. prove that grunge is the best form of music.

58. According to the passage, all the following were grunge bands EXCEPT
  a. Mudhoney.
  b. Soundgarden.
  c. Alice in Chains.
  d. Poison.

59. Based on information in the passage, the author likely believes
  a. grunge bands were short on substance.
  b. Britney Spears ended the grunge movement.
  c. Nirvana is a better band than Mötley Crüe.
  d. the American mainstream public cares about music deeply.

60. As used in the passage, the word *ephemeral* most nearly means
  a. passing.
  b. constant.
  c. brilliant.
  d. popular.

Read the following passage. Then answer questions 61 through 65.

No trip to New York City is complete until you've visited one of New York's famed Jewish food stores or delicatessens to nosh on treats of northern and central European Jewish origin: bagels and lox, Romanian pastrami on rye, chopped liver, cheesecake, or matzoh ball soup. Many classic Jewish delis, such as Reuben's, have now closed their doors, but the famous Katz's Delicatessen and the Second Avenue Deli still offer traditional Jewish specialty foods to a grateful clientele of native New Yorkers and international tourists.

If you're in the mood for a Jewish appetizing treat, visit Barney Greengrass's The Sturgeon King, or Russ & Daughters, for smoked or pickled fish, kippered salmon, whitefish, lox, and herring in sour cream sauce. If you're in the mood for a frothy, thirst-quenching beverage, visit the East Village's Chocolate Bar for a delicious chocolate egg cream. The egg cream is a classic New York treat that was *concocted* by Jewish candy store owner Louis Auster in Brooklyn, New York, in 1890.

Regardless of your personal taste, there's a Jewish specialty food that is perfect for you. The next time you visit New York City, be sure to indulge in a puffy, hot knish or a warm and tasty brisket sandwich for lunch. If you're really hungry, go for the gold! Sink your teeth into a towering, overstuffed corned beef, chopped liver, and coleslaw sandwich at Katz's Deli. Are you hungry yet?

61. The author's reason for writing this passage was to
  a. persuade the reader.
  b. describe a delicatessen.
  c. narrate a story.
  d. entertain the reader.

62. The writer most likely uses the word *nosh* in the first sentence, rather than words such as eat, *snack*, or *munch*, because
  a. the writer is trying to appeal to readers with strong vocabularies.
  b. *nosh* is a word that lends authenticity to the passage.
  c. the writer wants you to look up unfamiliar words in the dictionary.
  d. the word *munch* is too informal for a passage such as this.

63. In the passage, the word *concocted* is closest in meaning to
  a. built.
  b. poured.
  c. created.
  d. drank.

64. The passage supports which of the following conclusions?
  a. Vegetarians may not want to eat most Jewish sandwiches.
  b. Matzoh ball soup is extremely difficult to make.
  c. There are few Jewish delicatessens left in New York City.
  d. An egg cream is a nutritious breakfast meal.

65. According to the passage, Louis Auster owned
  a. Katz's Delicatessen.
  b. The Sturgeon King.
  c. Chocolate Bar.
  d. a candy store.

Read the following passage. Then answer questions 66 through 70.

Abraham Lincoln served as the sixteenth president of the United States, yet he never went to college. In fact, Lincoln had nearly no formal education whatsoever, attending schools for less than a year throughout his childhood. Yet this should not be construed to mean that Lincoln was ignorant or unlearned; on the contrary, he was one of the most well-read leaders of the time. The fact is that Abraham Lincoln educated himself by studying books of religion, philosophy, and literature, and he continued his voracious reading throughout his life.

A lack of public school education did not prevent Lincoln from becoming a great leader. He led the United States through four years of civil war, which threatened to divide the nation into two separate countries. He was a powerful opponent of slavery, and it was largely through his leadership that slavery was abolished in this country.

Lincoln's determination to educate himself through diligent reading also led to his reputation as a great *orator*—and even today his speeches are quoted and studied worldwide. He serves as an example of a great leader—and a great reader. His love of books and good literature enabled Abe Lincoln to rise to world renown.

66. Which sentence best summarizes the main idea of the passage?
  a. Abraham Lincoln served as the sixteenth president of the United States.
  b. Although Abraham Lincoln had no formal education, he was an extremely intelligent leader and man.
  c. Abraham Lincoln read books about religion, philosophy, and literature.
  d. Abraham Lincoln both led the United States through the Civil War and abolished slavery.

67. According to the passage, Abraham Lincoln got an education by
  a. attending college.
  b. leading the country.
  c. giving great speeches.
  d. reading books.

68. As used in the passage, the word *voracious* is closest in meaning to
  a. eager.
  b. clumsy.
  c. measured.
  d. jealous.

69. According to the passage, the American Civil War lasted for
  a. two years.
  b. four years.
  c. six years.
  d. eight years.

70. As used in the passage, the word *orator* is closest in meaning to
   a. leader.
   b. speaker.
   c. trooper.
   d. teacher.

Grammar—Questions 71 through 80
Select the best choice for each question.

71. Which of the following is NOT a complete sentence?
   a. Come over here.
   b. While cooking the soup, Ricardo thought he smelled something burning.
   c. Instead of going to the baseball game with Marcia.

72. Select the sentence that is written most correctly.
   a. Milo saw sequoias, oaks, spruces, and sycamores at the arboretum.
   b. Milo saw sequoias, oaks, spruces, and, sycamores at the arboretum.
   c. Milo saw sequoias oaks spruces and sycamores at the arboretum.

73. Select the sentence that is written most correctly.
   a. Would you like to go bowling with Miriam and I?
   b. Would you like to go bowling with Miriam and me?
   c. Would you like to go bowling with I and Miriam?

74. Select the sentence that is written most correctly.
   a. Many paintings in that museum, such as Vincent van Gogh's *A Starry Night*, are very famous.
   b. Many paintings in that museum, such as Vincent van Gogh's *A Starry Night*, is very famous.
   c. Many paintings in the museum, such as Vincent van Gogh's *A Starry Night*, is very famous.

75. Select the sentence that is written most correctly.
   a. Mrs. Harold my next-door neighbor has lived on this street for 45 years.
   b. Mrs. Harold, my next-door neighbor, has lived on this street for 45 years.
   c. Mrs. Harold my next-door neighbor, has lived on this street for 45 years.

76. Select the sentence that is written most correctly.
   a. When will Mr. and Mrs. wu be visiting again?
   b. When will Mr. and Mrs. Wu be visiting again?
   c. When will Mr. and Mrs Wu be visiting again?

77. Select the sentence that is written most correctly.
   a. Sheriff Bollock will be returning to this precinct on december 2nd.
   b. Sheriff Bollock will be returning to this precinct on December 2nd.
   c. Sheriff Bollock will be returning to this Precinct on December 2nd.

78. Select the sentence that is written most correctly.
  a. A good friend of mine wrote that novel.
  b. That novel was written by a good friend of mine.
  c. A good freind of mine wrote that novel.

79. Select the sentence that is written most correctly.
  a. The compact was much smaller in size than the station wagon we used to own.
  b. The compact was much smaller than the station wagon we used to own.
  c. The compact was much smaller in size than the station wagon we used to own before the compact.

80. Select the sentence that is written most correctly.
  a. Throughout its history, Japan has had a culture quite different from any other country.
  b. Throughout its history, Japan had a culture quite differently from any other country.
  c. Throughout its history, Japan had a culture quite different from that of any other country.

Section 3: Civil Service Skills

Customer Service—
Questions 81 through 85
Select the best answer for each question.

81. After visiting the contact page of an agency's website, the customer should be able to
  a. link to web pages that address similar issues.
  b. know the names of everyone who works for the agency.
  c. understand the agency's history.
  d. call the agency directly.

82. A customer who walks into an agency without an appointment should be
  a. informed that he or she must have an appointment and asked to leave.
  b. sent to the person with whom the customer wishes to meet immediately.
  c. greeted by a receptionist who informs the customer of his or her approximate wait time.
  d. given a magazine to read while waiting for his or her meeting.

83. The term FAQ stands for
  a. fast action queries.
  b. first answer questions.
  c. find accurately, quickly.
  d. frequently asked questions.

84. In the event a customer call is being recorded, the customer should
  a. speak clearly for the recording device.
  b. understand that a transcript of the call may be posted on the Internet.
  c. be informed that the call is being recorded for training or quality assurance.
  d. not know that he or she is being recorded.

85. A customer who is having trouble with an agency's website should be told that
  a. you are sorry he or she is having a problem and would be happy to help resolve the issue.
  b. the website has been designed in accordance with the CSLIC.
  c. navigating a website is not that difficult but you'll help the customer if it's really necessary.
  d. you are transferring the customer to a representative who is more qualified to resolve the issue.

Memory—Questions 86 through 90

Take five minutes to study the following picture. Then, answer questions 86 and 87 without looking back at the picture.

86. What is this bus's destination?
   a. Newport Mall
   b. Via St.
   c. NJ Hospital
   d. Park Ave.

87. How many cars in the lane behind the bus are visible in this photo?
   a. 0
   b. 1
   c. 2
   d. 3

Take five minutes to study the text that follows. Then, answer questions 88 through 90 without looking back at the text.

The following is the text that appears on a sign for a pay parking lot.

U-Park Co.
1221 George Washington Parkway
555-555-8349
up to 1 HR $3
up to 2 HRS $5
Max to Close $10
Monthly $200
OPEN 6 A.M.–7 P.M.
ALL DAY—$10

88. What is the cost of parking up to 2 hours?
   a. $3
   b. $5
   c. $10
   d. $200

89. What time does the parking lot close?
   a. 6 A.M.
   b. 12 P.M.
   c. 6 P.M.
   d. 7 P.M.

90. What is the name of this business?
   a. George Washington Parking
   b. GW Parking Inc.
   c. U-Park Co.
   d. Open All Day Parking

Coding—Questions 91 through 100

To answer questions 91 through 95, refer to the following scenario.

A municipal office maintains a log of all correspondence it receives. Each correspondence is coded according to the following rules.
1. Three letters indicating the first three letters of sender's last name
2. Six digits indicating date (mm/dd/yy) correspondence was sent
3. One letter indicating correspondence type
     E = e-mail
     P = posted mail
     T = telephone call
4. Two digits indicating nature of correspondence
     01. complaint
     02. employment inquiry
     03. general comment
     04. general inquiry
     05. violation report
     06. other

91. On February 4, 2011, the office received a call from Martha Lennon about obtaining a job interview after she spotted a help wanted ad in that morning's paper. How should her correspondence be coded?
   a. ML02042011
   b. LEN24201102
   c. Len020411T02
   d. MLen020411T2

92. Harrison Pilcher sent a letter reporting illegal activity in his neighborhood on March 7, 2012. The letter arrived at the office on March 10. How should his correspondence be coded?
   a. Pil030712P05
   b. HP030712PP5
   c. Pilcher372012
   d. Pil031012P5

93. Stella Richards would like to know the office's hours of operation. On October 10, 2009, she e-mailed the office to inquire about this information. How should her correspondence be coded?
   a. Ste10102009E
   b. Ric101009E04
   c. SR200910P01
   d. Ric101009E0

94. Which of the following describes the person who sent a correspondence coded Lee122011T01?
   a. Lee Davidson, who sent an e-mail of complaint on February 12, 2011
   b. Lester Ericson, who sent a letter of complaint via the U.S. mail
   c. Peter Lee, who made a telephone call of complaint on December 20, 2011
   d. Tim Leeson, who made a telephone call of complaint on January 1, 2001

95. The person whose correspondence was coded Bri091510T06 sent it in order to
a. report a violation in his district.
b. complain about a rude employee at the office.
c. ask whether the office is open on holidays.
d. make an appointment to repaint the office.

To answer questions 96 through 100, refer to the following scenario.

A state assigns numbers to commercial driver's licenses using the following code:
2 letters = licensee's initials
(e.g., Tina Lewy = TL)
4 digits = month and day of birth
(e.g., April 2nd = 0402)
3 letters = licensee's county of residence
(e.g., Bergman County = BER)
1 digit = vehicle class
3 letters = randomly assigned

96. Gary Bachman was born on August 22, 1969. He now lives in Crenshaw County, and drives a class 7 truck for a living. What is his commercial driver's license number?
a. BAC822CRE7IYG
b. GB0822CRE7PAK
c. GAR822CRE7MALP
d. GB0822CRE7

97. Julia Fielding resides in Nassau County. She drives a class 4 truck professionally. Her birthday is November 14, 1979. What is her commercial driver's license number?
a. JF1114NAS4GHY
b. JFNAS41114VSD
c. FIE1114NAS4TTR
d. 1114NAS4 JF

98. Jack Townshend drives a class 6 truck from his home in Trevor County every day. On May 29, he took the day off to celebrate his birthday. What is his commercial driver's license number?
a. GTDJT0529TRE6
b. JTTRE05296YUD
c. TO0529TRE6XDR
d. JT0529TRE6XDR

99. A commercial driver's license with the number ME0813HAB8DDT could belong to an individual named
a. Melissa King.
b. David Trotter.
c. Michelle Ewing.
d. Harry Beck.

100. A commercial driver's license with the number VW1008CHA5RAY could belong to an individual who lives in
a. Charming County.
b. Rayburn County.
c. Van Wick County.
d. Oslow County.

Answers

Section 1: Mathematics

1. b. Convert an improper fraction to a mixed number by dividing the denominator into the numerator; this will result in a whole number and a remainder, the latter of which is expressed as the numerator of a fraction with the same denominator as the original improper fraction. Doing so yields $\frac{41}{6} = 6\frac{5}{6}$. Choice **a** does not interpret the improper fraction correctly. This mixed number actually equals $\frac{25}{6}$. Choice **c** is incorrect because you do not interpret a mixed number as multiplying the whole part times the fractional part. The whole part is incorrect in choice **d**.

2. b. To reduce a fraction to lowest terms, write the numerator and denominator as products of their factors, and cancel all those that are common to both the numerator and denominator: $\frac{18}{108} = \frac{\cancel{18} \cdot 1}{\cancel{18} \cdot 6} = \frac{1}{6}$. Choice **a** subtracts the numerator from the denominator, which is not the correct way to simplify a fraction. In choice **c**, the fraction is not completely reduced. Choice **d** is incorrect because you cannot cancel like digits—they must be fractions.

3. a. First, subtract $\frac{3}{4} - \frac{1}{2}$. Rewrite each fraction over a common denominator 4 to get $\frac{3}{4} - \frac{1}{2} = \frac{1}{4}$. Next, subtract $32 - 15$, which equals $17\frac{1}{4}$. So, the correct answer is $17\frac{1}{4}$. Choice **b** is incorrect because it is the result of subtracting the fractions incorrectly. Choices **c** and **d** are incorrect because it is the result of subtracting the whole numbers incorrectly.

4. c. Transform all fractions to equivalent ones with a denominator of 48, and then add the numerators: $\frac{13}{16} + \frac{2}{3} + \frac{5}{8} = \frac{39}{48} + \frac{32}{48} + \frac{30}{48} = \frac{39+32+30}{48} = \frac{101}{48} = 2\frac{5}{48}$. Choice **a** adds the numerators and denominators without first getting a common denominator. Choice **b** is incorrect because after getting a least common denominator, it adds the numerators and denominators—you should keep the denominator fixed when adding fractions. Choice **d** is the reciprocal of the correct answer.

5. b. $4\frac{1}{4} \times 2\frac{2}{17} = \frac{17}{4} \times \frac{36}{\cancel{17}} = \frac{36}{4} = 9$. Choice **a** is the reciprocal of the correct answer. Choice **c** divides the fractions instead of multiplying them. Choice **d** incorrectly interprets the mixed numbers: $4\frac{1}{4} \neq 4 \times \frac{1}{4}$.

6. b. $\frac{4}{7} \div 7 = \frac{4}{7} \times \frac{1}{7} = \frac{4}{49}$. Choice **a** multiplies the numbers instead of dividing them. Choice **c** is the reciprocal of the correct answer. Choice **d** multiplies the numbers, and then takes the reciprocal; this should be done in the reverse order.

7. d. $2\frac{4}{5} \times \frac{5}{14} = \frac{14}{5} \times \frac{5}{14} = 1$. Choice **a** treats the mixed number incorrectly—$2\frac{4}{5} \neq 2 \times \frac{4}{5}$—and takes the reciprocal of the product. Choice **b** also treats the mixed number incorrectly. Choice **c** divides the fractions instead of multiplying them.

8. b. $250\% = 2.50$. So, 250% of 1.8 is $2.50(1.8) = 4.5$.

9. c. Align the decimal points and subtract as you would whole numbers, keeping the location of the decimal point.

```
  5.30
 −1.97
  3.33
```

Choice **a** does not borrow correctly when subtracting the whole parts and the tenths place. Choice **b** does not borrow correctly when subtracting the tenths place. Choice **d** adds the decimals instead of subtracting them.

10. c. $\frac{21}{40} = 0.525$. To find the percent, multiply 0.525 by 100 and write the % sign. This is 52.5%, which is the correct choice. Choice **a** is incorrect because after converting the fraction to a decimal, it moves the decimal point two places to the left instead of to the right. Choice **b** does not move the decimal point enough places to the right. Choice **d** does not move the decimal point to the right when converting to a percent.

11. a. To divide 0.5 by 100 to get 0.005. So, 0.5% = 0.005. Choice **b** is incorrect because you need to move the decimal point one more place to the left. Choice **c** is incorrect because you need to move the decimal point two places to the left when converting a percent to a decimal. Choice **d** is incorrect because you moved the decimal point two places to the right instead of to the left.

12. d. Subtract the weight registered when the bag of peaches is removed from the scale from the original reading: $17.03 - 6.87 = 10.16$ ounces. Choices **a** and **b** do not borrow correctly. Choice **c** is incorrect because instead of subtracting the decimals, it adds them.

13. c. Add the three fractions together: by adding the whole numers and then the fractional parts:
$$2\frac{1}{4} + 1\frac{1}{3} + \frac{3}{8} = (2+1) + \left(\frac{1}{4} + \frac{1}{3} + \frac{3}{8}\right)$$
$$= 3 + \frac{6}{24} + \frac{8}{24} + \frac{9}{24}$$
$$= 3 + \frac{6+8+9}{24}$$
$$= 3\frac{23}{24}$$

Choice **a** does not include the whole wheat flour. Choice **b** adds the fractional parts incorrectly. Choice **d** forgets to include the buckwheat flour.

14. c. Write the 15% tip as the decimal 0.15. To calculate the tip, multiply 27.25 by 0.15 to get 4.0875. Then, add this amount to the lunch bill to get $27.25 + 4.0875 = 31.3375$, which rounds to $31.34. This is the correct choice. Choice **a** is incorrect because it is the actual tip.

15. c. $\frac{80 - 68.20}{68.20} = \frac{11.80}{68.20} = 0.173$. So, the tip was about 17.3%. Choice **a** is the difference in dollar amounts—you must divide this by the amount of the bill in order to get the percent. Choice **b** divides the difference in dollar amounts by 80, not 68.20. Choice **d** is incorrect because 20% of 68.20 is 13.64, and so when it is added to 68.20, the sum exceeds 80.

16. a. Let x be the number of feet he pedals in 1 minute ($= 60$ seconds). Set up the following proportion: $\frac{8 \text{ feet}}{2 \text{ seconds}} = \frac{x \text{ feet}}{60 \text{ seconds}}$. To solve for x, cross-multiply: $8(60) = 2x$. This simplifies to $2x = 480$, so that dividing both sides by 2 yields $x = 240$ feet. Choice **b** assumes he moves 8 feet in 1 second, not 2 seconds. Choice **c** multiplies both sides by the coefficient of x instead of dividing by it. Choice **d** assumes he moves 8 feet in 4 seconds, not 2 seconds.

17. c. Multiply the number of rows by the number of trees per row: $22(48) = 1{,}056$. Choice **a** is incorrect because you added the number of rows and number of trees per row instead of multiplying them. Choice **b** is incorrect because you rounded each of the numbers to the nearest ten before multiplying—this produces an inaccurate count. Choice **d** is incorrect because you multiplied by the tens place incorrectly.

18. c. If 16% of the workers are part-time, then 100% − 16% or 84% are full-time. Calculate 84% of 450: $(0.84)450 = 378$ full-time employees. Choice **a** represents part-time workers.

19. c. Use the formula $D = R \times T$ in the form $R = \frac{D}{T}$: $R = \frac{17.08 \text{ miles}}{2.8 \text{ hours}} = 6.1$ miles per hour. Choice **a** subtracts the time from the distance traveled instead of dividing. Choice **b** rounds down—this is not an accurate speed. Choice **d** rounds each quantity before dividing, which is incorrect.

20. a. Multiply the two fractions: $\frac{5}{8}(2\frac{1}{4}) = \frac{5}{8} \times \frac{9}{4}$ $= \frac{45}{32} = 1\frac{13}{32}$ pounds. Choices **b** and **c** divide the fractions instead of multiplying them. Choice **d** subtracts the fractions instead of multiplying them.

21. d. Since 1 pound = 16 ounces, it follows that 3 pounds 4 ounces = 52 ounces. Divide this by 13 to determine the number of ounces per package: $\frac{52}{13} = 4$ ounces. Choice **a** is the weight of the entire bag. Choice **b** misinterprets 13 packages as 13 ounces per package. Choice **c** assumes there are 26 packages, not 13.

22. a. Since $\frac{3}{10} = 30\%$, it follows from what we are given that 45% of 9 hours is devoted to non-routine work. Since there are 60 minutes in 1 hour, the number of minutes to which this corresponds is $0.45 \times (60 \times 9) = 243$ minutes. So, the number of minutes spent completing routine work is $540 - 243 = 297$ minutes. Choice **b** does not subtract the time spent participating in off-site workshops. Choice **c** is the amount of time spent participating in off-site workshops. Choice **d** is the amount of time spent doing non-routine work.

23. c. Since 1 hour = 60 minutes, $\frac{1}{3}$ of an hour equals 20 minutes, so $1\frac{1}{3}$ hours equals 80 minutes. Forty percent of 80 minutes equals $0.40(80) = 32$ minutes. Adding this to the 80 minutes she routinely spent studying prior to the increase yields 112 minutes. Choice **a** is the number of additional minutes of study time. Choice **b** forgets to include the fractional part of $1\frac{1}{3}$. Choice **d** is incorrect because 40% does not equal 40— you must compute 40% of $1\frac{1}{3}$ hours.

24. b. Let x be the number of inches corresponding to $10\frac{1}{4}$ miles. Set up the following proportion: $\frac{1\frac{1}{4} \text{ inches}}{2\frac{1}{2} \text{ miles}} = \frac{x \text{ inches}}{10\frac{1}{4} \text{ miles}}$. Convert all fractions appearing in the numerators or denominators as improper fractions: $\frac{\frac{5}{4} \text{ inches}}{\frac{5}{2} \text{ miles}} = \frac{x \text{ inches}}{\frac{41}{4} \text{ miles}}$. To solve for x, cross-multiply: $\frac{5}{4}(\frac{41}{4}) = \frac{5}{2}x$. Now, multiply both sides by $\frac{2}{5}$ to isolate x on the right-side; then, simplify: $x = \frac{\cancel{2}}{\cancel{5}} \times \frac{\cancel{5}}{\cancel{4}_2} \times \frac{41}{4}$ $= \frac{41}{8} = 5\frac{1}{8}$. Choice **a** is incorrect it leaves out the fractional part in the conversion. Choice **c** makes an arithmetic error. Choice **d** solves for x incorrectly once the proportion is set up.

25. c. First, rewrite 1.5 hours in minutes by multiplying 1×60 minutes = 60 minutes and multiplying $0.5 \times 60 = 30$ minutes, for a total of 90 minutes. At $0.15 per minute, data sharing is 90 minutes $\times$ 0.15 = $13.50.

26. c. Subtract the sum of the fractions from 1 to obtain the fraction of the restaurant devoted to traditional table seating arrangements: $1 - (\frac{1}{5} + \frac{1}{3}) = 1 - (\frac{3}{15} + \frac{5}{15}) = 1 - \frac{8}{15} = \frac{7}{15}$. Choice **a** forgets to account for the fraction devoted to private banquet-style seating. Choice **b** forgets to account for the fraction devoted to bar seating. Choice **d** adds the fractions incorrectly—you must get a least common denominator before adding fractions.

27. b. If the student sleeps 18 out of 24 hours, then the student is awake for 6 hours of the day. To find this percentage, divide 6 by 24 to get $\frac{1}{4}$, which is 25%.

28. b. Use the fact that 1 mile = 5,280 feet, 1 foot = 12 inches, and 1 hour = 60 minutes to change the units, as follows:

65 ~~miles~~	5,280 ~~feet~~	12 inches	1 ~~hour~~
1 ~~hour~~	1 ~~mile~~	1 ~~foot~~	60 minutes

Pay particular attention to the canceling of units. Multiplying through gives 68,640 inches per minute. Choice **a** is the number of inches per second. Choice **c** is the number of feet per minute. Choice **d** is the approximate number of feet per second.

29. a. Add the numbers together and divide by 4: $\frac{65.2°F + 66.1°F + 65.3°F + 65.7°F}{4} \approx 65.585°F \approx$ 65.6°F. Choice **b** is the median temperature, not the average temperature. Choice **c** is the minimum temperature. Choice **d** is the maximum temperature, not the average temperature.

30. a. The *x*-axis is the horizontal axis in the graph, and it displays the month. Choice **b** is information conveyed on the *y*-axis. Choice **c** is not formally displayed on the graph. Choice **d** is not contained within the data.

31. a. This month had a percentage of 25%, which is the largest of all months shown in the graph. Choice **b** is incorrect because there is one month with a higher percentage. Choice **c** is the month with the lowest percentage. Choice **d** is incorrect because there are two months with a higher percentage.

32. b. Subtract the smallest percent (0) from the largest percent (25): 25 – 0 = 25. Choice **a** is the minimum percentage, not the range. Choice **c** is the percentage that occurs most often, not the range. Choice **d** is the average percentage, not the range.

33. b. This is the part of the graph that describes the meaning of the two types of bars—this, by definition, is the legend of the graph.

34. d. Add the sum of the heights of the bars for Monday and Tuesday for Emma: 90 + 30 = 120 minutes. Choice **a** is Hugh's overtime. Choice **b** is only Emma's overtime for Tuesday. Choice **c** is only Emma's overtime for Monday.

35. a. The total number of minutes overtime for the five employees is 210 for Monday and 195 for Tuesday. So, they work 210 – 195 = 25 minutes more overtime on Monday than on Tuesday. Choice **b** is the total overtime for Tuesday—you did not subtract it from Monday. Choice **c** is the total overtime for Monday—you did not subtract the overtime for Tuesday from it. Choice **d** is incorrect because there is more overtime on Monday than on Tuesday, so the difference cannot be zero.

36. c. Subtract the smallest value (40) from the largest value (76): 76 – 40 = 36 degrees. Choice **a** is the range for bending the torso, not the elbow. Choice **b** is the median, not the range. Choice **d** is the maximum value, not the range.

37. c. Add the eight values in the right column and divide the sum by 8 to get an average of 65 degrees. Choice **a** is the average number of degrees the elbow can bend over the 8-week physical therapy treatment. Choice **b** is the range, not the average. Choice **d** is the mode, not the average.

38. c. To find the average expenses, add up the slices of the pie chart and then divide by the total number of slices. So, ($3,700 + $3,000 + $2,000 + $1,300) = $\frac{\$10,000}{4}$ = $2,500.

39. a. $\frac{3,700}{10,000}$ = 0.37, so 37%. Choice **b** corresponds to the combined expenses for site maintenance and electronic payment. Choice **c** corresponds to the manufacturer fees. Choice **d** is the percentage of the expenses NOT devoted to site maintenance.

40. a. $\frac{3,000}{2,000}$ = $\frac{3}{2}$, so the ratio is 3:2. Choice **b** is written backwards—this is the ratio of shipping and handling fees to manufacturer fees. Choice **c** is the ratio of shipping and handling fees to electronic payment fees. Choice **d** is the ratio of site maintenance to manufacturer fees.

Section 2: Written Communication

41. c. The main purpose refers to the most important points of a passage while avoiding details not present in it. Choice **c** accomplishes this well. The first sentence of the passage states that a backdraft is only "One of the most hazardous conditions a firefighter will ever encounter," which means choice **a** is incorrect. Choice **b** only refers to a single detail in the passage and fails to capture all its main purposes.

42. d. According to the first paragraph, unburned carbon particles are causes of a backdraft, not a warning sign that one might occur. These signs are all listed in paragraph 2.

43. b. The first paragraph states "A backdraft can occur in the hot-smoldering phase of a fire when burning is incomplete." The paragraph contradicts choice **a**. Although backdrafts are also known as smoke explosions, two names is hardly several, so choice **c** is incorrect. Choice **d** describes information in the final paragraph, not the first one.

44. c. The final paragraph states "suddenly breaking a window or opening a door is a mistake, because it allows oxygen to rush in, causing an explosion." Choice **a** is a good way to prevent a backdraft. Choices **c** and **d** are not ways to prevent backdrafts.

45. a. Reread the sentence, substituting each choice for the word *sustain*. Of the four choices, only choice **a** makes sense in context.

46. c. The main purpose refers to the most important points of a passage while avoiding details not present in it. Each paragraph describes a different improvement in the bicycle. Choice **a** only describes the first paragraph, not the entire passage. The author never implies that the bicycle is the best form of transportation, so choice **b** is incorrect.

47. b. According to paragraph 3, the velocipede was nicknamed "the bone shaker" because it was so jarring to ride. This means it shook a lot, which was probably very uncomfortable.

48. a. According to the passage, after Pierre and Ernest Michaux made their own adjustments to the bicycle, James Starley "made several innovations that revolutionized bicycle design." This suggests Starley's bicycle was better than the Michaux brothers'. Choices **b** is contradicted by information in paragraph 4. Choices **c** and **d** are contradicted by information in the final paragraph.

49. c. Reread the sentence, substituting each choice for the word *durable*. Of the four choices, only choice **c** makes sense in context.

50. d. Baron Karl de Drais de Sauerbrun was the very first person to conceive of the bicycle, which means he was an incredible innovator.

51. b. A good summary touches on all the most important points of a passage while avoiding details not present in it. Choice **b** accomplishes this well. Choice **a** only describes paragraph 2 and choice **d** only describes paragraph 4. Choice **c** is not mentioned in the passage at all.

52. a. Paragraph 4 states that chemicals the walnut tree exudes can kill fruit trees, so it is hardly likely walnut trees could fertilize fruit trees. Choice **b** is incorrect because paragraph 1 states that walnut wood can be used to make furniture. Choice **c** is incorrect because paragraph 3 states that the walnut husk can be used as a wood stain. Choice **d** is incorrect because walnuts can be used to make several kinds of bread.

53. c. Reread the sentence, substituting each choice for the word *luster*. Of the four choices, only choice **c** makes sense in context.

54. b. According to paragraph 3, the inner shell of the walnut can be used to clean jet engines, but the walnut tree cannot be used to make engines. Paragraph 1 lists "fine furniture, flooring, and even gunstocks" as some things that can be made with walnut wood.

55. b. According to paragraph 2, "just about every part of the walnut is unusually hard and strong. The nut of the tree is encased inside a very hard shell, which itself is enclosed in a leathery outer covering called a husk."

56. d. Reread the sentence, substituting each choice for the word *ostentatious*. Of the four choices, only choice **d** makes sense in context.

57. b. The entire passage traces the start, popularity, and eventual demise of grunge. Choice **a** is a single detail in the passage. Choice **c** is incorrect because the grunge movement occurred in the late 1980s and the early 1990s.

58. d. Paragraph 1 defines Poison as a "glam rock or hair metal" band, which is the kind of band against which grunge was a reaction.

59. c. In paragraph 1, the author describes hair metal bands, such as Mötley Crüe, as "shallow, short on substance, and musically inferior." In the next paragraph, the author states that Nirvana had "thought-provoking lyrics." Based on this information, the author seems to prefer Nirvana. This information also contradicts choice **a**. Choice **b** is incorrect because the author states that grunge had already ended by the time Britney Spears became popular. The final sentence of the passage seems to contradict choice **d**.

60. a. Reread the sentence, substituting each choice for the word *ephemeral*. Of the four choices, only choice **a** makes sense in context. Choice **b**, *constant*, means the opposite of *ephemeral*.

61. a. The author addresses the reader directly, stating that "Regardless of your personal taste, there's a Jewish specialty food that is perfect for you" and asking "Are you hungry yet?" These direct statements and questions are designed to persuade the reader to visit New York's Jewish food stores or delicatessens.

62. b. The word *nosh* is Yiddish for *snack*. The writer uses it to lend authenticity to a passage about Jewish food stores or delicatessens.

63. c. Reread the sentence, substituting each choice for the word *concocted*. Of the four choices, only choice **c** makes sense in context.

64. a. All the sandwiches described in the passage are made with meat or fish: kippered salmon, lox, pastrami, corned beef, and so on. A vegetarian would want to avoid such sandwiches. No information in the passage supports choice **b**. The first paragraph states that "Many classic Jewish delis, such as Reuben's, have now closed their doors," but then goes on to describe some that are still in business, so choice **c** is incorrect. According to the passage, an egg cream is not a breakfast meal; it is a chocolate-flavored drink, so choice **d** is incorrect.

65. d. The last sentence of paragraph 2 states that Louis Auster, the inventor of the egg cream, owned a candy store. Although one can get an egg cream at Chocolate Bar, the passage does not indicate that Louis Auster owned it, so choice **c** is incorrect.

66. b. An expression of the main idea should focus on the most important ideas throughout the entire passage. All the details in this passage support the idea that Abraham Lincoln was extremely intelligent even though he had no formal education. Choices **a**, **c**, and **d** all refer to details that do not capture the most important idea running throughout the entire passage.

67. d. Paragraph 1 describes how Abraham Lincoln educated himself by reading many books on many topics. The paragraph contradicts choice **a** directly. One would need some education before becoming president or giving a great speech, so choices **b** and **c** are incorrect.

68. a. Reread the sentence, substituting each choice for the word *voracious*. Of the four choices, only choice **a** makes sense in context.

69. b. The second sentence of paragraph 2 states that Abraham Lincoln "led the United States through four years of civil war."

70. b. Reread the sentence, substituting each choice for the word *orator*. Of the four choices, only choice **b** makes sense in context.

71. c. This is a sentence fragment because it is missing a clause explaining who performed an action *instead of going to the baseball game with Marcia.*

72. a. When you write a list of items, such as the trees in these sentences, separate each item on the list with a comma, including the item preceding the word *and*. There should be no comma after the word *and*, as there is in incorrect choice **b**.

73. b. Choices a and c incorrectly use I where they should use me. Omit *Miriam* from the sentence to see why; would you say *Would you like to go bowling with I?* Because the sentence calls for an indirect object, the word *me* should be used, not *I*.

74. a. Choices **b** and **c** contain a subject-verb agreement error; the subject *paintings* requires a singular verb, not the plural verb *are*.

75. b. In choice **a**, the phrase *my next-door neighbor* is an appositive that should be set apart with commas. Choice **c** makes a similar error, failing to begin the appositive phrase with a comma.

76. b. The word *wu* in choice **a** is a proper name, so it should be capitalized. The abbreviation *Mrs.* in choice **c** should end with a period. Only choice **b** is correctly capitalized and punctuated.

77. b. The names of months should be capitalized, and choice **a** fails to capitalize *December*. Choice **c** capitalized the word *Precinct* incorrectly.

78. a. Choice **b** uses the passive voice when a better alternative in the active voice—choice **a**—is available. Choice **c** uses the incorrect spelling of the word *friend*.

79. b. Sentence **a** contains the redundant phrase *in size*, and choice **c** does not need the words *before the compact*.

80. c. Choice **a** makes an incorrect comparison, comparing Japan's culture to other countries. A properly formulated sentence should compare Japan's culture to other cultures. Choice **b** is awkwardly and confusingly worded; choice **c** is a much better formulation of the same idea, so it is the best answer.

Section 3: Civil Service Skills

81. b. An agency's contact page should include all essential information for contacting that agency. This includes the agency's telephone number.

82. c. Government agencies should always provide a front-desk receptionist to handle any customer issue, whether that customer has an appointment or has walked into the office without an appointment. The receptionist should greet walk-in customers politely and inform them of how long they will likely have to wait for an appointment.

83. d. An agency's official website should include an FAQ, or frequently asked questions, to provide answers to general information a customer should not have to call the agency to know.

84. c. Sometimes an agency will record customer calls either to monitor the quality of the customer service agent or for use in future training sessions. The customer's privacy is extremely important, and he or she should be informed whenever a call is being recorded.

85. a. Politeness is one of the key aspects of customer service, even if you personally think the problem is not very important. Choice **a** indicates a polite response to a basic question. Choice **b** is not an adequate response to a customer with a simple problem, who probably does not know what the CSLIC is. Choice **c** is condescending and a bit rude. Passing the buck is never a good customer service practice, so choice **d** is incorrect.

86. a. The sign above the windshield indicates that this bus's destination is *Newport Mall*. While the bus will reach this destination via Park Ave., Park Ave. is not the destination, so choice **d** is incorrect.

87. b. The front end of a single white car is visible directly behind the bus in this photo.

88. b. The sign indicates *up to 2 HRS $5*.

89. d. The sign indicates OPEN 6 A.M.–7 P.M.

90. c. The title at the top of the sign reads *U-Park Co. George Washington* is the parkway on which the lot is located, so choice **a** is incorrect.

91. c. This correspondence code should indicate the first three letters of Martha Lennon's last name (*Len*), six digits indicating she sent her correspondence on February 4, 2011, (*020411*), a letter indicating she made a telephone call (*T*), and two digits indicating hers was an employment inquiry (*02*). Only choice **c** presents all this information in the correct order.

92. a. Only choice **a** correctly codes the name, date, correspondence type, and nature of correspondence correctly. The six digits indicating *date of correspondence* should refer to the date the correspondence was sent, not the date it was received. So choice **d**, which also uses a single digit to code the nature of correspondence mistakenly, is incorrect.

93. b. Correspondence asking for hours of operation would fall under the *general inquiry* designation, which should be coded *04*. Only choice **b** includes this code.

94. c. The three letters *Lee* indicate a last name that begins with those letters, so choices **a** and **b** can be eliminated. The six digits that follow, *122011*, indicate the correspondence was sent on *December 20, 2011*, so choice **d** can be eliminated, leaving choice **c** as the correct answer.

95. d. This code ends with the digits *06*, which indicates *other*—a correspondence that does not fall under any of the natures listed in the rules. Since none of the *nature of correspondences* listed could describe office redecoration, a correspondence about it must be coded *06*. Choices **a**, **b**, and **c** could all be indicated by more specific *nature of correspondences*.

96. b. Choice **b** is correctly coded with Gary Bachman's initials (*GB*), four digits indicating he was born on August 22 (*0822*), three letters indicating he lives in Crenshaw County (*CRE*), one digit indicating he drives a class 7 vehicle (*7*), and three letters assigned randomly (*PAK*). Choice **d** is incorrect because it fails to include these three random letters.

97. a. Choice **a** is correctly coded with Julia Fielding's initials (*JF*), four digits indicating she was born on November 14 (*1114*), three letters indicating she lives in Nassau County (*NAS*), one digit indicating she drives a class 4 vehicle (*4*), and three letters assigned randomly (*GHY*). Choice **b** is incorrect because it arranges these details in the order they are presented in the question rather than the way they are supposed to be arranged according to the rules at the beginning of this section.

98. d. Choice **d** is correctly coded with Jack Townshend's initials (*JT*), four digits indicating he was born on May 29 (*0529*), three letters indicating he lives in Trevor County (*TRE*), one digit indicating he drives a class 6 vehicle (*6*), and three letters assigned randomly (*XDR*).

99. c. The first two letters of the license number indicate the licensee's initials. The only answer choice with the initials ME is **c**, *Michelle Ewing*.

100. a. The three letters placed after the two indicating the licensee's initials (*VW*) and the four digits indicating the licensee's month and day of birth (*1008*) indicate her or his county of residence. The only answer choice that begins with the letters *CHA* is choice **a**.

8 ▶ CIVIL SERVICE PRACTICE EXAM 7

This final practice exam will continue to prepare you for the types of questions you will see on your civil service exam. The 100 multiple-choice questions that follow will test your knowledge of math, reading, spelling, grammar, civil service, memory, and coding.

Remember to read the entire answer explanation thoroughly, regardless of whether you answered the question correctly. Compare your score on this test to tests 1 through 6. Are there areas in which you need more improvement?

Civil Service Practice Exam 7

1.	ⓐ	ⓑ	ⓒ	ⓓ
2.	ⓐ	ⓑ	ⓒ	ⓓ
3.	ⓐ	ⓑ	ⓒ	ⓓ
4.	ⓐ	ⓑ	ⓒ	ⓓ
5.	ⓐ	ⓑ	ⓒ	ⓓ
6.	ⓐ	ⓑ	ⓒ	ⓓ
7.	ⓐ	ⓑ	ⓒ	ⓓ
8.	ⓐ	ⓑ	ⓒ	ⓓ
9.	ⓐ	ⓑ	ⓒ	ⓓ
10.	ⓐ	ⓑ	ⓒ	ⓓ
11.	ⓐ	ⓑ	ⓒ	ⓓ
12.	ⓐ	ⓑ	ⓒ	ⓓ
13.	ⓐ	ⓑ	ⓒ	ⓓ
14.	ⓐ	ⓑ	ⓒ	ⓓ
15.	ⓐ	ⓑ	ⓒ	ⓓ
16.	ⓐ	ⓑ	ⓒ	ⓓ
17.	ⓐ	ⓑ	ⓒ	ⓓ
18.	ⓐ	ⓑ	ⓒ	ⓓ
19.	ⓐ	ⓑ	ⓒ	ⓓ
20.	ⓐ	ⓑ	ⓒ	ⓓ
21.	ⓐ	ⓑ	ⓒ	ⓓ
22.	ⓐ	ⓑ	ⓒ	ⓓ
23.	ⓐ	ⓑ	ⓒ	ⓓ
24.	ⓐ	ⓑ	ⓒ	ⓓ
25.	ⓐ	ⓑ	ⓒ	ⓓ
26.	ⓐ	ⓑ	ⓒ	ⓓ
27.	ⓐ	ⓑ	ⓒ	ⓓ
28.	ⓐ	ⓑ	ⓒ	ⓓ
29.	ⓐ	ⓑ	ⓒ	ⓓ
30.	ⓐ	ⓑ	ⓒ	ⓓ
31.	ⓐ	ⓑ	ⓒ	ⓓ
32.	ⓐ	ⓑ	ⓒ	ⓓ
33.	ⓐ	ⓑ	ⓒ	ⓓ
34.	ⓐ	ⓑ	ⓒ	ⓓ
35.	ⓐ	ⓑ	ⓒ	ⓓ

36.	ⓐ	ⓑ	ⓒ	ⓓ
37.	ⓐ	ⓑ	ⓒ	ⓓ
38.	ⓐ	ⓑ	ⓒ	ⓓ
39.	ⓐ	ⓑ	ⓒ	ⓓ
40.	ⓐ	ⓑ	ⓒ	ⓓ
41.	ⓐ	ⓑ	ⓒ	ⓓ
42.	ⓐ	ⓑ	ⓒ	ⓓ
43.	ⓐ	ⓑ	ⓒ	ⓓ
44.	ⓐ	ⓑ	ⓒ	ⓓ
45.	ⓐ	ⓑ	ⓒ	ⓓ
46.	ⓐ	ⓑ	ⓒ	ⓓ
47.	ⓐ	ⓑ	ⓒ	ⓓ
48.	ⓐ	ⓑ	ⓒ	ⓓ
49.	ⓐ	ⓑ	ⓒ	ⓓ
50.	ⓐ	ⓑ	ⓒ	ⓓ
51.	ⓐ	ⓑ	ⓒ	ⓓ
52.	ⓐ	ⓑ	ⓒ	ⓓ
53.	ⓐ	ⓑ	ⓒ	ⓓ
54.	ⓐ	ⓑ	ⓒ	ⓓ
55.	ⓐ	ⓑ	ⓒ	ⓓ
56.	ⓐ	ⓑ	ⓒ	ⓓ
57.	ⓐ	ⓑ	ⓒ	ⓓ
58.	ⓐ	ⓑ	ⓒ	ⓓ
59.	ⓐ	ⓑ	ⓒ	ⓓ
60.	ⓐ	ⓑ	ⓒ	ⓓ
61.	ⓐ	ⓑ	ⓒ	
62.	ⓐ	ⓑ	ⓒ	
63.	ⓐ	ⓑ	ⓒ	
64.	ⓐ	ⓑ	ⓒ	
65.	ⓐ	ⓑ	ⓒ	
66.	ⓐ	ⓑ	ⓒ	
67.	ⓐ	ⓑ	ⓒ	
68.	ⓐ	ⓑ	ⓒ	
69.	ⓐ	ⓑ	ⓒ	
70.	ⓐ	ⓑ	ⓒ	

71.	ⓐ	ⓑ	ⓒ	
72.	ⓐ	ⓑ	ⓒ	
73.	ⓐ	ⓑ	ⓒ	
74.	ⓐ	ⓑ	ⓒ	
75.	ⓐ	ⓑ	ⓒ	
76.	ⓐ	ⓑ	ⓒ	
77.	ⓐ	ⓑ	ⓒ	
78.	ⓐ	ⓑ	ⓒ	
79.	ⓐ	ⓑ	ⓒ	
80.	ⓐ	ⓑ	ⓒ	
81.	ⓐ	ⓑ	ⓒ	ⓓ
82.	ⓐ	ⓑ	ⓒ	ⓓ
83.	ⓐ	ⓑ	ⓒ	ⓓ
84.	ⓐ	ⓑ	ⓒ	ⓓ
85.	ⓐ	ⓑ	ⓒ	ⓓ
86.	ⓐ	ⓑ	ⓒ	ⓓ
87.	ⓐ	ⓑ	ⓒ	ⓓ
88.	ⓐ	ⓑ	ⓒ	ⓓ
89.	ⓐ	ⓑ	ⓒ	ⓓ
90.	ⓐ	ⓑ	ⓒ	ⓓ
91.	ⓐ	ⓑ	ⓒ	ⓓ
92.	ⓐ	ⓑ	ⓒ	ⓓ
93.	ⓐ	ⓑ	ⓒ	ⓓ
94.	ⓐ	ⓑ	ⓒ	ⓓ
95.	ⓐ	ⓑ	ⓒ	ⓓ
96.	ⓐ	ⓑ	ⓒ	ⓓ
97.	ⓐ	ⓑ	ⓒ	ⓓ
98.	ⓐ	ⓑ	ⓒ	ⓓ
99.	ⓐ	ⓑ	ⓒ	ⓓ
100.	ⓐ	ⓑ	ⓒ	ⓓ

Section 1: Mathematics

1. $5\frac{2}{3} =$
  a. $\frac{17}{3}$
  b. $\frac{52}{3}$
  c. $\frac{15}{2}$
  d. $\frac{10}{3}$

2. $\frac{56}{12} =$
  a. $4\frac{1}{3}$
  b. $8\frac{2}{3}$
  c. $6\frac{2}{3}$
  d. $5\frac{1}{3}$

3. $4\frac{1}{9} - 2\frac{1}{3} =$
  a. 2
  b. $\frac{9}{16}$
  c. $2\frac{2}{9}$
  d. $1\frac{7}{9}$

4. $3\frac{4}{15} - (\frac{3}{5} + 1\frac{2}{3}) =$
  a. 1
  b. $2\frac{4}{15}$
  c. $2\frac{4}{30}$
  d. 0

5. $9 \div \frac{2}{3} =$
  a. 6
  b. $\frac{2}{27}$
  c. $13\frac{1}{2}$
  d. $8\frac{1}{3}$

6. $3\frac{3}{5} \times \frac{25}{6} =$
  a. $7\frac{1}{2}$
  b. $\frac{108}{125}$
  c. $\frac{1}{15}$
  d. 15

7. $\frac{3}{8} \div \frac{8}{9} =$
  a. $\frac{1}{4}$
  b. $\frac{27}{64}$
  c. $2\frac{10}{27}$
  d. 3

8. 150% of 14 is
  a. 1.5
  b. 21
  c. 29
  d. 36

9. $5.25 \div 0.05 =$ _____.
  a. 5.30
  b. 0.2625
  c. 1.05
  d. 105

10. What is the percent equivalent of 0.034?
  a. 3.4%
  b. 0.034%
  c. 34%
  d. 0.00034%

11. What is the decimal equivalent of $3\frac{39}{50}$?
  a. 339
  b. 3.39
  c. 3.78
  d. 378

12. Jamie purchased a new DVD for $19.95 and a CD for $11.99. Assuming that tax was included in the prices of these items and he gave the cashier a $50 bill, how much change does he get back?
   a. $19.16
   b. $18.06
   c. $19.06
   d. $30.05

13. The distance from the bank to the coffee shop is $1\frac{3}{4}$ miles. Rick covered $\frac{2}{3}$ of this distance before he stopped at the bakery. How much further must he walk to cover the entire distance?
   a. $1\frac{1}{6}$ miles
   b. $1\frac{1}{12}$ miles
   c. $1\frac{7}{12}$ miles
   d. $\frac{7}{12}$ miles

14. A family closes on a $435,500 home. If the real estate agent is paid 3% on the sale, what is the real estate agent's fee from this sale?
   a. $136.50
   b. $1,365.00
   c. $13,065.00
   d. $130,650.00

15. The listed price of a vintage video game posted by an online vendor is $46.55. The vendor charges 5% sales tax and a 2.6% shipping and handling fee. What is the total cost of the game?
   a. $48.88
   b. $50.09
   c. $47.76
   d. $3.54

16. A printer can produce 12 color pages every 45 seconds. At this rate, how long would it take to print 50 color pages?
   a. 3 minutes 7.5 seconds
   b. 4 minutes 10 seconds
   c. 3 minutes
   d. 2 minutes 30 seconds

17. When laying tile on a kitchen floor, it is observed that 18 rows, each consisting of 14 tiles, are needed. How many tiles, total, are needed?
   a. 90
   b. 252
   c. 32
   d. 200

18. In a typical 8-hour day, 30% of a secretary's time is devoted to responding to e-mail. How much time does this correspond to?
   a. 2 hours 4 minutes
   b. 3 hours 12 minutes
   c. 2 hours 24 minutes
   d. 5 hours 36 minutes

19. Pete jogs at a rate of 1 mile every $11\frac{2}{3}$ minutes. If he jogs for 1 hour, how many miles will he have gone?
   a. $4\frac{6}{7}$ miles
   b. 5 miles
   c. $5\frac{5}{11}$ miles
   d. $5\frac{1}{7}$ miles

20. Pia buys a curtain panel that is $17\frac{5}{6}$ inches long. If she trims off $1\frac{1}{2}$ inches from the bottom, how much of the panel does she have left?
   a. $16\frac{1}{2}$
   b. $17\frac{1}{3}$
   c. $16\frac{8}{6}$
   d. $18\frac{1}{3}$

21. Three thousand four hundred flyers must be distributed prior to the big weekend sale. Twenty people divide the flyers equally among themselves. How many flyers does each person distribute?
a. 17
b. 170
c. 340
d. 3,400

22. A restaurant is revamping its menu, which is comprised of 80 items. Twenty percent of the menu consists of breakfast items, and one-fourth of the menu is devoted to lunch items. How many items are not designated for breakfast or lunch?
a. 16
b. 20
c. 44
d. 36

23. The value of a stock at the beginning of the day was $7.40 per share. By the end of the day, the price rose by 60%. What was the value per share of the stock at the end of the day?
a. $11.84
b. $8.00
c. $10.36
d. $4.44

24. A surfboard rental shop charges $4.25 per half hour. How much would a 6-hour rental cost?
a. $25.50
b. $51.00
c. $48.00
d. $76.50

25. You bought a 32.6 ounce bottle of dishwasher detergent, on sale. Each complete load of laundry requires the use of 1.4 ounces of detergent. How many complete loads of dishes can you wash using one bottle?
a. 23
b. 24
c. 32
d. 45

26. Marcus has a large computer game collection. If three-fourths of the games are role playing, one-third of the games are sports, and the remaining games are adventure, what fraction of the collection are adventure games?
a. $1\frac{3}{4}$
b. $\frac{5}{12}$
c. $\frac{7}{12}$
d. $1\frac{1}{12}$

27. A lacrosse team played 28 games and lost 4. Approximately what percentage of games did the team win?
a. $\frac{24}{28}$%
b. 86%
c. 14%
d. 28%

28. A professional tennis player can serve a ball at 120 miles per hour. At how many feet per hour does such a serve move?
a. 2,112 feet per hour
b. 176 feet per hour
c. 10,560 feet per hour
d. 633,600 feet per hour

29. Andrew worked late several times this week past his 5:00 P.M. stop time. On Monday, he worked until 5:50 P.M. On Tuesday, he worked until 6:30 P.M. On Thursday, he worked until 5:45 P.M. On Friday, he worked until 5:31 P.M. On average, how many minutes did Andrew work overtime for these 4 days?

    a. 45
    b. 50
    c. 54
    d. 216

Refer to the following graph for questions 30 through 32.

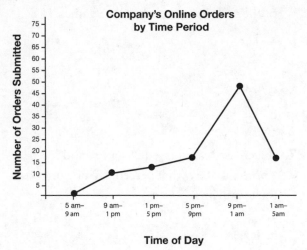

30. The time of day is represented by the
_____.

    a. scale
    b. *y*-axis
    c. *x*-axis
    d. legend

31. The average number of online orders submitted per 4-hour time period is
_____.

    a. 20
    b. 24
    c. 70
    d. 30

32. What is the peak time period for online orders?

    a. 5 A.M. to 9 A.M.
    b. 1 P.M. to 5 P.M.
    c. 9 P.M. to 1 A.M.
    d. 1 A.M. to 5 A.M.

Refer to the following chart for questions 33 and 34.

COST AND TYPICAL BATTERY LIFE FOR COMPUTERS (BY BRAND)		
COMPUTER BRAND	PRICE	BATTERY LIFE
D-Lux 3000	$2,500	7 hours
Comput-o-Magix 2x	$2,000	6 hours
Gen-R-ick v2	$1,650	5 hours
Looz-R v#	$ 900	3 hours

33. What conclusion is best supported by the data in the table?
   a. The more the computer costs, the longer its battery life.
   b. There is no correlation between price and battery life.
   c. The main factors in determining price are preinstalled software and screen size.
   d. Most people value battery life more than price.

34. What is the range of cost of the computers presented in the table?
   a. $1,762.50
   b. $2,500
   c. $900
   d. $1,600

Refer to the following chart for questions 35 through 37.

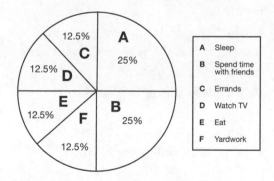

Ellen's 48–Hour Weekend Schedule

A	Sleep
B	Spend time with friends
C	Errands
D	Watch TV
E	Eat
F	Yardwork

35. How many hours does Ellen spend doing errands?
   a. 42
   b. 12
   c. 12.5
   d. 6

36. Which of the following conclusions is best supported by the chart?
   a. Ellen spends equal amounts of time on all six categories.
   b. Ellen spends half of her time either sleeping or spending time with friends.
   c. Ellen prefers doing yardwork to watching TV.
   d. If Ellen had more time, she would spend more time eating.

37. What does the legend of the chart tell you?
   a. what constitutes Ellen's weekday activities
   b. Ellen's ordered preferences of activities
   c. which categories correspond to which portions of the pie chart
   d. time devoted to each category

Refer to the following graph for questions 38 through 40.

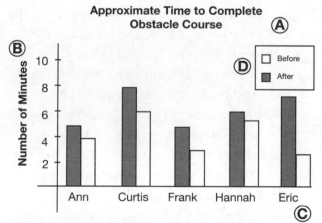

38. The information provided in D is the _____.
   a. legend
   b. x-axis
   c. y-axis
   d. title of the graph

39. Whose time improved the most after training?
   a. Ann
   b. Curtis
   c. Hannah
   d. Eric

40. Which of the following is a valid conclusion that can be deduced from the graph?
   a. Males showed more improvement than females by completing the training.
   b. Males and females improved by the same amount.
   c. Females liked the training, while males did not.
   d. Training had no effect on performance.

Section 2:
Written Communication

Reading Comprehension—
Questions 41 through 60

Read the following passage. Then answer questions 41 through 45.

The coconut is an unusual food for many reasons. It is technically a seed, produced by the coconut palm tree, and as such is one of the largest edible seeds produced by any plant. Its unusual contents also make it unique in the seed world—the interior consists of both "meat" and "water." The meat is the white pith with which we are all familiar, as it is used extensively for cooking and flavorings; the coconut water is a white liquid that is very sweet and thirst-quenching.

Portuguese explorers gave the nut its name in the fifteenth century, referring to it as coco, meaning "ghost" in their language. The three dimples and the hairy texture reminded them of a ghost's face, and the tree has retained that name ever since.

The coconut has many varied uses. It is used to make margarine as well as various cooking oils, and these cooking oils are used by fast-food restaurants around the world to make such diet staples as French fries. The coconut fluid is a favorite drink in hot climates,

providing a cool and refreshing beverage right off the tree. This water is also used by manufacturers of various sports drinks because of its isotonic electrolyte properties.

The coconut is also useful in many ways that have nothing to do with food. Coconut oil is used for cosmetics, medicines, and can even be used in place of diesel fuel. The shell has many uses, including cattle food and fertilizer. Dried coconut shells are used in many countries as a tool, such as a buffer for shining wood floors. The shells are also used for shirt buttons, and are commonly found on Hawaiian clothing. They are even used for musical instruments and birdhouses!

And all these are only some of the uses found for the coconut fruit. The coconut palm tree, which produces the nut, also produces countless useful items. It's no wonder that the coconut palm has been called "the tree of life."

41. Which of the following would be the best title for the passage?
   a. *The Ghostly Coconut*
   b. *Making Buttons from the Coconut Shell*
   c. *The Delicious Coconut*
   d. *The Many Uses of the Coconut*

42. According to the passage, the coconut can be used for all the following EXCEPT
   a. a drink.
   b. flooring material.
   c. a tool.
   d. birdhouses.

43. According to the passage, the coconut reminded Portuguese explorers of a ghost because
   a. the meat is white.
   b. the milk is transparent.
   c. it is dimpled and hairy.
   d. it is very oily.

44. As used in the passage, the word *staples* is closest in meaning to
   a. essentials.
   b. fasteners.
   c. clips.
   d. pins.

45. According to the passage, the coconut's isotonic electrolyte properties make it a good
   a. cattle food.
   b. cosmetic.
   c. sports drink.
   d. diesel fuel.

Read the following passage. Then answer questions 46 through 50.

Arteries of the heart blocked by plaque can reduce the flow of blood to the heart, possibly resulting in heart attack or death. Plaque is actually fat and cholesterol that accumulates on the inside of the arteries. The arteries of the heart are small and can be blocked by such accumulations. There is a medical procedure that creates more space in the blocked artery by inserting and inflating a tiny balloon into the blood vessel. It is called coronary balloon angioplasty. Angioplasty means "blood vessel repair." When the balloon is inflated, it compresses the plaque against the wall of the artery, creating more space and improving the flow of blood.

Many doctors choose this technique because it is less invasive than bypass surgery. Yes, both involve entering the body cavity, but in bypass surgery, the chest must be opened, the ribs must be cut, and the section of diseased artery must be removed and replaced. To replace it, the patient's body is opened, once again, to acquire a healthy section of artery. Usually, this comes from an artery located in

the calf of the leg. This means the patient now has two painful incisions that must heal at the same time. There is far more risk in such bypass surgery than in angioplasty, which involves threading a thin tube, called a catheter, into the circulatory system and working it to the damaged artery.

Angioplasty may take between 30 minutes and 3 hours to complete. It begins with a distinctive dye that is injected into the bloodstream. A thin catheter is then inserted into the femoral artery of the leg, near the groin. The doctor monitors the path of the dye using X-rays. He or she moves the tube through the heart and into the plaque-filled artery. The doctor then inflates the balloon, creating more space, deflates the balloon, and removes the tube. It is important to note that the plaque has not been removed; it has just been compressed against the sides of the artery. Sometimes, a stent, a tiny tube of stainless steel that is expandable when necessary, may be implanted. Its function is to keep the artery open.

46. What is the primary purpose of this passage?
   a. to prove angioplasty is the best way to deal with artery blockage
   b. to explain methods of removing artery blockage.
   c. to establish how the angioplasty first came into use
   d. to describe the dangers of angioplasty

47. According to the passage, a balloon is used in angioplasty to
   a. open the chest.
   b. locate the calf.
   c. cut the ribs.
   d. improve blood flow.

48. As used in the passage, the word *monitors* is closest in meaning to
  a. machines.
  b. controls.
  c. observes.
  d. pulls.

49. The passage supports which of the following conclusions?
  a. The time it takes to perform an angioplasty varies.
  b. Angioplasty removes artery blockage.
  c. Angioplasty does not involve entering the body cavity.
  d. The only way to ensure survival of a heart attack is angioplasty.

50. According to the passage, a stent is
  a. a thin catheter.
  b. an expandable stainless steel tube.
  c. a tiny inflatable balloon.
  d. a dye used in x-raying.

Read the following passage. Then answer questions 51 through 55.

The film *Lawrence of Arabia* may be somewhat dated by modern special effects standards, but it remains a high-water mark in the annals of filmmaking. The movie was filmed using real people who really performed the action. The long, slow scenes of camels walking in the desert may seem dull to the modern animation-jaded viewer, but those willing to pay attention to the underlying themes will be well rewarded by the movie's message.

And it is the theme of *Lawrence of Arabia* that really stays with a viewer, even some 50 years after it was released. That theme is the age-old story of hubris—the pride of a man, which raises him above his peers, only to dash him on the rocks of self-indulgence by the end.

We see this tragic <u>foible</u> of mankind worked out fully in the character of Lawrence himself, who begins the film as a genius who is eager to get involved in the desert conflicts of World War I. His cocky attitude irritates his superiors and amuses the Arabs fighting alongside the British, but his brilliance for details and strategy soon overcome all obstacles. Only Lawrence could have accomplished his victory at the Suez Canal, and his self-sacrifice and commitment to his followers display the best of his character.

Unfortunately, the baser elements of that character gradually take control as the film moves along, and Lawrence slowly declines into a dangerous blend of despair and self-assurance. The problem gradually becomes evident: Lawrence has grown to believe that he is a god who both gives life and takes it away again.

51. The author's main purpose in writing this passage is to
  a. analyze a movie.
  b. describe a historical figure.
  c. explain how films are made.
  d. show how modern audiences differ from older ones.

52. As used in the passage, the word *foible* is closest in meaning to
  a. effect.
  b. fault.
  c. genius.
  d. feature.

53. According to the passage, a quality Lawrence displays at the Suez Canal is
  a. hubris.
  b. cockiness.
  c. godliness.
  d. self-sacrifice.

54. The passage supports which of the following conclusions?
   a. *Lawrence of Arabia* involves numerous complex special effects techniques.
   b. Most modern audiences have never heard of the film *Lawrence of Arabia*.
   c. Lawrence experiences a radical change over the course of *Lawrence of Arabia*.
   d. *Lawrence of Arabia* shows a man's accomplishments over a series of wars.

55. According to the passage, scenes in *Lawrence of Arabia* that may not appeal to modern audiences involve
   a. camels.
   b. war.
   c. special effects.
   d. the Suez Canal.

Read the following passage. Then answer questions 56 through 60.

Medical waste has been a growing concern because of recent incidents of public exposure to discarded blood vials, needles (sharps), empty prescription bottles, and syringes. Medical waste can typically include general refuse, human blood and blood products, cultures and stocks of infectious agents, laboratory animal carcasses, contaminated bedding material, and pathological wastes.

Wastes are generally collected by gravity chutes, carts, or pneumatic tubes, each of which has its own advantages and disadvantages. Chutes are limited to vertical transport, and there is some risk of exhausting contaminants into hallways if a door is left open during use. Another disadvantage of gravity chutes is that the waste container may get jammed while dropping, or it may be broken upon hitting the bottom. Carts are primarily for horizontal transport of bagged or containerized wastes. The main risk here is that bags may be broken or torn during transport, potentially exposing the worker to the wastes. Using automated carts can reduce the potential for exposure. Pneumatic tubes offer the best performance for waste transport in a large facility. Advantages include high-speed movement, movement in any direction, and minimal intermediate storage of untreated wastes. However, some objects cannot be conveyed pneumatically.

Off-site disposal of regulated medical wastes remains a viable option for smaller hospitals (those with less than 150 beds). Some preliminary on-site processing, such as compaction or hydropulping, may be necessary prior to sending the waste off site. Compaction reduces the total volume of solid wastes, often reducing transportation and disposal costs, but it does not change the hazardous characteristics of the waste. Compaction may not be economical if transportation and disposal costs are based on weight rather than volume.

56. As used in the passage, the word *exhausting* is closest in meaning to
   a. tiring.
   b. weakening.
   c. using up.
   d. blowing.

57. With which of the following statements would the author most likely agree?
   a. All medical waste disposal methods have their failings.
   b. Chutes are better for disposing medical waste than pneumatic tubes.
   c. Every hospital should dispose of medical waste on site.
   d. There is no real risk in exposure to discarded blood vials or syringes.

58. According to the passage, the best method of transporting medical waste is
  a. gravity chutes.
  b. carts.
  c. compactors.
  d. pneumatic tubes.

59. Which of the following would be the best title for the passage?
  a. *Disposing of Medical Waste with Gravity Chutes*
  b. *The Methods and Challenges of Medical Waste Disposal*
  c. *Public Exposure to Medical Waste*
  d. *Compaction and Hydropulping*

60. As used in the passage, the word *viable* is closest in meaning to
  a. unlikely.
  b. possible.
  c. vital.
  d. formal.

Spelling—Questions 61 through 65
Select the choice that is spelled correctly.

61. The bookkeeper was in charge of keeping track of all the company's _____.
  a. expendatures
  b. expenditures
  c. expenditoures

62. The _____ boy always performed well on his exams.
  a. studious
  b. studeous
  c. studius

63. Which of the following words is spelled correctly?
  a. napsack
  b. magnatude
  c. qualification

64. Which of the following words is spelled correctly?
  a. withold
  b. yearn
  c. repeel

65. Which of the following words is spelled correctly?
  a. livelihood
  b. maleable
  c. hospitible

Vocabulary—Questions 66 through 70
Select the best answer for each question.

66. Find the word that is closest in meaning to the underlined word.
  an <u>opportune</u> prospect
  a. favorable
  b. immense
  c. baffling

67. Find the word that is closest in meaning to the underlined word.
  a <u>verdant</u> forest
  a. barren
  b. distant
  c. leafy

68. Find the word that is most nearly the opposite of the word.
  a <u>limpid</u> pool
  a. cloudy
  b. dense
  c. crowded

69. Find the word that best completes the sentence.
His excessively emotional speech was nothing
more than a _____ display.
  a. genteel
  b. histrionic
  c. buoyant

70. Find the word that best completes the sentence.
The book was _____ of any
truly useful information.
  a. permeated
  b. devoid
  c. invincible

Grammar—Questions 71 through 80
Select the best choice for each question.

71. Which of the following is a complete sentence?
  a. A hurricane was brought on by the
formation of an intense low-pressure area
over a warm spot in the Atlantic Ocean.
  b. The formation of an intense low-pressure
area over a warm spot in the Atlantic Ocean
brought on a hurricane.
  c. The formation, over a warm spot in the
Atlantic Ocean, of an intense low-pressure,
brought on a hurricane, area.

72. Select the sentence that is written most
correctly.
  a. The colors in this tapestry match those in
our living room perfectly.
  b. The colors in this tapestry matches those in
our living room perfectly.
  c. The colors in this tapestry match that in our
living room perfectly.

73. Select the sentence that is written most
correctly.
  a. Before we even finished the soup course the
waiter brought our entrees
  b. Before we even finished the soup course, the
waiter, brought our entrees.
  c. Before we even finished the soup course, the
waiter brought our entrees.

74. Select the sentence that is written most
correctly.
  a. Has everyone brought his or her textbook to
class today?
  b. Has everyone brought their textbooks to
class today?
  c. Has everyone brought their textbook to
class today?

75. Select the sentence that is written most
correctly.
  a. I did'nt go golfing on Saturday because I
could'nt find my clubs.
  b. I didnt go golfing on Saturday because I
couldnt find my clubs.
  c. I didn't go golfing on Saturday because I
couldn't find my clubs.

76. Select the sentence that is written most
correctly.
  a. The brown dog barked at the black dog, and
it was running across the lawn.
  b. The brown dog barked at the black dog; the
dog was running across the lawn.
  c. The brown dog barked at the black dog,
which was running across the lawn.

77. Select the sentence that is written most correctly.
   a. Next Saturday Kevin, Joe, and I are going to band practice.
   b. Next Saturday, Kevin, Joe, and I are going to band practice.
   c. Next Saturday, Kevin Joe and I are going to band practice.

78. Select the sentence that is written most correctly.
   a. Whenever my Uncle Stan comes to town, my entire family has dinner at the Polish restaurant across the street from Garwood's Stationery Supplies.
   b. Whenever my uncle Stan comes to town, my entire family has dinner at the Polish restaurant across the street from Garwood's Stationery Supplies.
   c. Whenever my Uncle Stan comes to town, my entire family has dinner at the Polish restaurant across the street from Garwood's Stationery supplies.

79. Select the sentence that is written most correctly.
   a. Beatrice asked me "if I was going to work on Sunday."
   b. Beatrice asked me if I was going to work on Sunday.
   c. Beatrice asked me "if I was going to work on Sunday?"

80. Select the sentence that is written most correctly.
   a. Emerging from the American South, the blues was one of the most influential forms of music of the twentieth century.
   b. Emerging from the American South, the twentieth century, the blues was one of the most influential forms of music.
   c. One of the most influential forms of music of the twentieth century, the American South produced the blues.

Section 3: Civil Service Skills

Customer Service—
Questions 81 through 85
Select the best choice for each question.

81. A customer who leaves a voicemail message should receive a response
   a. immediately.
   b. within an hour.
   c. within a day.
   d. within a week.

82. If a customer service agent is unable to deliver a response to a customer's e-mail query, the agent should
   a. attempt to resend the response at least two more times.
   b. assume the customer has already received a response.
   c. pass the problem over to an Internet technician.
   d. respond with any answer the customer might want to hear.

83. The term *BOT* refers to

  a. a web page that provides an agency's telephone number, e-mail address, and postal address.

  b. a comprehensive list of links to other agencies' websites.

  c. response software programmed to answer customer queries automatically.

  d. a program that allows customer service representatives to chat with customers on the Internet.

84. Before transferring a customer on the telephone, the customer needs to be told all the following EXCEPT

  a. to whom he or she is being transferred.

  b. the reason for the transfer.

  c. the extension of the person to whom the customer is being transferred.

  d. the number of times the customer can expect to be transferred over the course of the call.

85. Agencies should use RSS technology to

  a. respond to customer telephone calls.

  b. inform customers when their web pages have been updated.

  c. answer Internet queries automatically.

  d. help their web pages to load quickly.

Memory—Questions 86 through 90

Take five minutes to study the following picture. Then, answer questions 86 and 87 without looking back at the picture.

86. How many people are visible in the photo?
  a. 1
  b. 2
  c. 3
  d. 4

87. Future Restaurant serves
  a. Chinese food only.
  b. Chinese and Mexican food.
  c. Italian food only.
  d. Mexican and Italian food.

Take five minutes to study the text that follows. Then, answer questions 88 through 90 without looking back at the text.

> You are about to interview 12 new candidates for a position at your agency. Before the interview process, you studied each person's personal information on his or her resume to help you remember their names during the interviews. The information is as follows:
>
> Bernadette Franklin: Caucasian, female, age 21
> Samuel Peters: Latino, male, age 53
> Grant Aubach: Caucasian, male, age 30
> Rita Ballard: African American, female, age 23
> Pat Blarney: Latino, female, age 38
> Chris March: African American, female, age 61
> Jo Robie: Caucasian, female, age 31
> Burt Lu: Asian, male, age 50
> Mariel Hooper: Asian, female, age 26

88. How old is Samuel Peters?
  a. 21
  b. 30
  c. 53
  d. 61

89. Chris March is
  a. an African American female.
  b. an Asian male.
  c. a Caucasian female.
  d. a Latino male.

90. Which is a complete list of Latino applicants?
  a. Bernadette Franklin, Pat Blarney, Mariel Hooper
  b. Samuel Peters, Pat Blarney
  c. Rita Ballard, Burt Lu
  d. Chris March, Grant Aubach, Rita Ballard

Coding—Questions 91 through 100

To answer questions 91 through 95, refer to the following scenario.

> A record of all employees, past and present, is maintained in a log at a particular government office. The following code is used to record the information. All letters and digits are coded in the following order:
> 1. first letter of employee's last name
> 2. six digits (mm/dd/yy) indicating employee's first date of work
> 3. six digits (mm/dd/yy) indicating employee's final date of work (current employees are coded with six zeroes)
> 4. first letter of the employee's department

91. On December 1, 2010, Shirley Hemphill worked her final day in the information technology office. She had worked there for 20 years. How should she be coded?
  a. H10019012011HR
  b. H100190H120110
  c. H100190120110H
  d. SH00190120110H

92. Mark Ransford has been working in the information technology department since March 2, 2001, and he plans to continue working there for many years to come. How should he be coded?
a. R030201030201I
b. R030201019284I
c. M030201000000I
d. R030201000000I

93. Since January 18, 1999, Patricia Barenstein had been a valued member of the public affairs team. On July 2, 2009, she worked her final day in that department. How should she be coded?
a. P011899070209P
b. B011899070209P
c. B070209011899P
d. PB011899070209P

94. A log entry reading L092108040512C could represent
a. Larry Denber, whose last day of work was September 21st.
b. an employee from the legal department who started work on September 21st.
c. Niles Lang, who worked in the customer service department.
d. an employee from the tax department whose last day of work was in 2012.

95. The following log entry for Ella Ford, who worked in the finance department from August 20, 1992, until November 11, 2007, was coded F082092111107FD. It contains which of the following errors?
a. The last year of work is miscoded.
b. The employee's name should be coded EF.
c. The first date of work should be coded 2092.
d. The employee's department is miscoded.

To answer questions 96 through 100, refer to the following scenario.

A city's property complaint department has issued a form for the reporting of neighborhood property nuisances. Each form is coded according to nature of the nuisance and the zone in which it occurred. The code follows the following rules.

Nature of nuisance (record all that apply)
1 = excessive noise
2 = graffiti
3 = high grass
4 = trash on property
5 = none of the above

Zone
zone 1 = black
zone 2 = blue
zone 3 = green
zone 4 = orange
zone 5 = purple
zone 6 = red
zone 7 = yellow

The zone color directly follows the number(s) indicating the nature of the nuisance(s).

96. A citizen calls the property complaint department to complain that a neighbor in zone 7 has not mowed his lawn for two years. How should this complaint be coded?
a. yellow3
b. yellow5
c. 5yellow
d. 3yellow

97. A clerk at the property complaint department receives a nuisance form from a citizen living next door to a person who has left rusted car parts scattered all over his property. The person who filed the form lives in zone 3. The clerk is responsible for coding the form. How should the form be coded?

    a. 4green

    b. 4orange

    c. 3green

    d. 3orange

98. The property complaint department receives a form indicating that a person in zone 6 has been throwing loud parties and allowing the party guests to spray paint tags on the garage door. How should this nuisance be coded?

    a. 1red

    b. 12red

    c. 1red2

    d. 2red

99. The code 5blue could refer to

    a. a lawn that needs to be mowed.

    b. a married couple that has loud arguments.

    c. an abandoned building covered in graffiti.

    d. a neighbor who allows her dog to wander around without a leash.

100. A person living in zone 2 has set up a workshop in his backyard. He runs a loud table saw at all hours of the day and discards the scrap wood on the sidewalk in front of his house. A neighbor files a complaint form against him. How should the form be coded?

    a. black4

    b. 1black

    c. 14blue

    d. 1blue4

Answers

Section 1: Mathematics

1. a. Convert a mixed number to an improper fraction by multiplying the denominator of the fractional part by the whole number, then add the numerator to it, and finally, put that number over the denominator of the fractional part. Doing so yields $5\frac{2}{3} = \frac{3(5) + 2}{3} = \frac{17}{3}$. Choice **b** multiplies the whole part of the mixed number by the fractional part, which is not a correct interpretation of a mixed number. Choice **c** divides 5 by the fractional part—this is not a correct interpretation of a mixed number. Choice **d** multiplies the whole part times the fractional part.

2. b. To find the mixed number, divide 56 by 12 to get 4 with a remainder of 8. Put the remainder over the denominator to get $4\frac{8}{12}$; $\frac{8}{12}$ reduces to $\frac{2}{3}$. The final answer is $8\frac{2}{3}$.

3. d. $4\frac{1}{9} - 2\frac{1}{3} = \frac{37}{9} - \frac{7}{3} = \frac{37}{9} - \frac{21}{9} = \frac{37-21}{9} = \frac{16}{9} = 1\frac{7}{9}$. Choice **a** subtracts the fractional parts incorrectly. Choice **b** is the reciprocal of the correct answer. Choice **c** subtracts the fractional parts in the wrong order.

4. a. $3\frac{4}{15} - (\frac{3}{5} + 1\frac{2}{3}) = \frac{49}{15} - (\frac{3}{5} + \frac{5}{3}) = \frac{49}{15} - (\frac{9}{15} + \frac{25}{15}) = \frac{49}{15} - \frac{34}{15} = \frac{15}{15} = 1$. Choice **b** does not compute the sum enclosed within the parentheses correctly. Choice **c** adds the fractions within the parentheses incorrectly—you must first get a least common denominator. Choice **d** does not treat the mixed number $3\frac{4}{15}$ correctly—it does not equal $\frac{34}{15}$.

5. c. $9 \div \frac{2}{3} = 9 \times \frac{3}{2} = \frac{27}{2} = 13\frac{1}{2}$. Choice **a** multiplies the fractions instead of dividing them. Choice **b** is the reciprocal of the correct answer. Choice **d** subtracts the fractions instead of dividing them.

6. d. $3\frac{3}{5} \times \frac{25}{6} = \frac{18}{5} \times \frac{25}{6} = \frac{\cancel{6} \cdot 3 \cdot \cancel{5} \cdot 5}{\cancel{5} \cdot \cancel{6}} = \frac{15}{1} = 15$.
Choice **a** multiplies the whole part and fractional part in the mixed number , which is not a proper interpretation of a mixed number. Choice **b** divides the fractions instead of multiplying them. Choice **c** is the reciprocal of the correct answer.

7. b. $\frac{3}{8} \div \frac{8}{9} = \frac{3}{8} \times \frac{9}{8} = \frac{27}{64}$. Choice **a** multiplies the fractions instead of dividing them. Choice **c** is the reciprocal of the correct answer. Choice **d** multiplies the fractions, and then takes the reciprocal.

8. b. Write 150% as a decimal by dividing 150 by 100 to get 1.5. Then, multiply: $1.5 \times 14 = 21$. Choice **a** is just the decimal representation of the percentage. Choice **c** adds 14 and 15, which is incorrect. Choice **d** adds 21 and 14, which is incorrect.

9. d. First, move the decimal point two places to the right in both the dividend and divisor to get the equivalent problem: $5.25 \div 0.05 = 525 \div 5$. Now, divide the numbers to get the quotient 105. Choice a adds the decimals instead of dividing them. Choice **b** multiplies the decimals instead of dividing them. Choice **c** does not move the decimal point in the dividend, but does in the divisor. You must move it in both numbers prior to dividing.

10. a. Move the decimal point two places to the right to get the percent equivalent of a decimal: $0.034 = 3.4\%$. Choice **b** is incorrect because you must move the decimal point two places to the right in the decimal for which you are trying to get the percent equivalent. Choice **c** moves the decimal point three places to the right instead of two. Choice **d** moves the decimal point two places to the left instead of to the right.

11. c. $3\frac{39}{50} = 3\frac{78}{100} = 3.78$. Choices **a** and **b** are incorrect because you must convert the fractional part to an equivalent fraction whose denominator is 100 in order to obtain the decimal equivalent in this manner. Choice **d** is incorrect because while 378% is equivalent to the given fraction, the corresponding decimal equivalent is 3.78.

12. b. Add the prices of the DVD and CD, and then subtract that sum from $50: $50 - ($19.95 + $11.99) = $50 - $31.94 = 18.06. Choice **a** does not borrow correctly when subtracting the sum of the prices of the DVD and CD. Choice **c** does not borrow from the ones place correctly when subtracting. Choice **d** forgets to subtract the cost of the CD.

13. d. Multiply the two fractions to determine how far he has walked: $\frac{2}{3}(1\frac{3}{4}) = \frac{2}{3} \times \frac{7}{4} = \frac{7}{6}$ miles. Now, subtract this from the entire distance that must be traveled to obtain the distance he must yet travel: $1\frac{3}{4} - \frac{7}{6} = \frac{7}{4} - \frac{7}{6} = \frac{21}{12} - \frac{14}{12} = \frac{21-14}{12} = \frac{7}{12}$ miles. Choice **a** is the distance he has already traveled. Choice **b** subtracts $\frac{2}{3}$ from $1\frac{3}{4}$ instead of multiplying them to get the distance traveled. Choice **c** does not subtract the whole parts.

14. c. Write the 3% fee as $\frac{3}{100}$. Then, multiply $\frac{3}{100}$ by 435,500 to get $\frac{1,306,500}{100}$, which is 13,065 when reduced. Therefore, the correct choice is $13,065. Choices **a**, **b**, and **d** miscalculate with the amount and location of the zeros.

15. b. The additional fees added to the list price come to 7.6% of the list price, which is $0.076($46.55) = 3.54. Adding this to the list price gives the total cost of the game: $46.55 + $3.54 = 50.09. Choice **a** forgets to include the 2.6% shipping and handling fee. Choice **c** forgets to include the 5% sales tax. Choice **d** is the total fees that must be added to the list price, not the total cost of the game.

16. a. Let x be the time it takes to produce 50 color pages. Set up the following proportion: $\frac{45}{12} = \frac{50}{x}$. To solve for x, cross-multiply: $12x = 45(50)$. This simplifies to $12x = 2{,}250$, so that dividing both sides by 12 yields $x = 187.5$ seconds. Since there are 60 seconds in one minute, this equals 3 minutes 7.5 seconds. Choice **b** assumes that the printer requires 1 minute to produce 12 color pages. Choice **c** forgets to include the fraction of a minute left over upon dividing. Choice **d** assumes that the printer produces 15 color pages every 45 seconds.

17. b. Multiply the number of rows (18) times the number of tiles needed per row (14): $18 \times 14 = 252$ tiles. Choice **a** multiplies by the tens place incorrectly. Choice **c** adds instead of multiplying. Choice **d** estimates each dimension before computing the product, which does not yield an accurate count.

18. c. First, compute 30% of 8 hours: $0.30(8) = 2.4$ hours. Since there are 60 minutes in 1 hour, 0.4 hours $= 0.4(60)$ minutes $= 24$ minutes. So, the total amount of time is 2 hours 24 minutes. Choice **a** does not convert "0.4 of an hour" to minutes correctly. Choice **b** assumes that 40% of the time was spent responding to e-mail. Choice **d** is the amount of time not devoted to responding to e-mail.

19. d. Let x be the number of miles Pete jogs in 1 hour (or 60 minutes). Set up the following proportion: $\frac{1 \text{ mile}}{11\frac{2}{3} \text{ minutes}} = \frac{x \text{ miles}}{60 \text{ minutes}}$. To solve for x, cross-multiply: $60 = (11\frac{2}{3})x$. Now, divide both sides by $11\frac{2}{3}$: $x = \frac{60}{11\frac{2}{3}} = 60 \div 11\frac{2}{3} = 60 \div \frac{46}{3} = 60 \times \frac{36}{3} = 5\frac{1}{7}$ miles. Choice **a** divides incorrectly. Choice **b** leaves off the remainder upon dividing. Choice **c** forgets to include the fractional part $(\frac{2}{3})$ of the time.

20. b. To subtract $17\frac{5}{6} - 1\frac{1}{2}$, first, rewrite the two fractional parts over a common denominator 6 to get $\frac{5}{6} - \frac{3}{6} = \frac{2}{6}$, which reduces to $\frac{1}{3}$. Next, subtract, $17 - 1$, which equals 16. Therefore, the correct answer is $16\frac{1}{3}$. Choice **a** is incorrect because it subtracts the fractions incorrectly. Choice **c** is incorrect because it adds the fractional parts. Choice **d** is incorrect because it adds the whole numbers instead of subtracting them.

21. b. Divide the total number of flyers by the number of people: $\frac{3{,}400}{20} = 170$. So, each person distributes 170 flyers. Choice **a** assumes 200 people were distributing the flyers, not 20. Choice **c** is twice the number each person will distribute. Choice **d** misreads the problem—each person does not distribute 3,400 flyers.

22. c. First, note that $\frac{1}{4} = 25\%$. So, the percentage of items on the menu that are either for breakfast or lunch is 45%. As such, the percentage *not* designated as breakfast or lunch is 55%. To find the number of such items, compute 55% of 80: $0.55(80) = 44$. Choice **a** is the number of items designated for breakfast. Choice **b** is the number of items designated for lunch. Choice **d** is the number of items designated for either breakfast or lunch.

23. a. Compute 60% of $7.40: $0.60(\$7.40) = \$4.44$. Now, add this to the original price per share to get the value per share at the end of the day: $\$7.40 + \$4.44 = \$11.84$. Choice **b** incorrectly interprets 60% as $0.60 and adds that incorrect value to the starting price of a share. Choice **c** adds 40% of the original value, not 60%. Choice **d** is the amount of the increase in value, not the total value.

24. b. Let x be the cost for a 6-hour rental. Set up the following proportion: $\frac{\$4.25}{\frac{1}{2}} = \frac{x}{6}$. To solve for x, cross-multiply: $6(\$4.25) = \frac{1}{2}x$. Now, multiply both sides by 2 to isolate x on the right side; then, simplify: $x = 2 \times 6(\$4.25) = \$51.00$. Choice **a** assumes the charge was per hour, not per half hour. Choice **c** assumes the cost was \$4 per half hour, not \$4.25 per half hour. Choice **d** assumes the charge was \$4.25 for every 20 minutes, not every half hour.

25. a. Divide the total number of ounces in a bottle by the number of ounces needed for a single load: $\frac{32.6}{1.4} = 23.28$. So, you can wash 23 complete loads. Choice **b** rounds up instead of down—a fractional load is not a complete load. Choice **c** assumes that each complete load of dishes requires the use of about 1 ounce of detergent, not 1.4 ounces. Choice **d** multiplies the two decimals instead of dividing them.

26. b. Marcus' game collection consists of $\frac{1}{4}$ role play, $\frac{1}{3}$ sports, and the remaining fraction are adventure. Let x represent the fraction of adventure games. The entire collection can be thought of as 1. Write an equation from the problem: $\frac{1}{4} + \frac{1}{3} + x = 1$. Add $\frac{1}{4}$ and $\frac{1}{3}$ by first rewriting each fraction over a common denominator 12 to get $\frac{3}{12} + \frac{4}{12} = \frac{7}{12}$. So, the resulting equation is $\frac{7}{12} + x = 1$. To solve this equation, subtract $\frac{7}{12}$ from both sides to get $x = 1 - \frac{7}{12} = \frac{5}{12}$.

27. b. Since the team lost 4 games of 28, they must have won 24 of 28. To find the percentage of games won, divide: $\frac{24}{28} = 0.857$. So, the team won approximately 86% of the games played. Choice **a** is incorrect because it does not convert the fraction to a percentage correctly. Choice **c** is the percentage of games lost, not won. Choice **d** is incorrect because the number of games played is not equal to the percentage of games won.

28. d. Use the fact that 1 mile = 5,280 feet to change the units, as follows:

120 ~~miles~~	5,280 feet
1 ~~hour~~	1 ~~mile~~

Pay particular attention to the canceling of units. Multiplying through gives 633,600 feet per hour. Choice **a** is the number of inches per second the ball is moving. Choice **b** is the number of feet per second the ball is moving. Choice **c** is the number of feet per minute the ball is moving.

29. c. To calculate the amount of overtime, subtract each time from 5:00 P.M. For Monday, subtract 5:50 – 5:00 to get 50 minutes. For Tuesday, 6:30 – 5:00 = 1:30. There are 60 minutes in 1 hour so 1:30 is 60 minutes + 30 minutes = 90 minutes. For Thursday, 5:45 – 5:00 is 45 minutes. For Friday, 5:31 – 5:00 is 31 minutes. The average time is (50 + 90 + 45 + 31), which is 216 minutes; divide 216 by 4 days to get 54 minutes. Choices **a** and **b** are the overtimes for Thursday and Monday, respectively. Choice **d** is the sum of the overtimes, not the average.

30. c. The time of day is represented on the horizontal axis of the graph, which is the x-axis. Choice **a** is the number of units each hash mark on the y-axis represents. Choice **b** is the number of orders submitted. Choice **d** is incorrect because there is no legend included in the graph.

31. a. Add the six numbers and divide by 6: $\frac{0 + 5 + 10 + 20 + 70 + 15}{6} = \frac{120}{6} = 20$. Choice **b** divides the sum of the numbers by 5, not 6. Even though one of the numbers is zero, you must include it in the total count by which to divide to get an accurate average over all time periods, not just those during which a positive number of orders took place. Choice **c** is the maximum number of orders, not the average. Choice **d** divides by 4 (length of each time interval), not the number of time intervals (6).

32. c. The most sales, by far, occur during this time period. Choice **a** is the worst time period, having 0 sales. Choices **b** and **d** are not the best time period—others have more sales.

33. a. This is the case because as the price goes down in the second column, the battery life goes down in the third column. Choice **b** is incorrect because this is not the case. Looking at the chart, as the price goes down in the second column, the battery life goes down in the third column. Choices **c** and **d** cannot be determined from what is provided.

34. d. Subtract the lowest price from the highest price: $2,500 − $900 = $1,600. Choice **a** is the mean price, not the range. Choice **b** is the maximum cost, not the range. Choice **c** is the minimum cost, not the range.

35. d. Compute 12.5% of 48: 0.125(48) = 6 hours. Choice **b** is the number of hours she spends not running errands. Choice **c** corresponds to 25% of her total time, not 12.5%. Choice **d** is the percentage of time she spends running errands, not the number of hours spent doing so.

36. b. The combined percentage of sleeping and spending time with friends is 50%. Choice **a** is incorrect because the graph indicates that she spends more time on activities A and B than she does on activities C, D, E, and F. Choices **c** and **d** are incorrect because the information provided in the graph does not support these one way or the other.

37. c. The legend tells you what each of the letters A, B, C, D, E, and F in the graph correspond to. Choice **a** is incorrect because the graph only describes Ellen's weekend activities. Choice **b** is incorrect because preference is not indicated in the graph. Choice **d** is incorrect because this is provided within the actual graph, not in the legend.

38. a. The legend tells you what each type of bar appearing in the graph represents.

39. d. Eric's time improved by 5 minutes (found by subtracting *before – after*), which is the most of anybody in the graph. Choice **a** is incorrect because Ann improved by only 1 minute, and others improved by more. Choice **b** is the second best, not the best. Choice **c** is the least improved person, showing only 0.5 minute improvement.

40. a. This is true because the difference in before and after times for males exceeded those of the females. Choice **b** is incorrect because the males' times actually improved by more than the females' times. Choice **c** is not supported by the graph. Choice **d** is incorrect because everyone actually improved after the training.

Section 2: Written Communication

41. d. A good title should give a strong idea of a passage's main idea. This passage describes the uses of the coconut, so choice **d** is the best title. Although the word coconut derives from the Portuguese word for ghost, the passage is not mainly about how coconuts are ghostly, so choice **a** is not the best title. The passage explains the coconut; it does not provide directions for making buttons out of its shell, so choice **b** is not a good title either. Choice **c** is incorrect because the passage is about more than the coconut's use as food.

42. b. Paragraph 4 mentions that the coconut can be used to buff wood floors, but it does not suggest that floors can actually be made from the coconut. The uses described in choices **a**, **c**, and **d** are all supported by information in the passage.

43. c. Although many people may not think of dimples or hair when they think of ghosts, these are the qualities that inspired Portuguese explorers to name the fruit after ghosts. This is explained in paragraph 2 of the passage.

44. a. Reread the sentence, substituting each choice for the word *staples*. Although all four choices can be used to mean staples, only choice **a** makes sense in this particular context.

45. c. Paragraph 3 explains that "This water is also used by manufacturers of various sports drinks because of its isotonic electrolyte properties."

46. b. This is an informative passage focused on explaining the purposes, benefits, and procedures of angioplasty and bypass surgery. Although the writer discusses the invasiveness of bypass surgery in paragraph 3, the passage's main focus is not to prove that angioplasty is better than bypass surgery. So choice **a** is incorrect. Choices **c** and **d** are never addressed in the passage.

47. d. Paragraph 1 directly states "When the balloon is inflated, it compresses the plaque against the wall of the artery, creating more space and improving the flow of blood." Choices **a** and **c** describe steps in bypass surgery, not angioplasty, which utilizes a balloon.

48. c. Reread the sentence, substituting each choice for the word *monitors*. Only choice **c** makes sense in this context.

49. a. The first sentence of paragraph 3 states "Angioplasty may take between 30 minutes and 3 hours to complete," which indicates that the time it takes to perform the procedure varies. Choices **b** and **c** are contradicted by information in the passage. Choice **d** is never suggested in the passage.

50. b. The final paragraph states, "a stent, a tiny tube of stainless steel that is expandable when necessary, may be implanted."

51. a. The author analyzes the making and themes of the movie *Lawrence of Arabia*. Although Lawrence of Arabia was a real historical figure, this is never indicated in the passage, which discusses a movie, so choice **b** is incorrect. Choices **c** and **d** are briefly mentioned in paragraph 1, but neither describes ideas that run throughout the entire passage, so they are incorrect.

52. b. Reread the sentence, substituting each choice for the word *foible*. Choice **b** makes the most sense in this context.

53. d. Paragraph 3 states "Only Lawrence could have accomplished his victory at the Suez Canal, and his self-sacrifice and commitment to his followers display the best of his character."

54. c. The author explains that Lawrence is a great leader at first because he puts his followers ahead of himself, but later allows his despair and self-assurance to control him. Choices **a**, **b**, and **d** are not supported by information in the passage.

55. a. In paragraph 1, the author states "The long, slow scenes of camels walking in the desert may seem dull to the modern animation-jaded viewer."

56. d. Reread the sentence, substituting each choice for the word *exhausting*. Although all four choices can be used to mean exhausting, only choice **d** makes sense in this particular context.

57. a. In paragraph 2, the author describes several methods of disposing of medical waste, and each method has its particular failing. Information in the paragraph contradicts choice **b**. The author acknowledges that on-site disposal is not an option for smaller hospitals, so choice **c** is not a very good answer.

58. d. Paragraph 2 states "Pneumatic tubes offer the best performance for waste transport in a large facility."

59. b. A good title should give a strong idea of a passage's main idea. This passage describes several methods of medical waste disposal, and the challenges each method faces, so choice **b** is the best title.

60. b. Reread the sentence, substituting each choice for the word *viable*. Choice **b** makes the most sense in this context.

61. b. The correct spelling is *expenditures*.

62. a. The correct spelling is *studious*.

63. c. The correct spelling is *qualification*.

64. b. The correct spelling is *yearn*.

65. a. The correct spelling is *livelihood*.

66. a. *Favorable* is the word that is closest in meaning to *opportune*.

67. c. *Leafy* is the word that is closest in meaning to *verdant*.

68. a. The word *limpid* means clear, so the word most nearly its opposite is *cloudy*.

69. b. Choices **a** and **c** can be eliminated because neither makes sense in the context of this sentence. The word *genteel* means *courteous* and *buoyant* means *floating*. When something is *histrionic*, it is excessively, melodramatically emotional.

70. b. *Devoid* means *completely lacking*. Choice **a**, *permeated*, means *flooded*. Choice **c**, *invincible*, means *unbeatable*.

71. b. Choice **a** uses the passive voice when a better alternative in the active voice—choice **b**—is available. Choice **c** is awkwardly and confusingly constructed.

72. a. Choice **b** contains an agreement error; the plural verb *matches* does not agree with the plural subject *colors*. Choice **c** contains a pronoun error; the pronoun *that* refers to *colors*, and therefore, should be plural rather than singular.

73. c. Choices **a** and **b** both contain punctuation errors. In choice **a**, there should be a comma between *course* and *the*. In choice **b**, the comma after *waiter* is confusing and ungrammatical.

74. a. Choices **b** and **c** contain pronoun errors; *everyone* is a collective pronoun that should take the singular pronoun *his or her*, not the plural pronoun *their*.

75. c. Choice **c** uses apostrophes correctly. In choice **a**, the apostrophes are misplaced in the words *didn't* and *couldn't*, and they are missing completely in choice **b**.

76. c. In choices **a** and **b**, it is unclear whether the pronouns refer to the brown dog or the black dog. Only choice **c** clearly identifies the antecedents to the pronouns.

77. b. The series commas in this sentence are in the correct spots, as is the comma following the introductory phrase *Next Saturday*.

78. a. Every proper noun in this sentence is capitalized correctly.

79. b. Choices **a** and **c** are incorrectly punctuated; because the sentence includes no direct quotes, the quotation marks are incorrectly used. The question mark in choice **c** is also grammatically incorrect, because the sentence is a statement of fact, not a question.

80. a. Choices **b** is confusingly worded. Choice **c** indicates that the *American South* was *One of the most influential forms of music of the twentieth century* rather than *the blues*. Only choice **a** is clearly and correctly constructed.

Section 3: Civil Service Skills

81. c. According to government agency policies, return calls for voicemail messages should be made no later than the next day.

82. a. Sometimes an e-mail response will get bounced back to a customer service agent. This may be because the customer is having some sort of temporary problem with his or her e-mail provider. The agent should attempt to resend the response at least two more times in the hope that the customer's problem with receiving e-mail has been resolved.

83. c. A BOT is a kind of response software programmed to answer certain customer queries automatically. Choice **a** refers to a contact page. Choice **d** refers to Web chat.

84. d. Choices **a**, **b**, and **c** all describe standard information a customer should receive before being transferred to another agent. Choice **d** is information the transferring agent probably does not know.

85. b. RSS (Really Simple Syndication) technology should be made available to provide information to customers over the Internet automatically, such as when an agency has updated its web page.

86. d. This photo shows two people sitting on a bench, one person sitting in a car, and one person standing on the sidewalk.

87. b. According to the awning over Future Restaurant, it serves Chinese and Mexican Food.

88. c. According to the information, Samuel Peters is a 53-year-old Latino male.

89. a. The information lists Chris March as "African American, female, age 61."

90. b. According to the information, both Samuel Peters and Pat Blarney are Latinos.

91. c. An employee is coded with a single letter indicating her or his last name, 12 digits indicating first and final days of work, and a single letter indicating the employee's current or former department. Only choice **c** is coded correctly.

92. d. The question suggests that Mark Ransford is still working in the information technology department, which means he is a current employee. The second six-digit string in the code is 000000 for current employees.

93. b. B011899070209P is the correct way to code an employee whose last name begins with B and worked in the Public Affairs Department from January 18, 1999, until July 2, 2009.

94. c. The code indicates an employee, whose last name begins with L, who worked in a department beginning with c from September 21, 2008, until April 5, 2012. Choice **c** is the only one that matches this description.

95. d. Only one letter should be used to code an employee's department, and the one in this question uses two. The correct code should be F082092111107F.

96. d. A lawn that has not been mowed for two years has unacceptably high grass. The digit indicates the nature of the nuisance, and since 5 indicates *none of the above*, choices **b** and **c** can be eliminated. The rules of the code state, "The zone color directly follows the number(s) indicating the nature of the nuisance(s)." Therefore, the code for a lawn with high grass in zone 7 is choice **d**, *3yellow*.

97. a. Rusted car parts strewn on one's property is an example of nuisance 4, *trash on property*. The two choices that do not include code 4, choices **c** and **d**, can be eliminated. Since the nuisance occurred in zone 3, which is coded with the color *green*, the only correct answer choice is **a**.

98. b. The instructions indicate that all numbers that apply to nuisances need to be recorded on the form. So if there is more than one nuisance that needs to be reported, the form should include more than one digit. The rules of the code state, "The zone color directly follows the number(s) indicating the nature of the nuisance(s)." So a form reporting both excessive party noise and graffiti needs to include both digits indicating these nuisances placed before the color indicating zone.

99. d. According to the instructions, the digit 5 indicates *none of the above*. Although high grass (choice **a**), excessive noise (choice **b**), and graffiti (choice **c**) all have their own codes in the instructions, animal-related offenses do not. Therefore, choice **d** falls under *none of the above*.

100. c. The man described in this question is guilty of excessive noise and discarding trash on his property. When coded together, these two nuisances are indicated with the digits 14. Those digits are placed before the color code indicating zone. Since the man lives in zone 2, the correct code is blue. Only choice **c** includes the correct digits and color placed in the correct order.

Using the code below, you'll be able to log in and access additional online practice materials!

Your free online practice access code is:
FVE0GBGX3643P658N42Q

Follow these simple steps to redeem your code:
- Go to **www.learningexpresshub.com/affiliate** and have your access code handy.

If you're a new user:
- Click the **New user? Register here** button and complete the registration form to create your account and access your products.
- Be sure to enter your unique access code only once. If you have multiple access codes, you can enter them all—just use a comma to separate each code.
- The next time you visit, simply click the **Returning user? Sign in** button and enter your username and password.
- Do not re-enter previously redeemed access codes. Any products you previously accessed are saved in the **My Account** section on the site. Entering a previously redeemed access code will result in an error message.

If you're a returning user:
- Click the **Returning user? Sign in** button, enter your username and password, and click **Sign In**.
- You will automatically be brought to the **My Account** page to access your products.
- Do not re-enter previously redeemed access codes. Any products you previously accessed are saved in the **My Account** section on the site. Entering a previously redeemed access code will result in an error message.

If you're a returning user with a new access code:
- Click the **Returning user? Sign in** button, enter your username, password, and new access code, and click **Sign In**.
- If you have multiple access codes, you can enter them all—just use a comma to separate each code.
- Do not re-enter previously redeemed access codes. Any products you previously accessed are saved in the **My Account** section on the site. Entering a previously redeemed access code will result in an error message.

If you have any questions, please contact Customer Support at Support@ebsco.com. All inquiries will be responded to within a 24-hour period during our normal business hours: 9:00 A.M.–5:00 P.M. Eastern Time. Thank you!

NOTES

NOTES

NOTES

NOTES

NOTES

NOTES